Photograph of the author by Lucinda Douglas-Menzies, taken for an exhibition in London called 'Luminaries'.

Autistic states in children

If the care of autistic children is to be humane, it needs to be based on a deep understanding of what lies behind the strange behaviour and impassive faces which mask their intense states of terror. In *Autistic States in Children* Frances Tustin gives the reader an insight into this terror and the children's attempts to shelter from it. This is done in an unsentimental way so that the children can be understood with compassion, but also with down-to-earth common sense.

In the first edition of *Autistic States in Children* Frances Tustin made a convincing, if controversial, case for the existence of psychogenic forms of autism which are most appropriately treated by psychotherapeutic methods, rather than behavioural techniques. Since the book was published, her findings have gained ground and there are now several clinics in America and Europe where work is based on her ideas. However, observations of early infancy by such researchers as Daniel Stern in the USA and Colwyn Trevarthen in Britain, together with her own clinical observations, have led the author to revise her understanding of the *etiology* of psychogenic autism. In this edition she has fully revised the original text, retaining the bulk of the invaluable clinical material, but setting it in a rather different theoretical context and taking account of the latest research findings.

Following her training in Child psychotherapy at the Tavistock Clinic, London, Frances Tustin worked from 1954–5 at the James Jackson Putnam Children's Center in Boston, USA, which, at that time was a research and treatment centre for autistic children. Her experiences there made a deep impression on her so that on her return to England she continued to study such children. At the outset, she was fortunate in that Dr Mildred Creak, the then consultant psychiatrist at Great Ormond Street Hospital for Children, who had a long-standing interest in autistic children, referred private patients to her and finally invited her to work at the hospital. As time went on, her own clinical experience was enriched by the supervision of clinicians from many other countries. She found that some of the young autistic children who had no detectible brain damage could be helped to normal functioning. In *Autistic States in Children* she describes the insights, the type of psychoanalytic therapy and the treatment conditions which enabled this to occur.

Frances Tustin died in 1994.

Autistic states in children

Revised edition

Frances Tustin

Brunner-Routledge
Taylor & Francis Group

HOVE AND NEW YORK

First published in 1981
by Routledge & Kegan Paul Ltd

Revised edition first published in 1992
by Routledge
11 New Fetter Lane, London EC4P 4EE

Simultaneously published in the USA and Canada
by Routledge
29 West 35th Street, New York, NY 10001

Reprinted 1997, 1999

Reprinted 2003
by Brunner-Routledge
27 Church Road, Hove, East Sussex, BN3 2FA
29 West 35th Street, New York, NY 10001

Brunner-Routledge is an imprint of the Taylor & Francis group

Typeset in Times by Intype, London
Printed and bound in Great Britain by
Biddles Ltd, Guildford and King's Lynn

British Library Cataloguing in Publication Data
A catalogue record for this book is available from the British Library

Library of Congress Cataloguing in Publication Data
Tustin, Frances.
  Autistic states in children / Frances Tustin. – Rev. ed.
  p. cm.
  Includes bibliographical references and index.
  1. Autism. 2. Autistic children. I. Title.
  [DNLM. 1. Autism – in infancy & childhood. WM 203.5 T965a]
  RJ506.A9T873   1992
  618.92′8982–dc20
  DNLM/DLC   91–36918
  for Library of Congress

ISBN 0–415–08128–9 (hbk)
ISBN 0–415–08129–7 (pbk)

To Adriano, Eleonora and Giuliana,
who have been such a stimulus to me
in our common task of trying to understand
psychotic children

Contents

Figures and tables

Acknowledgements

This book originally arose out of a series of working papers given by me at conferences in the Institute of Childhood Neuropsychiatry at the University of Rome. This institute had a unit for the psychotherapeutic treatment of psychotic children which was in the care of Professor Adriano Giannotti. The book was not a collection of the papers given at the conferences but was the result of the thinking stimulated by preparing these papers and the discussions aroused by them. In dedicating this book to the three pioneer members of the psychotherapy unit, I acknowledged this debt. I was also grateful to those dedicated workers from many countries who over the years had brought their clinical work and papers to discuss with me. In particular, I mentioned Dr Geneviève Haag, Leni Iselin and Dr Anik Maufrois from France, Dr Izelinda Garcia de Barros from Brazil, Dr Vicky Subirana from Spain and Dr Susannah Maiella from Italy.

I also acknowledged my debt to Miss Sandra Stone who, from the background of her many years of work with psychotic children at the Putnam Center, Boston, Massachusetts, carefully read the whole of the first draft of the book and made many constructive comments. The final draft owed much to all the people who have been mentioned, as well as a continuing debt to my husband, Professor Arnold Tustin, whose stringent criticism has resulted in the constant use of a blue pencil, that indispensable tool for all writing. My debt to Dr W. R. Bion and Dr S. Leigh was also a continuing one, for helping me to establish an earthy base from which my own thinking could grow. Also, what I had learned from the courageous child patients and their equally courageous parents was acknowledged with respect and gratitude.

In addition, I thanked Dr Herbert Rosenfeld and Dr Donald Meltzer, whose supervision had enabled me to continue working through an upsetting period and to emerge from it to a more authentic way of working. Finally, my thanks were due to the editor, Mr David Godwin, who had patiently steered the book to publication.

For help in preparing this new edition, I should like to thank the following people: Maria Rhode with whom I exchanged letters and telephone calls which were important in supporting me in the re-writing: Mrs Helen High who generously allowed me to use her carefully recorded observations of autistic children which comprise Chapter 1; the editors of the *International Journal of Psycho-Analysis* for permission to use parts of my paper 'Revised Understanding of Psychogenic Autism' (Tustin, 1991) in Chapter 2; Mrs Shirley Hoxter for sending me Bernice Rubens's allegorical novel *Spring Sonata* (London, 1979); Sue Norrington for sending me Joyce McDougall's books, *Theatres of the Mind* (London, 1986) and *Theatres of the Body* (London, 1989), and for drawing my attention to Henry Moore's sculpture 'Mother and Child: Block Seat', reproduced by kind permission of the Henry Moore Foundation. I would also like to thank the editor, Edwina Welham, for the meticulous care she has taken in preparing this revised edition for publication. This enabled me to make the revisions reassured that this second edition was in good hands.

Finally, I want to take this opportunity to thank the friends from all over the world who contributed to the retirement present for me initiated by Dr Victoria Hamilton and Dilys Daws. This enabled me to revise this book in financial comfort.

Preface to the revised edition

In this second edition of *Autistic States in Children* I have made many revisions to the text and also incorporated changes that have occurred in my thinking since the first edition was originally published by Routledge & Kegan Paul in 1981.

The most significant change is that I now longer use the concept of 'normal primary autism', and no longer see the pathology of autistic childhood disorders as being a regression to such an early stage. I discuss the reasons for this change in Chapter 2, entitled 'A revised understanding of the etiology of psychogenic autism'. All the following chapters that were part of the first edition have been revised so that what is said there now takes cognisance of this new thinking.

Clinical material from autistic children is difficult for us as differentiated human beings to 'take in' because it is so different from our own experience. For this reason, although I discovered repetitions on re-reading the book, I have allowed some of them to remain so that the reader can consider the same finding in a different context, and perhaps understand it more fully.

Finally, but most important, I have inserted a new chapter on observational studies of autistic children at the beginning of the book, so that the reader will 'see' the sort of child I am trying to understand.

Frances Tustin
June 1991

Introduction

Chapter 1

Observational studies of autistic children

The sort of children this book is about

On re-reading the first edition of this book, I realised that it lacked a detailed description of the type of psychotic child with whom it was primarily concerned. I therefore decided to include in the second edition a series of detailed observations of autistic children generously given to me by Mrs Helen High. These were made when Mrs High, who is now a child psychotherapist, was working as an educational psychologist. They were part of a lecture on childhood autism she gave in that capacity.

Mrs High's observations are preceded by a short extract from Leo Kanner's original description of the syndrome he called Early Infantile Autism, a syndrome he pioneered, differentiating it from other forms of mental handicap. Here is Kanner's description of such a child whom he called Paul:

> There was on his side, no affective tie to people. He behaved as if people as such did not matter or even exist. It made no difference whether one spoke to him in a friendly or harsh way. He never looked at people's faces. Whether he had any dealings with persons at all, he treated them or rather parts of them, as if they were objects.
>
> (Kanner, 1943)

AN EDUCATIONAL PSYCHOLOGIST'S OBSERVATIONS OF AUTISTIC CHILDREN

I looked after six-year-old Jimmy one day at the Child Guidance Clinic while his mother was being interviewed by another member of staff. I will describe his reactions for the first fifteen minutes he was with me.

I took him into my room where I had a small table and chair ready and some play materials in the cupboard. I sat down and spoke to him, taking out a pegboard and coloured pegs and showing them to him. He did not respond to what I said, or look at me, and did not show by any sign that he was aware of my presence. He went round the room touching the walls, cupboard and window, smelling and licking things and making clicking noises with his tongue and fiddling with the catch on the window. He wandered into the corridor continuing to explore by touch and smell. When I took him by the arm to lead him back to my room, his arm pulled away from me, but I found that if I grasped him firmly by the waist from the back and steered him, he responded by going in the direction in which I steered him. Back in my room I steered him over to the table and pegboard and showed him the pegs, putting one in his hand. He picked up the pegs one at a time and licked them. When I put the pegs in the pegboard and made a lot of gestures to show what I was doing, he imitated me and eventually he arranged the pegs in rows according to colour. This was a task he had learnt at school. When I 'swapped' some of the pegs into different rows I got the first show of any feeling from Jimmy; he waved his arms in the air and squealed and put the pegs back in their rows of the same colour. This happened again each time I 'swapped' the pegs. He became aware of me and showed a reaction of annoyance to me when I interfered with his design of the pegs, but it was not until then that he showed any reaction to me as a person. Even then he did not look at me. He did not speak during all this time and very rarely does at all.

This gives a glimpse of the reaction of an autistic child to a stranger. Perhaps I could compare Jimmy's response to that of a normal baby of, say, eight or nine months. A baby of this age on being brought into the room with a stranger, who then talks to the baby, will look the stranger in the face, and may cry or smile or stare or look away and then look back again. The baby shows marked signs of awareness of another person. But Jimmy at six years old, who could in fact do jigsaw puzzles as well as most other six-year-olds, showed much less awareness of another person than an eight-month-old baby.

This failure to respond to other people is not just with strangers. The greatest handicap and the most consistent one amongst autistic children is the impairment in the ability to make emotional relationships with other people. They fail to make contact or play with other children, as well as lacking responsiveness to adults. They sometimes use people or parts of them in an unusual way. A characteristic gesture of an autistic child is to get hold of someone's arm, place the person's hand on the knob of a door, and then try to use the hand to turn the doorknob and open the door.

An autistic child seems to lack a sense of himself as a separate person. He does not seem clear about the difference between himself and the world of objects around him. Autistic children show various sorts of confusion which suggest they have this difficulty. For example, when Jimmy fell and bumped his knee on the ground he would kiss the spot on the ground where he had bumped his knee to make it better, as if he were not sure which was his knee and which was the ground. Also some children persist in behaviour which is physically injurious to them as if unaware of inflicting the injury on themselves. One little girl I saw in a hospital unit had to have padded mittens tied round her wrists because she had a habit of banging her hands on the floor, table, wall etc, and bruised them badly and persistently unless they were protected.

The confusion between themselves and other people is shown in the speech of some autistic children who get the words 'I' and 'you', or 'me' and 'you' the wrong way round, saying for instance, 'Do you want a drink of water?' when they mean, 'I want a drink of water'. Another instance was when I heard a girl say 'thank you' after she had given some of her chocolate to a boy in her class (that is, she said 'thank you' to the boy to whom she had given the chocolate!).

Speech is one of the main problems. Some autistic children do not speak at all and have never developed speech; others have learnt to speak up to a point, and then have gone back in speech, losing some of the speech they had acquired. Others stick at an early stage in speech and often have odd speech habits and mannerisms. Some children say the same phrase or phrases over and over again parrot fashion, or imitate a remark they have heard someone say a long time afterwards and quite irrelevantly, and apparently meaninglessly.

Unusual patterns of movement are often shown by autistic children. Many of them have odd rituals or mannerisms such as rocking backwards and forwards on a chair. I have seen one child who tipped the whole chair backwards and forwards as he rocked vigorously, the legs making a rhythmic clatter to and fro. Spinning is another mannerism; I remember seeing a girl who spun round and round in circles on the floor endlessly. Other children will spin an object round and round. One little girl goes rigid at times and her arms tremble. A boy I observed used to hold one fist closed and the other hand open, banging hand and fist together rapidly, and uttering a high-pitched squeal and screwing up his face at the same time.

Some of the children are preoccupied or obsessed with certain objects, or certain aspects of the objects, which are often unconnected with the way the thing is usually used. Sometimes the mannerisms of movement and the object go together. For instance, one boy had a bootlace that he waved about in the air from time to time, and another child had a piece of mirror that she liked because it was shiny, reflecting the light into her eyes; but she appeared not to notice her reflection in it. I saw a little boy who had a tin box, not to put things in, but to wave about in the air to tap his fingers on, and to point to, and to show people with great excitement and repeatedly. The boy who banged hand and fist together had a stage when he held an old metal toy in the closed fist while doing this; he called it his 'shrieking toy'. When asked why, he said, 'because I shriek with it'.

Of course, normal children of three, four and five years old or thereabouts often have an object or toy they cling to, but the normal child's object is usually a soft, cuddly, comforting one like a piece of old blanket or a teddy bear or other cuddly thing. The objects autistic children use usually seem anything but cuddly (such as a tin box, metal toy, piece of iron, bootlace), and they do not seem to be for the same purpose as the normal child's cuddly object. Although, like the child with the cuddly object, the autistic child will become distressed if his object is lost or removed, he usually replaces it with another one quite quickly. This is very different from the normal child's reaction to the loss of his treasured cuddly transitional object.

Autistic children resist change, being upset if their usual routine is altered. Jimmy protested when I changed the pattern of his rows of coloured pegs. He also went through a stage which was very difficult for his mother when he screamed with protest if she tried to put a new or clean pair of trousers on him. He would only wear the pair of trousers that he was used to.

Autistic children show unusual responses to things seen or heard. Some children show a lack of response to sounds, for instance, and others an exaggerated response. Some autistic children are thought to be deaf at first because they do not react to sounds, do not blink, flinch or turn their head at a loud noise. This, combined with failure to speak, naturally leads to doubts about their hearing. Usually, however, it is proved that they hear normally, but they do not respond normally to the sounds they hear. On the other hand, I remember an autistic child clapping his hands over his ears and rushing round the room in some distress when the other children began to sing, as if the sounds which the other children were enjoying were too much for him. Some children show an inconsistent reaction to sounds. One child in a nursery playgroup was imitating the sound of a far-away machine whose rhythmical noise could only be heard faintly and was only picked out with difficulty by an adult who was studying the sounds autistic children make spontaneously. At the same time as picking out this faint background noise, the child was apparently oblivious to the noisy play of several other children alongside him.

The same inconsistencies apply to vision as to hearing. Autistic children often do not focus with their eyes; they do not seem to look at things or people. When occasionally they do look towards you, this lack of focus makes it seem as if the child is looking right through you, which gives one a strange feeling. The autistic child may not notice visual changes in his surroundings. Michael did not notice that a room he was very familiar with at the clinic, having seen it once a week for two years, had been redecorated. It had changed from dingy pink walls with blue paintwork, to bright yellow walls with white paintwork, but, when asked, he said he did not notice anything different about the room. He did, however, immediately notice a small Plasticine model of an octopus, made by another child, on the top of the bookcase as soon as he came into the room. On a visit to Jimmy's school, he did not seem aware of me during the morning I spent with the small group of six children he was in, until playtime when another child asked me to chase him. Jimmy then suddenly started to chase after me, becoming more interested in me as a moving object, although he had not reacted to me as a person.

Another problem with autistic children is acute, excessive anxiety, sometimes for no understandable reason. Here communication is a difficulty, for how do you reassure a panic-stricken child when he can't tell you, and you don't know how to find out, what he is frightened about? Sometimes ordinary things or events seem terrifying, but on the other hand, the autistic child may lack a sense of appropriate fear in the face of real danger. The anxiety mostly tends to be set off by changes in environment or routine. For example, Michael joined in skipping round the room to music, but accidentally bumped his toe against a tower of wooden bricks some of the children had built earlier. The tower collapsed and he went into a screaming panic and was inconsolable for half an hour before calming down. Also, Jimmy showed panic and cried in terror when it started to rain heavily while his class were out for a walk.

Linda went for a day's visit to her teacher during the school holidays. She seemed happy on the journey there and during the day, but had a screaming outburst on the train on the way home after she and her teacher had rushed down the stairs onto the platform and into the last carriage of the train just before it started off. Linda kicked and hit out in terror. We can only guess why this was, and it was quite unexpected as Linda usually likes train journeys. It may have been the suddenness of the change in her environment that frightened her. One moment she was walking down the station steps to the platform; the next moment she was inside the train, which was noisy and jerked about.

Autistic children are often very patchy in their abilities, sometimes seriously backward in most things, but in one thing at average level; other children are nearer average in general ability but outstanding at one skill. Examples are a five-year-old who could not speak at all, but who was outstandingly good at jigsaw puzzles, better than most six-year-olds. Also a seven-year-old had not learnt to read or do sums but had a great deal of knowledge about prehistoric monsters. He could accurately name pictures of any prehistoric monster you could show him. He could also draw them accurately and knew factual details about them, for example, which was 'flesh-eating', which 'vegetarian', etc.

(Recently, a programme on television described autistic Stephen Wiltshire, who can draw complicated buildings in fantastic detail from memory, but who cannot cross the road or find his way about. – F. Tustin 1991.)

The foregoing observations are of autistic children, with whom this book is predominantly concerned.

Chapter 2

A revised understanding of the etiology of psychogenic autism
General implications

INTRODUCTION

Over the intervening years since this book was first published, my ideas concerning the etiology of childhood autism have undergone considerable revision. These revisions were recently embodied in a paper published in the *International Journal of Psycho-Analysis* (1991). The editors of that journal have generously given me permission to use parts of that paper in this chapter.

In the light of those revisions, the first chapter of the original version of this book has been rewritten, and throughout the rest of the book changes have been made in the text, so that what is said there is in keeping with the revisions. The rewritten first chapter of the original book (now Chapter 3) will deal with the theoretical implications of these changes. This present chapter will deal with the more general implications of the changes.

REASONS FOR THE REVISIONS

After many years of working with a certain type of autistic child, and after attempts to digest this experience by writing books and papers, I have come to the conclusion that I made a mistake in following the general trend of psychoanalytical writers is using the term 'autism' for an early stage of infantile development, as well as for a specific pathology. I now realise that it is more correct, and leads to clarity in our thinking, if the term 'autism' is solely reserved for a specific spectrum of disorders in which there is an absence of human relationships and gross impoverishment of mental and emotional life – these impairments being the result of the blocking of awareness by an early aberrant development of autistic procedures. Also, this has the additional recommendation that it is in keeping with the way the meaning of the word 'autism' has been developing over the years. For example, it is no longer used in the way that Bleuler (1913), who initiated this term, used it. In inventing the name

Early Infantile Autism for the syndrome he differentiated from other forms of mental handicap, Leo Kanner (1944) directed its meaning towards psychopathology.

Recent observational studies of babies by writers such as Brazelton (1970), Bower (1978), Trevarthen (1979) and Stern (1986) have shown us that, in normal development, there are periods of lively, alert awareness and active questing even from the beginning of life. This has been confirmed by the detailed baby observations reported by Perez-Sanchez (1990) and Michel Haag (private circulation), both of whom were supervised by Dr Esther Bick (1964), and in the book inspired by her work, *Closely Observed Infants* (Miller *et al.*, 1989). Use of the concept of 'normal primary autism', as implying that there is a stage in earliest infancy when the normal infant is totally unaware of being separate from the mother's body, is incorrect in view of the objective findings of those infant observers who have just been cited. It also seems to me to be similarly untenable in terms of the different, and more subjective, timeless, non-sequential, unconscious processes as they are experienced during psychoanalytical treatment. In this situation, I have realised that the extrapolation from pathological conditions, to see them as being an exact reproduction of features of *normal* early infancy, inevitably leads to error.

I realise that those workers who have used the scheme of understanding based on pathological autism as being a regression to, or halt at the stage of 'normal primary autism' will find it difficult to accept this new formulation; but, in my experience, the revised understandings which are to be described lead to greater freedom and clarity of one's thinking. The essence of these revised understandings is that autism is an early developmental deviation which occurs in the service of dealing with unmitigated terror. This means that from earliest infancy, the child's psychological development in terms of human relationships is massively diverted in an unduly auto-sensual direction which increases as the years go by. If this is not modified it affects all development. As Ogden (1989) expresses it, early psychological states co-exist dialectically with one another and affect each other in a non-linear fashion.

THE AUTHOR'S PRESENT VIEWS

The clinical material of the patients on whom the ensuing findings are based can be found in various books and papers (Tustin, 1966; 1972; 1984; 1987; 1990). These findings have come from the type of autistic child who has responded to the kind of psychoanalytic therapy that was used. (In this, the *infantile transference* played an important part.) I have come to term their autism 'psychogenic autism', since psychogenic factors seem to have been most operative, although some of the children may have had minimal organic damage which could not be detected by the investigative methods at present available. If this had been present, it would seem that it would have been possible to modify it by the type of psychotherapy that was used.

I have come to realise that autism may arise in several different situations: for example, *organic autism* can be a reaction to brain damage or sensory defect, whereas *psychogenic autism* is the reaction to a delusory traumatic situation which seems to threaten life and limb. The latter is the type of autism I have treated with a certain amount of success. The pathologies in which organic factors predominate, and those in which psychogenic factors are most operative, seem to use the same kind of protective mechanisms, so that on a superficial inspection, it is difficult to tell the difference between them because they manifest similar behavioural characteristics.

FINDINGS ABOUT PSYCHOGENIC AUTISM

My first discovery came from the first autistic child I treated. This was four-year-old John, who had no discernible brain damage but who showed me unmistakably that his infantile awareness of bodily separateness had been traumatic, and had been experienced as a 'black hole' associated with elemental panic and rage about the seeming loss of part of his body. Dr Victoria Hamilton, who has usefully defined the term 'trauma', writes as follows:

> The word trauma should be reserved for responses to events which arouse in most of us intense feelings of horror, a sense of outrage and very often *a feeling of revulsion and turning away. We would rather not know or hear.*
>
> (Hamilton, 1989, p. 74; emphasis added)

In these terms, autism can be seen as a massive 'not-knowing' and 'not-hearing' provoked by traumatic awareness of bodily separateness. As such, it would seem to be an intensification and entrenched exaggeration of an in-built set of reactions which are specific to trauma. It is of the nature of a post-traumatic stress disorder. It is also a survival mechanism.

Clinical material indicates that, in the type of autistic child I have treated, the traumatic stress which had provoked the autistic reactions had been experiences of unbearably sudden and painful awareness of bodily separateness from a mother with whose body they had previously felt fused and equated. Prior to the alarmingly unexpected awareness of bodily separateness they had not been aware of a mothering person, as such. They had taken her bodily presence for granted. They only realised that 'it' had been there when they felt that 'it' had gone. When awareness of their separateness from the mother's body was suddenly experienced, it was as if they had lost a part of their own body. This brought home to them their vulnerability; they felt unprotected and at risk. Autism became an impenetrable protection which shut out the frustrating and terrifying awareness of bodily separateness. But this prevented the development of a sense of individual identity, since awareness of bodily separateness is a necessary precursor for that development. (The nature of autism will be discussed later.)

I have come to see that the delusory state of fusion which existed prior to the catastrophic awareness of bodily separateness was not a normal early infantile stage but an abnormal state with which both mother and child had colluded, and for which there may have been a genetic susceptibility in both of them, as well as environmental pressures which provoked it. Inevitably, since there was felt to be no space between them, this undue closeness hampers the development of 'object relations'. This means that cognitive and emotional developments are impeded. The 'closing down' nature of autism is a further impediment.

THE IMPEDIMENTS OF AUTISM

Autistic children are not fully born – they still feel part of the mother's body; to exist, to 'be', seems fraught with danger. Thus, they are very immature and have many deficits, a crucial one being that the early panic-stricken fusional 'clinch' between mother and infant means that normal primary relations between mother and infant are prevented. Also, the abnormal 'hot-house' state of fusion with the mother is very enervating. The autism increases this weakness still further, because the infants have no practice in dealing with the exigencies of life. Although in reality they are weak, the 'adhesive equation' (Tustin, 1990) with the mother's body will have increased the early infantile sense of omnipotence. This means that when the omnipotence is assailed by awareness of bodily separateness, and their weakness is momentarily brought home to them, such awareness is unbearable and traumatic. They have no 'background *presence* of primary identification' (Grotstein, 1980), no 'background of safety' (Sandler, 1960). These lacks prevent them from 'breasting' this crisis. Instead, it is dealt with by autistic reactions, but the effects of this trauma lie encapsulated and intact in the depths of the somatic psyche like an unexploded bomb. As they recover, this pent-up explosive situation may be released and expressed in psychosomatic manifestations such as boils or other skin eruptions. This can be an attempt to process and to come to terms with the traumatic experience(s).

In short, the blocking of early normal processes of psychological development by an unnatural degree of fusion with the mother has meant that the child was not psychologically strong enough to cope with awareness of bodily separateness. This is the essence of the pathology of autism.

Autism is not functional in terms of long-term psychological develop-ment, but it is a protective measure which prevents the marasmus and death such as befell the institutionalised infants described by Spitz in his poignant film *Grief*.

Insulated by the autism, the unhealthy omnipotence becomes mon-strous, so that when they begin to talk, autistic children will say such things as 'I am God' or 'I am a King'. Indeed, these children are 'monsters' (see Sandra Stone's patient, Sam, who became a monster called Earthlifter, in Chapter 16). They sap the mother's life-giving energy and undermine her often already inadequate self-confidence. In her remarkable allegorical novel *Spring Sonata*, Bernice Rubens visual-ises such an overgrown infant who was not born to term but stayed within the mother's womb, growing and becoming ever more monstrous. The synopsis on the dust-cover describes him thus:

> Buster was not happy. He was a gifted violinist but he feared that his ambitious, greedy family would exploit and destroy his talent. His confused mother, his possessive grandmother and his weak father were already quarrelling over his future. But he had one protection they could never violate – *he had not yet been born. So began Buster's long and eventful siege against the outside world.*
>
> (emphasis added)

(When they recovered, all the psychogenic autistic children I have treated were musical or artistic or good with words.) Bernice Rubens graphically describes the destructive *folie à deux* which developed between Buster and his mother, Sheila. Finally, Rubens writes of the death of Buster and Sheila:

> Buster put down his violin, and softly began to hum to himself the adagio melody that was so cruelly cut off in mid-phrase. Sheila heard, and softly hummed with him, as if in begging reminder *that they were one*. He wept for her. She had no part in the treachery, he was sure. But she housed him, and that house *had now become his prison*, and Samson-like he must destroy her too . . . Then he took his bow in one hand, and in the other, the umbilical cord. . . . and he sawed the cord. . . . At last, he sawed it through. Then he lay back . . . cut off from his life-line.
>
> (p. 212; emphasis added)

As Buster died, 'Sheila's head dropped gently on to her chest, in a movement quieter than death itself' (p. 213). In the epilogue Rubens writes:

> When all the post mortem investigations were over, the official cause of death was registered as heart-failure, due to excessive overweight.

For myself, I was convinced that Sheila Rosen died quite simply of a broken heart, which woefully lost its beat when her love-object withdrew.

(p. 215)

Autistic children break their mothers' hearts because they feel heart-broken. They will break the heart of their therapist also, unless he or she is aware of this and protects against it. Protection is to be realistic about their destructive monstrousness, and not to try to satisfy the desire for an unrealistic perfection and indulgence which is not humanly possible to achieve. This was the mistake made by psychoanalytical therapists in the early days of treating these children. These therapists were far too indulgent, in the mistaken belief that they had to compensate for inadequate nurturing by a mother who had been 'cold, intellectual and rejecting'.

Awareness of bodily separateness is the heartbreak at the centre of all human existence, but when it occurs to those undifferentiated infants who have been unduly close to the mother, it is agonisingly intense. This is the crux of our work with autistic children. To be able to help them, we need to have worked through our own omnipotent romanticism and our all-or-nothing quest for unrealistic total perfection. Sublime primal unity is a transient state which cannot exist in an absolute form for normally differentiating human beings. Quietly, patiently and compassionately we need to help the children to accommodate to this inevitable fact of existence. Our approach to these children needs to be rooted in down-to-earth common sense, but yet it should not dismiss more sublime states of being, so long as these are tempered by the effort to acquire the skills to express them through the containing and processing media of play, communication and aesthetic and/or religious activities. Otherwise such states, if they become uncontrolled and excessive, can become an impediment to living as a developing human being.

The epilogue to *Spring Sonata* ends with the following passage:

Central on the upper lip of every human being, is a small mark of indentation, a birthmark as obligatory as the navel. It is said that when we struggle into birth, an angel presses his finger on our lips, and seals them from retelling of our pasts. That indentation is his finger-print, and it condemns us to repeat our former follies, and to live out once again our human frailty. We must, for if we dodge that finger, we would, all of us, be gods.

(p. 215)

Intuitively, Bernice Rubens realised that the mouth, with its sense of loss of the suckling attachment to the mother, is the place where the realisation of our human frailty begins. Ordinary acts such as kissing revive this attachment and help us to bear our human situation. It brings with it the joy of reunion and helps us to bear our separateness. Handshakes and hugs have the same effect of accepting our dependency on other human beings, and of acknowledging our neediness and weakness. Autistic children are debarred by their pathology from such healing reunions.

Rubens also hints at the dire effects which result from weakness of the father's influence. Clinical work shows that undue fusion with the mother's body, and the resulting autism, mean that the father's influence is lacking in an autistic child's psychological development (or, rather, lack of such development). Such children do not experience the discipline of sharing the mother with the father. This means that excessive omnipotence is not checked. Underneath their passive exteriors, and often angelic appearance, autistic children are extremely wayward, wilful, and tyrannical. Work with them brings home to us the value of the 'Oedipus complex' in giving structure and discipline to the personality, whether this be conceived of as a very early oedipal situation as described by Melanie Klein, or as a pre-oedipal situation as described by classical Freudians.

And now, with the help of a writer and an artist, let me evoke in 'picture language' the situations which precipitate the swaddling protections of autism.

A STATE OF FUSION

Joyce McDougall has given us a graphic description of fusional interlocking. In her books *Theatres of the Mind* (1986) and *Theatres of the Body* (1989) she has described how, in certain circumstances, a mother may unwittingly use her infant as an inanimate object – as what McDougall calls 'a cork child' – to fill the hole of her emptiness and loneliness. In my experience, such a mother is under-confident, bewildered, deprived, and/or depressed, or she may have experienced a shock, tragedy or bereavement around the time of the child's birth. Such a mother cannot make her presence felt. For example, one mother told me that she felt like 'a non-person' for months after her baby was born. Some such situations have been operative in the early mother and infant fusion of the autistic children I have encountered, although some of the children seem to have experienced the trauma of separateness at the moment of birth itself, the foetus having been unduly experienced by the mother as a solace for her loneliness and sense of deprivation. Birth in such a situation was unusually traumatic for both mother and baby and precipitated a panic-stricken 'clinch' which, if not modified by subsequent nurturing, would result in the catastrophic consequences of feeling torn apart when awareness of bodily separateness could no longer be avoided.

Dr Esther Bick (1986) has vividly described this in her paper 'Further Considerations of the Function of the Skin in Early Object Relations'. She writes the following of a child patient: 'The desperate clinging for survival was mounted in the face of experience of lacerating separation which would let her life leak away like a liquid substance' (p. 293).

The result of traumatic separateness

A Henry Moore sculpture (shown in Figure 2.1 and on the cover of my recent book, *The Protective Shell in Children and Adults*, 1990) poignantly expresses the effect of separation from such a state of absolute fusion. (It is known that Moore had an over-close relationship with his mother.) In what was Moore's last great work, 'Mother and Child: Block Seat', mother and child are each swathed and enveloped, and are thus out of contact with each other's bodies. The mother's unswathed left breast has a black hole where the nipple should have been. The infant, although sitting on her lap, is cut off from touching her by the swathes which cover its body. Instead of a mouth, it has a cork-like protrusion. This protrusion would block the flow of milk from the breast instead of being a means of sucking at it. The realistic function of both breast and mouth has been occluded. In my experience, such a perversion of natural functions lies at the root of autism. Thus, in my present view, autism is a protective system of perverse reactions, provoked by a traumatic experience of bodily separateness, and is *not* a defensive regression to a so-called normal autistic stage of infantile development.

AUTISM AS A PROTECTIVE REACTION

Influenced by papers by David Rosenfeld (1986) and by Yolanda Gampel (1988), I have come to realise that autism has a protective and preservative function. I now see it as an elemental 'proto-mental' state (to use Bion's useful term (1979)), which is an automatic, psychochemical reaction to traumatic stress. (The term 'psychochemical' is used to indicate elementary mental states which are closely associated with and affected by body chemistry.) The psychological development of such an infant has been shocked into developing autistic protections. Normal on-going psychological development has been halted in a way that is either well-nigh total, as in an autistic child, or partial, as in neurotic, borderline and even relatively normal individuals who have a 'pocket' of autism. This fusional closeness between mother and infant is far more common than we realise. Why in relatively rare cases almost total autism develops is not understood, but in such a rare syndrome one would expect that there would be an exceptional conjunction of factors which led to the final tragic outcome.

Figure 2.1 'Mother and Child: Block Seat', Henry Moore, 1983
(Reproduced by kind permission of the Henry Moore Foundation.)

There are a few autistic children, the so-called 'idiots savants', who develop an isolated talent along a narrow line in an obsessive way to a remarkable level of achievement although in other respects – for example in toilet training – they may be quite immature. Such an unusual development seems, to some extent, to help ensure that they live in a controllable, predictable world, in order to save them from a re-evocation of the alarmingly unexpected experience of bodily separateness from which they had recoiled.

By contrast with the autistic child, through the containing medium of his art Henry Moore had been able to tolerate, objectivise and depict the 'black hole' catastrophe of sudden and alarming awareness of separateness from the body of a mother with whom there had been fusion and a sense of being inanimate. Perhaps Moore had always been working against 'this backward pull to the inanimate', as Freud expressed it (1920), but for Moore it had been a stimulus for creativity rather than for the development of autism. Again, why in some individuals the undue sense of fusional closeness with the mother should lead to total 'shut down', and why other individuals can emerge from it to a life of achievement and satisfaction, is not understood. Is there perhaps a stronger drive to integration in these children?

Autistic phenomena

Clinical material demonstrates that when bodily separateness from the mother is experienced traumatically, the gap between their two bodies is experienced by such infants as being filled with rivalrous and predatory other sucklings who threaten to annihilate them and to push them out of existence in order to take their place. (The father is sometimes experienced as a particularly dangerous rival.) Thus, to exist becomes a life-or-death struggle. For such children to exist – to have an individual identity – becomes fraught with horrific dangers. The reaction to these existential dangers is an endogenous auto-sensuousness which generates what, in an effort to conceptualise these unconceptualised sensation-dominated reactions, I have called 'autistic sensation objects' (1980) and 'autistic sensation shapes' (1984). These seem to swathe such children in a sensual protective 'shell'. This autogenerated protection is made up of autistic sensation objects, which make the child feel strong and safe, and autistic sensation shapes (Tustin, 1984), which are calming and tranquillising. These are not objective visual shapes, but are tactile endogenous swirls of sensation. Similarly, it is not so much the *object* that they carry that is responded to, but the sensations on the skin that are aroused. These sensations distract attention away from unbearable bodily separateness and assuage the terrors which beset these children, but they have deleterious side effects. (These will be discussed in detail in the next chapter.) Such children's sensation-engendering activities are more primitive than masturbation in that they are not associated with fantasies. They are a kind of autogenerated hypnosis which makes the child feel safe and comfortable. I have often wondered whether they stimulate the development of endorphins in the brain. They certainly result in the 'attention deficits' so characteristic of autistic states. If their 'spell' is disturbed, the child will break into inconsolable grief.

Paradoxically, these attempts to avoid awareness of bodily separateness result in such children becoming increasingly separate, alienated and 'cut-off', a situation of which such patients are unaware until when, and if, they begin to emerge from their protective autistic shell. To us, as observers, these autogenerated, auto-sensual protective reactions appear in external behaviour as what are usually called 'stereotypes' (rocking, hand flapping, finger flicking, twirling, object twirling, toe walking, etc.). Such stereotypes are a ubiquitous feature of autistic children's overt behaviour. When and if the endogenous protective manoeuvres are abated, these stereotyped activities cease to be behavioural characteristics.

Autism as a reaction to unbearable stress

Clinical work has brought home to me that when these automatic, sensation-dominated reactions to infantile trauma are used persistently and exclusively, psychological development becomes increasingly pathological. Autism becomes an entrenched way of life. This means that it is increasingly difficult to ameliorate it as the child grows older. It also means that at a certain point in the analysis, the enclaves of autism that are to be found in neurotic, borderline, and even relatively normal patients become an obstinate barrier to psychoanalytic work with them (S. Klein, 1980; Tustin, 1987; Gomberoff, et al., 1990).

My work with autistic children has made me realise that the way in which the frustration arising from awareness of bodily separateness is handled, and the way the infant reacts to it, are critical for future psychological development. This is particularly so with regard to the sense of individual identity and the development of self-confidence, in that it affects the degree of panic, rage and anguished feelings of weakness that 'well up' as stressful situations in later life are encountered. For example, unventilated, unprocessed explosive panic, rage and 'black hole' anguish can manifest themselves in psychosomatic and phobic conditions of various kinds (S. Klein, 1980; Taylor, 1987; McDougall, 1974, 1982, 1986, 1989; Tustin, 1987, 1990). It is a turning point in psychotherapeutic treatment when, as it were, the cork comes out and this bottled-up tantrum of rage and terror is exploded by the patient, to be received and understood, to some extent at least, by the therapist. In these states, actions speak louder than words, both on the part of the therapist and the child. Such an outburst usually comes in relation to separations from the therapist due to holidays, illnesses and suchlike inevitable breaks in treatment. Prior to therapy, if these tantrums had been expressed, they would have vapoured away into a void and would not have been caught and held in an understanding person's thinking and concern. Such understanding can help the patient to digest and come to terms with these experiences.

Childhood autistic syndromes would seem to constitute different sections on a continuum of autistic disorders. For example, as well as constituting the Kanner syndrome of Early Childhood Autism and variants of this, autistic phenomena can also be seen in Asberger's Syndrome (Asberger, 1944; Wing, 1981; Gillberg, 1989; Barrows, 1988). They are at the root of schizoid personalities (Weil, 1953; Wolff and Barlow, 1979; Wolff and Cuth, 1986; Wolff and Chick, 1980). Indeed, once they have been intractably set in train, autistic reactions will be manifested and may become intensified at all the critical phases of life such as teething, weaning, walking, talking, entry into latency and adolescence, the mid-life crisis, old age and ultimately, in death – this final event inevitably bringing acute awareness of bodily separateness and the threat of loss of bodily existence.

THE NATURE OF AUTISM

The trouble in writing about autism is that one has to think thoughts that, for the patient, have been unthinkable, and to find concepts for what were unconceptualised states. Such a patient is not 'object related', does not objectivise, and is asymbolic, although some of them may use 'symbolic equations' as described by Hanna Segal (1957). This equation of objects affects everything that autistic children do. For example, in classification, that basis for cognition, two objects – although different in many respects – will be equated on the basis of a single superficial similarity. These are not similes or metaphors; the two objects are felt to be one and the same. There is no discrimination of differences. Similarly, fantasies are not present; only things that can be touched and handled to produce sensations are meaningful to autistic children who have been found to have no capacity for empathy (Hobson, 1986) and to lack imagination (Frith, 1985). Also, as is to be expected, such children do not play (Tustin, 1988; 1990). They have little inner life and are predominantly an auto-sensual shell. They have also missed the ebb and flow of states of 'flowing-over-oneness' flexibly interspersed with states of separateness. These alternating flexible states, which have been described by both Grotstein (1980) and Ogden (1989), gradually prepare the infant for an awareness of bodily separateness which is bearable.

The abnormal fusional states with the mother are perseverating and rigid. In such states, awareness of bodily separateness is unbearable in that it comes suddenly, unexpectedly and traumatically. This precipitates aberrative autistic reactions. These children lack a 'psychic floor' and are very dependent upon external support. This is because their 'sensory floor', as described by Ogden (1989), and the 'psychic envelopes' described by Anzieu (1990) have become distorted and perverted by the use of inanimate autistic sensation objects, which are described in this book, and also autistic sensation shapes, which have been described in an earlier book (Tustin, 1987). Thus, these children have no internal regulator for the feelings associated with object relations because their early skin-to-skin sensuousness has been so disturbed. This leads me to a discussion of normal primary sensuousness and auto-sensuousness.

PRIMARY SENSUOUSNESS AND AUTO-SENSUOUSNESS

To make more specific Freud's statement that the ego 'is first and foremost a body ego', we could say that 'the ego is first and foremost a sensation ego', since sensations seem to be the basis for psychological development. Thus, what happens in the early sensation life of the infant has a profound interactive effect on all later cognitive and conative developments.

Normal infants alternate between sensuousness directed towards the body of another, and sensuousness directed towards their own body, or other bodies experienced as if they are the infant's own body. For example, Winnicott (1958) has described two babies feeding at the breast. He intuits that one baby is experiencing the breast as being part of its mouth, whereas the other baby is experiencing the nipple as being separate from its mouth. We could apply those two experiences to one baby, and say that, at one moment, the baby experiences the nipple as being part of its mouth, whilst at another moment, the same baby experiences the nipple as being separate from its mouth. At one moment, the baby's mouth is *equated* with the breast, whereas at another moment, because the baby is aware (however dimly) of the separateness between its mouth and the breast, there are the possibilities for *identifying with* the breast. This latter situation fosters on-going development.

If the situation of being equated and fused with the breast predominates and persists, infantile omnipotence becomes intensified. In such a situation, awareness of separateness is not sufficiently experienced for need-satisfying people to be recognised as such – they are experienced as being part of the baby's body. This is what has happened with autistic children. The mother has not been able to make her presence sufficiently felt to modify this situation. Auto-sensuousness gets out of bounds. Perhaps it is this situation which has led to theories about there being a state of normal primary autism but, as will be obvious from the foregoing, it is, in fact, an abnormal situation. Almost total auto-sensuousness is not normal. In normal infancy, auto-sensuousness alternates flexibly with sensuous satisfactions which are recognised as flowing from other people. In normal development, there is a sensuous ebb and flow which promotes adaptability.

However, in an insecure nursing situation (for example, an under-confident or grieving mother and a hypersensitive baby), the baby's autogenerated sensations can take the dominant role. This was well illustrated by an audio-tape recording, made by a student of mine, of the breast-feeding of her first grandchild from birth up to two months of age. This baby had been born into somewhat stressful circumstances which, in the interests of confidentiality, I will not go into here. Also, the father was away, and the mother of the baby had to live with her own parents, the grandmother being the student who made the recording. The recording illustrated strikingly that, at first, the infant's irregular rhythms of breathing and sucking were superimposed upon those of the breast and, indeed, impeded the baby's use of the breast. This was partly because this was a first baby and the mother was under-confident and lacked experience (she may also have been affected by the tape-record-ing, although the student was sure that this was not so), but it was also because she was unhappy about the baby's father being away. When he returned home, she became happier. Almost immediately, the infant's rhythms of breathing and sucking, and the rhythms of the flow of milk from the breast, became more co-ordinated. All that could be heard in the tape recording was a quiet 'glug, glug', as mouth and breast worked together harmoniously and effectively. This was in great contrast to the stormy, unhappy period when baby and mother had not synchronised with each other. This was a robust baby, and a basically happy mother, so that they adjusted to each other and rhythmical co-operation was achieved. This was, to some extent, dependent on their recognising their separateness from each other.

It will be obvious that the state of mind of the mother and that of the baby will affect all their activities together – feeding, bathing, nappy-changing, playing, etc. – and in this early state of mind, sensuousness plays a major role. An unhappy mother and baby will cling together to get comfort and support from each other; when this becomes an adhesive fusion with each other, their own identities become lost or confused. This failure to achieve self-identity was well exemplified in Mrs High's observations of autistic children which appear in Chapter 1.

The theoretical implications of the foregoing generalised descriptions will be discussed in the next chapter.

Part I

Childhood psychosis

Childhood psychosis is a state in which the child is massively out of touch with a reality that is shared by other children of the same age. In terms of this definition childhood autism is a psychotic condition.

In this book autistic syndromes are the main focus of my attention, but for purposes of differentiation and comparison another group of psychotic children in whom commonly agreed reality is obscured and evaded in ways other than by autism is discussed and investigated. This group of children is introduced and described in Chapter 3.

Chapter 3

Theoretical aspects of psychogenic childhood psychosis

For organic psychiatrists, the concept of 'psychogenic' childhood psychosis is a controversial one, for they see all childhood psychoses as inevitably being the result of organic damage. However, in the psychotic children I have treated by psychotherapy, no brain damage could be detected by the investigative techniques then available, so a psychogenic hypothesis seemed tenable.

In this connection, it is interesting that in a paper concerning an obviously organic type of childhood psychosis, four organicists have written: 'It is often difficult to distinguish those cases of childhood psychosis which are associated with organic conditions from those that apparently are not' (Corbett, *et al.*, 1977). This implies that these writers accept that, in some forms of childhood psychosis, an organic etiology is not apparent and a psychogenic one is a possibility. However, even in relation to the children in whom psychogenic factors seem to be the most operative, the cautious child psychotherapist would not rule out the possibility that such children may have minimal neurological impairments or metabolic imbalances which cannot be detected by the physical investigative techniques at present available. This is an area where co-operation with medical colleagues is indispensable. On first sight, it is difficult to know whether the 'triggers' for the development of psychosis have been predominantly organic or predominantly psychogenic. To some extent, the degree of organic damage will affect the degree to which psychotherapy can be effective. However, Sandra Stone (see her observations in Chapter 16) has witnessed substantial improvements as the result of psychotherapy with some predominantly organic children. She makes the important point that such children use psychological modes of protection to cope with their organic disabilities, and these can be affected by psychotherapy. However, the possibilities for the outcome of psychotherapy with the predominantly psychogenic children will not be restricted by a 'ceiling' set by organic impairments, although if the psychosis has gone on for too long it will have become a way of life that is usually impossible to modify.

CLASSIFICATION

In psychiatric schemes of classification, two main types of childhood psychosis are diagnosed: *childhood autism* and *childhood schizophrenia*. Such classification is on the basis of presenting appearance and behavioural characteristics. However, when investigated at the deeper level that is possible in psychotherapeutic treatment, we find that the psychotic children in whom psychogenic factors predominate have been overwhelmed by a tumult of feelings associated with awareness of bodily separateness. Bodily separateness is the prelude to individuation and self-identity. Both types of psychotic child have failed to achieve these developments satisfactorily.

When there has been pathological fusion between mother and baby, such as was discussed in the previous chapter, both mother and baby are in a hypersensitised state when, due to a variety of occurrences, awareness of their bodily separateness is suddenly forced upon them. Their hypersensitised state makes the experience particularly sharp and upsetting. When working with such children it becomes clear that, in a vulnerable state, they had felt pitch-forked into a dangerous outside world. For them, to be psychologically born meant being bombarded by painful sense impressions and flooded by turbulent feelings, for which their psychological-cum-physiological apparatus was not ready and for which, for various reasons that will be discussed later, the parental support and sheltering had not seemed adequate. As will be discussed in a later chapter, their psychological birth had been a psychological catastrophe. Their reaction had been to develop safe havens but, as a recovering previously autistic child expressed it, 'my sanctuary became my prison'. In this reaction, emotions became an anathema. Endogenous sensations were mustered to keep them out. Thus, both types of psychotic child had dealt with the trauma of bodily separateness (the 'psychotic depression', as Winnicott (1958) has called it) by the over-development of auto-sensual protections, but of different kinds. Let me differentiate between them.

(a)   For the *childhood autistics* these protections take the form of being enfolded by the autogenerated sensations of their *own* body. In terms of their mode of protection, I call these children *encapsulated* children.

(b)   The *childhood schizophrenics* generate a protective illusion of being enfolded inside a body other than their own (usually that of the mother), this other body scarcely being experienced as alive. Cultivating the illusion of sheltering inside someone else's body means that these children feel confused and entangled with other people. This is not a genuine relationship, although to the superficial observer it might look like one. In terms of their mode of protection, I call them *confusional entangled* children. (Margaret Mahler called them *symbiotic*.) With these children, since there is some awareness of bodily separateness, patchy and confused psychological development takes place. However, this is not the case with the childhood autistics, with whom psychological development has virtually stopped (except in those rare cases where it takes place along an isolated, restricted line).

Some children use a mixture of these two forms of protection. Also as treatment proceeds autistic encapsulated children may begin to use confusional entanglement.

A COMMON FACTOR IN CHILDHOOD PSYCHOSIS

Dr James Anthony (1958) attempted to find a significant diagnostic feature common to all types of childhood psychosis. To do this, he analysed the records of one hundred psychotic children seen by him at the Maudsley Hospital in London. After several abortive attempts with other features, and after careful trials, he decided that *autism* was the common feature he had been looking for. Anthony was using the term 'autism' to designate a set of processes which excluded reality, and so produced the clinical picture we term 'psychotic'. In the light of the way in which the use of the term 'autism' has been evolving over the intervening years since James Anthony wrote his paper, and the present tendency to restrict the use of this term to designate specific syndromes centred around childhood autism, I would suggest that it is more specific to say that overdeveloped *auto-sensuousness* is *the* common diagnostic feature in psychogenic childhood psychosis. In psychotherapy, when working at depth, we find that this over-development of auto-sensuousness has developed to deal with the endogenous 'psychotic depression' arising from traumatic experiences of bodily separateness.

In the early days of work with psychotic children, childhood autism and childhood schizophrenia were often not clearly distinguished from each other; this was the case, for example, with Dr Mildred Creak's well-known 'seven points of autism' (1961). However, as Sheila Spensley (1989) has pointed out, in recent years the differences between these two psychotic disorders have become increasingly recognised. Spensley writes:

Kanner, himself, was interested in the similarities between the withdrawal states of schizophrenia and those found in autism, and he even expressed the view that the two would ultimately be linked. Far from supporting this prediction subsequent research has, conversely, drawn attention increasingly to the many differences and contradictions existing between the two. That schizophrenia throws little light on autism has been firmly established. *However, it does not necessarily follow that autism cannot illuminate schizophrenia*

(Spensley, 1989, p. 237; emphasis added)

(In the above passage, Spensley is using the term 'autism' to designate specific psychotic syndromes centred around Early Childhood Autism.)

I have found that childhood autism *can* illuminate childhood schizophrenia, in that the auto-sensuousness of the encapsulated autistic child is much simpler than that of the confusional entangled schizophrenic-type child, whose auto-sensuality is much more confused. In the course of psychotherapy of the kind described in this book, the auto-sensuality of autistic children is laid bare, and its origins can be traced and deduced. This study of the origins of auto-sensuality highlights the role of primary sensuousness in the psychological development of human relationships.

PRIMARY SENSUOUSNESS

Psychotherapeutic work with autistic states in children indicates that the flux of sensations which constitute the infant's primary sense of being has two main head-streams. There is *sensuousness*, which is directed towards the body of other human beings who are experienced as responsive and alive; and there is *auto-sensuousness*, which is directed towards the subject's own body, or parts of other bodies experienced as if they were parts of the subject's body. As was indicated in Chapter 2, infant observation suggests that in normal development, from the beginning of life, the consciousness of the very young infant flits, in a flexible way, between these two states. But trouble is in store if auto-sensuousness becomes over-reactive and over-developed. Such abnormal over-reactive auto-sensuous developments mean that primary sensuousness is distracted away from becoming focused on succouring nurturant figures, and thus from developing relationships with them. The tragic state of autistic children brings home to us the importance to psychological development of primary co-operative sensuous relationships. One of the first co-operative interactions of the human infant is sucking at the breast (or bottle). This is the basis for later co-operative relationships. Feeding difficulties are invariably reported in the early infancy of autistic children, and later on they are 'faddy' feeders; for example, one feeding difficulty often observed is that of eating only soft foods and rejecting hard lumps. An outstanding characteristic of all autistic children is that they cannot or will not co-operate with anybody. Some of them are very malleable in a catatonic way, and will allow their limbs to stay in the position in which they are arranged by other people, or they will stay sitting in the position in which they have been put down. But this is not co-operation. Co-operation is not part of the pattern of their responses, for this requires some awareness of bodily separateness, and autistic children have developed auto-sensuous protections to avoid experiencing this.

This lack of co-operation is obviously a serious lack in terms of the ontogenetic development of these children, but it is a lack in evolutionary terms also. Human beings are tribal animals, and the ability to co-operate with other members of the tribe has been an essential feature in our successful evolution. At depth, we find that autistic children are 'red in tooth and claw', and have a dread of pre-conceptual rivals who seem similarly vicious. (In *Autism and Childhood Psychosis* (1972) I used the term 'innate forms' for such pre-conceptual in-built constellations.) The terror of these 'pre-conceptual rivals' is a devastating hindrance to their psychological development. Without the civilising support of the ability to co-operate with other members of their human 'tribe', these children are at the mercy of these in-built 'preconceptions' of primeval rivals who could never exist in reality, but who nevertheless exert a devastating influence which keeps autistic children trapped in a state of terror. Pathological auto-sensuousness develops to insulate them from these 'things' which seem to threaten their very existence. This means that they do not develop co-operation with nurturant figures, in particular with the suckling mother. Instead, their pathological auto-sensuous addiction to idiosyncratic, inanimate objects (to be exemplified and discussed in detail in later chapters) becomes a serious perversion, and is the source of many damaging deficits. These will now be discussed.

THE DEFICITS ARISING FROM OVER-DEVELOPED AUTO-SENSUOUSNESS

Stein (1967) and Fordham (1976) have suggested that autism is akin to auto-immune reactions on the part of the body to reject or annihilate alien tissues. They suggest that autistic children have reacted by rejecting or annihilating 'not-me' experiences which are felt to be alien and dangerous. This has damaged their development as individuals, in that to have a sense of being a 'me' requires some sense of the 'not-me'.

The over-development of auto-sensuousness is also damaging in another way, in that it blocks normal sensuous experiences with other people. This is as damaging to psychological development as is actual damage to the brain. Indeed, it may even damage the brain, for post-mortem investigation of apes who, as infants, had been barred from sensuous co-operative interactions with their mothers has revealed that neural dendrites in the cerebellum had become atrophied. Also, recent work is indicating that stress can produce hormones which damage the brain. This interaction between psychological and physiological factors in the states which are operative in childhood psychosis is one of the factors which makes diagnosis so difficult. As psychotherapists, our study concerns the psychogenic aspects of childhood psychosis. However, we must not be blind to the fact that neurological and hormonal factors may be lurking in the wings.

Now I will continue with the discussion concerning the deficits arising from the pathological over-development of auto-sensuousness.

Deficit in nurturing

Excessive auto-sensuous reactions prevent the child from receiving the nurturing which is almost invariably available, although in varying degrees. Since these children presented a picture of being unnurtured, some workers who observed them in the early days of studying autistic children thought that the parents had been cold and neglectful. My findings show that the actual situation is infinitely more complicated and subtle, and varies from child to child. Most autistic children have not experienced coldness, neglect or physical violence from their parents. For a great variety of reasons, different in each child and intrinsic to the constitutional nature of each, these children have retreated to the sensual fastness of their own bodies and have become insulated from outside influences. Inbuilt patterns with which they were endowed have become operative in a bizarre way unmodified by nurturing influences. Such children become more and more out of touch with any reality which they can share with other human beings. They become increasingly isolated in a state of insulation dominated by their idiosyncrasies and stereotypes. Thus, they present the clinical picture we term 'psychotic'.

As will be discussed in Chapter 11, it is not that these children are innately under-responsive, as some workers have alleged, nor, as other workers have suggested, are they over-responsive children who have been 'snubbed' by cold, unresponsive mothers. Rather, it seems that, for some of a large variety of reasons, pathological auto-sensual reactions have been set in train which either stopped or confused normal psychological development.

THE BLOCKING OR CONFUSING OF EARLY PSYCHOLOGICAL PROCESSES

Projection, introjection and projective identification

The normal processes of *projection* and *introjection* do not get underway in encapsulated autistic children, and are confused and hampered in confusional entangled schizophrenic-type children.

In autistic children, as the result of the encapsulation made by their auto-sensual manipulations, nothing can seem to get in or get out. These are 'bottled-up' children. When in psychotherapeutic treatment, as the result of the disturbance to their auto-sensual protections, the cork seems to come out of the bottle, there is a volcanic eruption of rage, terror, agony and despair in a seizure or a tantrum. With autistic children such eruption and evacuation takes place instead of the psychological process of projection; these take the form of physiological modes of discharge as in actual spitting, vomiting, sneezing, coughing, etc.

The schizophrenic-type children use projection as well as the physiological release of tension used by autistic children. These schizophrenic-type children were studied intensively by Melanie Klein, and it is from them that she learned about the process of *projective identification* and its ramifications (Klein, 1950; 1963). W. R. Bion (1962b) carried this thinking further and differentiated what he called 'hypertrophy of projective identification'. This was an over-reaction which was characteristic of schizophrenic functioning. He differentiated this psychotic form of projective identification from the processes of projective identification as used by normal and neurotic individuals. He showed that normal projective identification was a non-verbal form of communication, in that feelings the subject wanted to communicate were evoked in other people, so that they could understand and identify with them. In everyday, non-technical language we refer to this as 'empathy'. By humane experimental work, Dr Peter Hobson (1986) has shown very convincingly that autistic children are not capable of empathy. This is to be expected, for the possibility of functioning in an empathic way requires some sense of bodily separateness. This lack of bodily separateness and of empathy also means that projection and projective identification do not get under way.

Adhesive equation and adhesive identification

To avoid awareness of bodily separateness, autistic children use a process that I have called 'adhesive equation'. This is a delusory state in which the child feels stuck to and 'at one' with the mother in a pathological unchanging way. (The normal state of 'flowing-over-at-oneness' does not have this rigid, unchanging quality.) Adhesive equation obviates awareness of bodily separateness, but it seriously stunts the child's psychological growth.

The schizophrenic-type children who have a modicum of awareness of bodily separateness, and thus a capacity for empathetic identification with other people, use the delusion of being stuck to and identified with other people in order to *diminish* awareness of bodily separateness. At the end of Esther Bick's paper (1986), Meltzer has called this process 'adhesive identification'; Esther Bick (1986) calls it 'adhesive identity'. All these pathological panic-stricken adhesive processes obstruct the development of *primary identification*.

Primary identification

In a letter to me, Dr James Grotstein brought this process to my attention. He wrote as follows:

> I believe that the concept of primary identification, described by Freud [1921a: 1921b] but not dealt with by anyone except Fairbairn [1941] constitutes a very important idea. In my conception, it has to do with an outgrowth of an idea by Heinz Lichtenstein [1961] about the identity theme of the infant which is inextricably and forever bound up with its relationship with its mother.

In the same letter Grotstein also wrote:

> Marasmic children, those that have faced infantile catastrophe, especially those from foundling homes, suffer from a deficit of *primary identification*. I have the notion that the same is true for what you are stating about autistic children.

I see primary identification as being associated with what I have called 'rootedness'.

Rootedness

When they begin to draw, borderline and psychotic patients often draw plants and trees without roots. They also say such things as, 'I am cut off from my roots'. In Chapter 16 Sandra Stone describes her work with Sam who, on one occasion, wanted to stand on her feet in order to get roots. (Such clinical work with child patients has led me to prefer the term 'rootedness' to 'bonding', a term which is often borrowed from the ethologists to refer to elemental processes of connection with the mother.) In common parlance, we often speak of a baby as 'rooting' for the nipple of the breast, and clinical work with autistic children has demonstrated to me that the nipple (or its substitute experienced in terms of an in-built preconception of a nipple-like sensation) is the primary focus of the infant's early sensuality. (See the clinical material on John in *Autism and Childhood Psychosis* (Tustin, 1972) and in *Autistic Barriers in Neurotic Patients* (Tustin, 1987).) Sensuous connection with the nipple of the breast seems to replace the ante-natal umbilical connection with the placenta of the mother. Clinical work which is informed by the *infantile transference* indicates that the constellation of nipple and tongue working rhythmically together with mouth and breast sets the feeling of rootedness in train. As well as demonstrating this situation to us, the infantile transference enables the 'unrooted' (or 'uprooted') patient to become rooted. This basic sense of being rooted sets the scene for the development of a sense of identity, security and self-confidence.

Lacking this sense of rootedness, the child's psychic life is dominated by feelings of 'nothingness'; the child feels unsupported and let down – 'falling endlessly', as Winnicott (1958) so well expresses it. This is experienced in a bodily way as a 'black hole'. (This black hole where the nipple of the breast should have been is tellingly exemplified in the Henry Moore sculpture shown in Plate 2.1 and discussed in Chapter 2.) Clinical work has shown that this sense of having a black hole arises from too sudden and too sharp awareness of bodily separateness from the mothering person. (As witness John (Tustin, 1972; 1987).) This frustration arouses paroxysms of rage, panic, despair and anguish which, finding no means of expression, are bottled-up and implode to make the black hole (as stated earlier, this is Winnicott's 'psychotic depression' (1958)). The tragedy is that this awareness comes so suddenly that such children do not have time to adjust to it, and they feel that they have no help in coping with it. (The analytic situation gives them time and help.)

Awareness of bodily separateness has been very little investigated, yet it is a crucial part of human development. It is an essential prelude to primary identification. The catastrophic effect of an undue sense of having a black hole is that, in later life, it results in suicidal feelings of lack and loneliness. (Those fortunate individuals who have grown adequate psychic roots will experience the *aloneness* of having a separate identity, but this stimulates the urge to relate to other human beings, and so is distinguished from *loneliness*.) Shocked, panic-stricken fusion of mother and baby, such as was described in Chapter 2, shuts out awareness of the mothering person as an alive presence with whom to become rooted and with whom to identify.

THE BACKGROUND PRESENCE OF PRIMARY IDENTIFICATION

In his letters Grotstein developed his ideas further by saying that, at one time, he used to speak of 'the background *object* of primary identification', but that in more recent years because of his 'growing dissatisfaction' with the term 'object', he has renamed it 'the background *presence* of primary identification'. I found this phrase illuminating in relation to psychotic children. A background presence with whom to connect and identify is just what they have lacked. I am also sympathetic to Grotstein's dissatisfaction with the term 'object' as it is commonly used in psychoanalytical writings viz 'object relations' as applied to living human relationships. When writing about the pathology of autistic children who use the alive mother as an inanimate object, to use the phrase 'object relations' to apply to their relationships with alive people becomes confusing. Grotstein's phrase 'the background presence of primary identification' prevents this confusion. It also corrects the undue concretisation of some psychoanalytical formulations and brings into focus that both types of psychotic child have lacked the sense of there being a living presence with whom co-operative interchanges could take place. An inanimate object, which is how they have experienced the nurturant figures of their early infancy, does not give them this possibility. It does not make them feel safe.

A sense of safety

Dr Grotstein wrote this letter to me as the result of my misattribution to him of the phrase 'the background presence of safety'. He ends his letter by saying, 'I am perfectly happy with the idea of "The Background Presence of Safety".' This background presence of safety is also something which both autistic and schizophrenic children have lacked and have compensated for with their auto-sensual modes of protection. This background feeling of safety would seem to come from sensuous rooting connections with the suckling mother, combined with the ambience of confidence and security surrounding this and other nurturant experiences, and also emanating from them. In this connection it is important to remember that, at first, it is not the milk that seems important to the baby but the sensuous connection with the nipple (or its substitute), which attracts the infant to the breast. Nature baits the hook, as it were, so that a life-giving activity is sought after. Work with autistic children highlights the importance of the nipple of the breast in this primary life-seeking situation.

The early importance of the nipple has many ramifications in later situations – for example, sensuous experiences with the constellations of 'nipple in mouth' seem to affect such later sensuous constellations as 'penis in vagina' and 'faecal stool in anus'. If early infantile development becomes aberrant at the suckling stage, and unresponsive, inanimate auto-sensuous artefacts (such as will be described in later chapters) become preferred, then future developments are in jeopardy. As Bion (1962b) so well says, the 'good-enough mother' (to use Winnicott's phrase) 'mediates sanity to the infant at the breast as well as life-giving milk'. She also gives the infant the confidence that it is safe to be a separate being – to become a 'me'.

A sense of 'me-ness'

The blocking or blurring of awareness of the outside world by auto-sensual manipulations causes other devastating deficits. For one thing, as was stated earlier, to become a 'me' there has to be awareness of the 'not-me'. But if awareness of the 'not-me' is insufferable, then awareness of 'me' is not born. Awareness of 'me-ness' seems to be associated with the sense of having a skin.

The sense of having a skin

The psychotic child's early pathological fusion with the mothering person means that awareness of bodily separateness is not experienced in slow and manageable degrees, as is the case in normal development; it comes suddenly and traumatically. This makes such infants feel vulnerable and exposed. The autistic reaction is to seem to cover their body with an autogenerated 'armour' of sensuous protection or, as in the schizophrenic-type children, to seek protection inside another body. In a meticulously detailed paper which combines infant observation with clinical material, Dr Esther Bick (1968) has discerned how such infants form what she calls a 'second skin' to protect their vulnerability. In a striking example, she describes how a baby she observed developed a particularly hard and strong musculature in order to withstand traumatic situations. In another paper, which again combined detailed observations of a baby with detailed clinical material from a psychotic child patient, Bick (1986) points out the importance of the subjective sense of having a *skin* in order to feel that the bodily parts which otherwise might seem to threaten to spill away felt contained within the body outlines. At the end of her paper, Dr Donald Meltzer (Bick, 1986) relates Bick's findings to Bion's work on the need for a 'container'.

W. R. Bion (1962a) has described how the mental capacity of the mother is important in helping her child to contain and cope with the stresses and strains of life. Through her maternal experience and understanding (her 'alpha function' as Bion has termed it), the mother transforms the raw elements of her child's naïve feelings (the 'beta elements' as Bion has called them) into assimilable form so that the child grows in the understanding of and the ability to cope with himself, with life and with the people in it. In William Blake's terms, she helps in the transformation of innocence into experience. In this, the creative interactions of the parents are important. Bick's thesis is that as the child feels 'contained' in this way, he develops the sense of having a skin which protects and holds him together. In the seminal work *Le Moi Peau*, Dr Didier Anzieu (1986) has also written about the importance of the sense of having a skin in giving the child a sense of 'me-ness', as outlined against the 'not-me-ness' of the outside world.

Objectively, we know that the skin receives and modulates sense impressions and that this is a very important function, but the infant has no such objective knowledge. From work with autistic children, it has seemed to me that when they begin to sense that they have a skin, they feel that they are inside something which makes them feel safe. It also makes them feel that there is a surface where their body comes to an end and where the outside world begins. Thus there is somewhere outside themselves into which unpleasant feelings can be pushed away. Thus, projection can begin. Before their autistic pathology is moderated they fear that their skin is not firmly attached to their body, and that it can peel away. Thus, they fear being bathed or showered. Also, they fear hair-washing in case their hair will be washed away.

Lacking an inner sense of creative conjunction, on the model of 'mouth with nipple', such children lack the creative notion of *growing*. Operating in their manipulative terms, they feel that their limbs are stuck onto them and can easily become detached. This makes them afraid of hand-washing, feet-washing, and bathing and showering. The notion of growing can dawn on them as a reassuring revelation. I shall never forget the occasion when the autistic patient I have called John came into the therapy room after having seen a baby feeding at the breast, saying in tones of astonished wonderment, 'The red button *grows* on the breast'. It was an important turning point in his recovery. The notion that the skin *grows* on their body and cannot peel away is a similar reassuring revelation. It would seem feasible that the feeling that babies have about their skin is dependent, in some measure, on the quality of holding (both mental and physical holding) that they have experienced with the mothering person. With the sense of having a skin, they develop the notion that as well as there being 'me' and 'not-me', there is an inside to their body which is separated from outside happenings. Bion has written about this in terms of an exo- and endoskeletal bodily structure (1963). I would suggest that this sense of having an inner container links the 'me' and the 'not-me' together in that it makes possible such activities as unconscious phantasizing and conscious fantasizing, thinking, playing, and the like. In terms of his approach, Winnicott (1958) has called this a 'transitional area'.

Unconscious phantasies

Prior to the development of the sense of being a container separated from the 'not-me' outside world, most autistic children seem to lack those rudiments of psychological functioning which psychoanalysts refer to as 'unconscious phantasies'. However, in-built pre-conceptions as described by Bion (1962a) are present. These are the most basic psychological elements. They form the seed-bed for unconscious phantasies, as well as affecting the more developed activities such as conscious fantasies and thoughts. All this will be illustrated by the clinical material presented in Chapter 17. By being contained the child feels that he has become a container. In therapy with young autistic children it is fascinating to see the 'birth' of these basic psychological ideas.

The genesis of self-hood

The very early processes which have just been described are essential to the genesis of self-hood. They have been abnegated in autistic children, and confused and blurred in schizophrenic children. To express this in a picturesque way, we might say that the psychological *marasmic* children stare emptily into a void, the *autistic* children avert their gaze from a 'black hole', whereas the *schizophrenic* children look through murky windows at a scene of chaos and disorder.

Esther Bick (1986) advises us that: '. . . such patients in analysis require a slow and firmly contained process with prolonged working through of each step forward in development' (p. 286). Psychotherapy with them requires that we firmly but gently establish the necessary limitations and boundaries to make this work possible.

THE ESTABLISHMENT OF LIMITATIONS AND BOUNDARIES

All children find that the 'not-me' outside world that will not let them have their own way is a source of frustration and disillusionment. Indeed, the story of the Garden of Eden and the subsequent 'fall' symbolises the story of the disillusionment which arises from the disappointment of infantile omnipotent expectations. For psychotic children this has been intolerable. By auto-sensual manoeuvres they make up a world that is more to their liking, but this becomes a snare and a delusion. Lacking a normal sensuous co-operative relationship with the sources of their nurture, such children do not transform sensations into percepts and concepts, and the basis for cognitive and emotional development is not established, or is only established very insecurely. In Ogden's term (1989), a 'sensory floor' is not laid down. In terms of Didier Anzieu's formulations, they have not developed 'psychic envelopes' (1990).

At this point the reader may think that what is being implied here is that, lacking sensuous experience, psychotic children need extra sensuous gratification in treatment. In the early days of psychotherapy with such children, the work was often based on this misconception. For example, in the 1950s in many units for autistic children, the children were treated with a great deal of indulgence and allowed a great deal of sensuous gratification. They were given lollipops and raisins and chocolate bits and allowed to wander from room to room in the clinic with very few limits being set as to what they were allowed to do. It was thought that this would compensate them for the sensuous satisfactions they had missed as the result of having the cold, 'refrigerator' mothers they were believed to have had. This was much too simplistic a view; on deeper investigation, it is found that although sensuous gratification actually comes from the outside, it is most often experienced by the children in an auto-sensual way, as if it had been brought about by their own manipulations.

To develop a 'me-skin' these children need outside boundaries to be established in a firm, consistent way. We need to talk to the children about what they are doing and to show that we understand and can help them with the terrors which gave rise to their recoil and retreat. After many temper tantrums about the frustration occasioned by the limitations and restrictions of these boundaries, and if the children are held with firmness and understanding through these important crises, they gradually begin to accept that there is a 'not-me' outside world which does not always accommodate their needs and wishes, but also that they are protected from the terrors which this gives rise to. This is a lesson we all have had to learn, but for psychotic children it has been a particularly difficult one. This may be due to constitutional factors, but these will have been affected by features in their early nurturing. Such interactions between nature and nurture will be discussed as the book proceeds. Let me now sum up the main features of psychogenic auto-sensuousness.

PSYCHOGENIC AUTO-SENSUOUSNESS

This is a pathological sensation-dominated state in which attention is focused almost exclusively on endogenous bodily rhythms and sensations. In this unregulated state, later sensuous developments are precipitated out of phase, so that sensuality becomes eroticised and inappropriately directed. Objects in the outside world may be attended to (often, as it seems, intently and in minute detail), but on close observation it becomes clear that these are experienced as being part of the body or very closely akin to it. People and things outside are scarcely used or seen as having a separate existence. They are experienced as an extension of bodily activity and in terms of the sensuous experience of them, particularly the sensuous experience of touch. Over-developed auto-sensuousness (or autism) characterises a state in which experience is not differentiated or objectivised to any appreciable extent.

In this state, massive automatic reactions are set in train which avoid or blur awareness of the upsetting 'not-me' mother (as the first represent-ative of the outside world). These auto-sensual reactions generate illusions of fusion or confusion with a mother who is experienced as a part of the child's body. The activities arising from these auto-sensual reactions become idiosyncratic because modifications from outside influ-ences and from other people are minimal. They also become rigid and intractable to a damaging degree. Thus, the pathology of psychogenic psychosis is set in train.

This means that obviating or entangling the 'not-me' mother in order to feel that everything is arranged in terms of comfort-making auto-sensuality becomes more important than developing the skills to control and manage their own potentialities, which will enable them to adjust to, and to use the possibilities of, the 'not-me' outside world. At a basic level, this fundamentally affects the child's relationships with other people. Instead of the 'not-me' becoming a stimulus which facilitates co-operation, learning and other on-going psychological activities, it becomes a focus for negation or confusion.

Negation and *confusion* are the two main types of reaction which come into operation in the service of this recoil from the 'not-me'. In the forthcoming chapters, the type of auto-sensual reaction which predominates will be used as a means of differentiating between psychogenic psychotic children, so that their particular needs can be met and necessary treatment measures and possibilities for outcome can be assessed. In treatment, we often find that the autistic negation has developed to avoid confusion and that, as the autism is modified, this confusion is exposed. The child then appears to be pre-schizophrenic.

Thus, to differentiate between these two types of protective mechanisms clarifies and facilitates psychotherapeutic treatment. This is the focus of the following chapters.

Chapter 4

Auto-sensuous aspects of psychogenic childhood psychosis

In autistic children, primary sensuousness has been disturbed. Sensuousness is closely linked to hormonal functioning in that it affects and is affected by it. Thus, hormonal dysfunction can be either a concomitant of the disorder or a precipitant. O'Gorman (1967) relates all autism to hormonal dysfunctioning. This hypothesis seems too sweeping but in some children it may have been a determining factor. There is much to be unravelled here that is not within my competence. Psychogenic factors are my professional concern and, like the cobbler, I must keep to my 'last'.

However, we need to be aware that, in some forms of childhood autism, psychological and physiological factors can be so closely intertwined that it is difficult to say which set in motion the vicious circle of over-developed auto-sensuousness. Infants with neurological impairments are likely to be more difficult to nurture, and are thus more liable to fall into bottomless pits and to show autistic features. In others, nurturant lacks can have occurred very early (even *in utero*, for example, as the result of toxaemia), and thus are indistinguishable from constitutional defects. Obviously, great discretion needs to be exercised in assessing whether an autistic child is likely to benefit from psychotherapy. However, the few autistic children who have recovered spontaneously, and those who have benefited from educational and psychotherapeutic techniques, must have found some way around any physiological and neurological impairments which may have existed.

In some cases the catastrophic breakdown of the infant's sensuous expectations may have been inevitable, for they were expectations which no human mother could satisfy. In other cases, it may have been that, for some of a great number of reasons, possibilities which should have been there were not present, or some children may have had too much sensuous gratification so that, when frustration inevitably came, they had not developed the inner organisation to cope with it. The detailed steps by which an infant becomes autistic are different in each case. Former slapdash diagnoses which invariably blamed early maternal nurturing are to be deplored. Also, since sensuousness affects metabolic functioning and is affected by it, no form of childhood psychosis can be attributed to purely psychogenic causes. At this elemental level, it is difficult to separate organic, metabolic and psychogenic factors, so it seems to me regrettable that the psychodynamicists and the organicists should be in opposite corners snarling at each other. The detailed records of psychotherapeutic work with these children might be useful to the organicists to see where to put their efforts, and similarly the organicists might help the psychotherapists to be more cautious in their conclusions.

In psychotherapy we deal with psychogenic factors and it has been my experience that certain autistic children can be helped by psychotherapy which modifies their autism. An important part of this modification is the understanding that the autistic child has encountered the 'not-me' in an unduly hurtful way. He has encountered the 'slings and arrows of outrageous fortune' (as Shakespeare called them), or 'impingements' (as Winnicott has termed them), in a state in which his neuro-mental structure was not sufficiently developed to cope with the strain.

As a result, he developed auto-sensuous reactions to protect the psychosomatic core of incipient self which was essential to his survival as a psychological being. But this resulted in the development of a 'false self', as described by Winnicott (1958). To help the child to abandon the fake artefacts such as autistic and confusional objects, which will be discussed in later chapters, and to get in touch with the authentic core of self at the centre of his being, is the major aim of treatment. As a result of this, the child is enabled to develop a core of sensuous integrations leading to an inner life of dreams, fantasies and symbolic activities. This is a long and difficult process which, in the light of our knowledge so far, is only possible for some children. But, as insights increase, more and more such children are being helped.

The organicists have a wide range of investigatory techniques available to them, and they have concentrated on diagnosis more than have the psychodynamicists, who have been more concerned with treatment. However, it seems to me that the time has now come for an attempt to be made to classify, in terms of treatment needs and prognosis, those psychotic children in whom psychogenic factors seem most operative. An attempt was made to do this in my earlier book *Autism and Childhood Psychosis* (Tustin, 1972). This new attempt is based on further and deeper experience. Although it has features in common with my previous attempt, certain significant revisions have been made.

BASIS FOR PSYCHOGENIC ASSESSMENT

The organicists seem to think of psychotherapy as being the abreactive technique of 'play therapy'. They do not realise that there is a growing body of psychotherapists who use a much more disciplined and rigorous technique than is usually implied by the term 'play therapy'. This disciplined psychotherapeutic technique can be as useful for investigating the psychogenic elements of psychosis as the physical techniques have been in investigating organic impairments.

The essence of this more disciplined type of psychotherapy is that the child is seen individually for a set period of time in the same room at the same times each week and that, in so far as is practically possible, the arrangement of the furniture in the room is kept the same from session to session. Each child has his own drawer of extremely simple toys to which no other child has access, the drawer being locked at the end of the session. This simple unchanging background provides a kind of projective test which enables the therapist to compare the individual responses of the children. The way in which the child uses the contents of his drawer also provides a useful indication of the use, misuse or non-use the child makes of provisions from sources outside himself. It is also extremely illuminating to see the child's responses to the inevitable limitations that have to be imposed in terms of his own safety and that of the contents of the room and the therapist's own person, which he has to share with other children. As such, the therapeutic situation is a research laboratory as well as a stringent treatment setting.

Workers who use treatment material for such research purposes need to have been trained to make detailed observations and to reflect deeply upon what they observe. This detailed observation is not an easy matter and needs practice and training (Bick, 1964). Infant and young child observation is an excellent preparation. Interpretation of the observation does not only depend on logical deduction but involves the capacity to empathise with the child without losing one's own identity. It also involves being able to observe with 'fresh eyes' and to free oneself from theoretical preconceptions and affiliations. One's loyalty should be to 'understanding' rather than to some particular doctrinal school. However, to be realistic, in the early days of working as a therapist, the protection of a professional training is a necessity for most of us. This means that there needs to be commitment to the theoretical 'school' of our choice, involving acceptance of the disciplines and limitations which this implies. As time goes by, we find that we can observe other phenomena than the ones we have been trained to observe. In this, the discipline of making detailed observations, which are recorded carefully and compared with those of other people, is what keeps us from making wild assertions. Thus, it will be seen that though the tools for physical investigation may be expensive in terms of material equipment and finance, those for psychogenic investigation are expensive in terms of time, patience and the capacity to bear extreme states of feeling.

CURRENT SCHEMES OF CLASSIFICATION

In the scheme of classification to be presented later, the type of pathological protective manoeuvre which predominates will be used as a basis for differentiating between the various types of childhood psychosis. This classification does not aim to replace the schemes in current use, but is specifically evolved for psychoanalytic therapists who are contemplating working with a psychotic child along lines similar to those described in this book.

The schemes of classification in most general use are those of Rimland (1964) and Mahler (1958). Although based on different premises, they both differentiate the Kanner-type of childhood psychosis from a type of childhood psychosis which has much in common with adult schizophrenia. Mahler distinguishes between autistic and symbiotic psychoses. Hers is a developmental hypothesis, in that she sees a stage of autism preceding a symbiotic stage in infantile development. (At the end of her life Mahler abandoned this notion of an early autistic stage, but she had no opportunity to write about it.) Thus, she implies that the age of onset determines the type of psychosis manifested by the child. This does seem to be operative in some cases, but in other cases Rimland's hypothesis also seems to be relevant. Rimland (who does not recognise psychogenic psychosis) distinguishes between autistic (Kanner-type) and schizophrenic children. He makes the suggestion that the features distinguishing the two groups would seem to be reminiscent of those for Kretschmer's (1936) categories of *cyclothymes* (the autistic group) and *schizothymes* (the schizophrenic group). This makes sense of my own clinical experience, since the children he would designate as autistic manifest manic-depressive mood swings as they come out of their autism during psychotherapy.

Tischler and Stroh (personal communication) grouped psychotic children into autistic, schizophrenic and sufferers from Stroh's Traumatic Psychosis (these are children who have been battered from early infancy onwards, and have seen violence between their parents). In reviewing his years of work with the parents of fifty psychotic children, Tischler (1979) found that the parents of the children in these three groups also fell into related categories. Parents in each category had marked common features in terms of personalities, life-histories, marriages and infant-rearing practices. There were also marked differences between the categories. The parents, particularly the mothers of autistic children had manic-depressive trends, and the mothers of schizophrenic children had schizophrenic tendencies. Thus, mother and child would seem to be the same personality type. Of course, a theory based on personality types does not exclude developmental hypotheses. It does, however, make the age of onset of less importance in diagnosis.

In some instances, theories about childhood psychosis have been put forward that are based on the type of psychotic child the particular worker has encountered. These theories have been given general relevance as applying to all types of psychotic child. For example, those who have worked a great deal with environmentally deprived children tend to propose that psychosis arises from actual nurturant deficiencies. Some childhood psychosis does arise from this, but in other children it has arisen as the result of their not being able to use the nurturing which was available for them to use. Again, many factors, including such constitutional factors as neurological and metabolic predispositions, bring about this state of affairs. The situation is complicated by the fact that these constitutional factors in the child intertwine with constitutional factors in the parents and with environmental happenings. Other workers have attributed the onset of childhood autism to depression in the mother in the child's early infancy. This certainly seems to have been the case with many of these children. Some workers have encountered the confusional, schizophrenic-type child, in whom the mechanisms of *disintegration* and *splitting* are especially operative. They have not encountered the *unintegration* of the Kanner-type child.

Another difficulty in the psychoanalytic field seems to be that findings concerning adult psychosis, such as those of Bion (1962a and b), Kohut (1971), Laing (1971) and Rosenfeld (1950), have been applied to childhood psychotics, without the realisation that the 'unintegration' which is characteristic of Kanner-type children does not occur in adults in the unmodified form in which it occurs in young children.

Another source of confusion is that amongst both organicists and psychodynamicists there has been a failure to realise that the same psychotic picture can arise as the result of very different precipitating circumstances and reactions. In the organic psychoses, the organic handicap will have prevented the child from making adequate use of early nurturing, so that pathological protective compensations will have come into play. These, combined with the neurological impairment, result in the child being grossly out of touch with reality. Thus, organic factors can lead to the same external appearance as psychogenic factors.

It is only by deep and careful physical and psychological investigations, which go behind the superficial presenting appearances, that useful classifications in terms of treatment possibilities can be made. In such work it is important that both organicists and psychodynamicists should co-operate and be able to communicate with each other. At the moment, at least in England, this is rarely the case. This has hampered the making of more precise and refined differential diagnoses between the various types of psychotic children. At the moment, in many institutions for their care, they are all 'lumped together' indiscriminately with very little distinction being made between the type of autism in which organic features predominate and those in which psychogenic factors seem most operative. This has had serious consequences in terms of expectations for their recovery. Psychotherapy is not effective to the same degree with organic factors as with psychogenic ones and, indeed, may not be effective at all. If it is helpful, results can often be seen very quickly, until the inevitable ceiling set by the organic damage is reached. As the result of this lack of distinction between the obvious 'organic' children and the apparently 'psychogenic' children, the erroneous conclusion is often reached that no autistic child can be helped to normal functioning.

This has not been my own experience, nor that of certain workers, both educationists and psychotherapists, dotted here and there throughout the world. In this first part of the present book, a scheme of classification, in terms of psychogenic factors which have impeded normal development, will be presented. It will be suggested that there are two main types of pathological reaction by which the psychotic child has avoided 'not-me' reality, and that these have to be understood if the child is to be helped to normal functioning. These are: (a) autogenerated encapsulation reactions, which shut out the 'not-me' outside world, and (b) confusional entangling reactions, which blur but do not completely shut out the 'not-me' outside world.

The next two chapters will give detailed descriptions of these two types of evasive reaction by which impingements from the outside world are made into 'me' or, are diluted to a degree which makes them feel sufficiently part of 'me' to seem manageable.

Chapter 5

Autogenerated encapsulation

EXTERNAL APPEARANCE OF ENCAPSULATION CHILDREN

These are the children whose psychological disorder is akin to the Kanner syndrome of Early Infantile Autism. (These are the children described in Chapter 1.) Almost invariably, these children have well-formed limbs and beautiful, 'other-wordly' faces. They often have such a translucent skin that they look like 'fairy children'. Their body movements are nimble and graceful, although they may walk on their toes. Sometimes they are fearlessly agile. For example, one child I observed at the Putnam Center, in Boston, Mass., could walk a tightrope placed very high from the ground. Although they may be clumsy at first, as treatment progresses, their fingers become very deft in that they can perform very fine finger movements. They have a feather-light touch and they may tap surfaces in this way. When touched or picked up, their bodies are usually stiff and often they do not 'body-mould', as Mahler terms it (although a few of them may do this).

They are fascinated by mechanisms and will look at the works of an object which they refuse to use. They spin certain objects obsessively, and they take hard toys (like metal trains and cars) to bed with them instead of the soft cuddly toys enjoyed by normal children. They are usually faddy about food. They will often use another person's hand to open doors or even to spin objects.

They are often mute and not toilet-trained. They avoid looking at people and may turn their heads to one side to avoid doing so. They are untestable by the usual intelligence test procedures and are often thought to be either deaf or mentally defective, although the tester often has the uneasy feeling that there is good intelligence lurking behind the child's seeming lack of capacity.

In these children psychological development has been halted at an early age because auto-sensuous reactions have been set in train which bring about the delusion of fusion with a hard sensation-giving object. Objects in the outside world which are idiosyncratic to the child himself may be used in an obsessive way to bolster this delusion. (These *autistic objects* will be discussed in detail in Chapter 10.) Hand and body stereotypes are also used. Outwardly the child seems cut off from contact with the parents and with the outside world.

To deal with the terrors associated with awareness of bodily separateness from the sensation-mother, autistic delusions of being encapsulated are set in motion. (These terrors will be discussed in more detail in later chapters.) The sensations aroused by their own bodily substances and movements bring about this delusion of encapsulation. There are two types of encapsulation: one is global and the other is encapsulation of segments. I refer to those children who use global encapsulation as *shell-type children*. This is a primary protective manoeuvre.

SHELL-TYPE CHILDREN

In this type of encapsulation, the child seems to us to be in a shell in which, in a global state of unintegration and undifferentiation, he lies dormant, waiting for more propitious conditions for his development. Later, when he can talk, he may tell us about feeling that he was in a shell, or he may draw it. These are the children described by Beata Rank as being 'a little sleeping prince or princess waiting to grow up' (personal communication). I suspect that the children described by Rimland who have recovered spontaneously, or those who have recovered after courageous and marathon efforts by their families, such as Ellie in *The Siege* (Park, 1972) and Ann in *For the Love of Ann* (Copeland, 1973), were this type of child. Preliminary assessment sessions with such a child, taken from my own notebooks, will now be presented.

SHELL-TYPE CHILD (PRIMARY ENCAPSULATION)

This is the record of my first interview with a shell-type encapsulated child, who was also a Kanner-type autistic child. Before seeing John I met the parents.

> Mother had large grey eyes and a pale face with no make-up. She had straight fairish hair. It was cut in a cap shape round her head. It is not abundant hair and adds to the waif-like impression she gives. This is also conveyed by her body, which is slight. On several occasions she said things to indicate that she is protected and cherished. For example, I said something about its being cold, upon which she wrapped her mink three-quarter-length coat around herself and said, 'I'm not cold in this.' As she did this, in spite of the mink, I was reminded of the Little Match Girl who warmed herself in the glow of a match.
>
> Later, at the door, father was very concerned to protect mother

with an umbrella as they began to walk to the car which they had left some distance down the road. It was only raining very slightly and mother said delightedly, 'He thinks I'm made of sugar.'

However, as I came to know mother better she has emerged as a person of considerable competence. Her movements are deft and efficient. She knits and sews in the waiting-room. I have the impression that she runs her house very efficiently and likes doing it. Her speech is extremely clear and she has an obvious feeling for words. She began to write poems after John started treatment. She has shown herself to be an accurate and astute observer.

The impression she gave me in the first interview, and this has been confirmed by later encounters, is of a sensitive girl who is very quick, intelligent and intuitive. However, underneath this I sensed a steel-like obstinacy to keep things arranged within the orbit of her prearranged schemes. It has emerged that she had a deprived childhood, the details of which I will not give here because of betraying confidentiality.

Father was a good-looking and extremely courteous man. It has emerged that he is very obsessional; for example, he has to go round the pillar-box several times before he can post a letter. He had a typical upper-middle-class upbringing.

What the parents told me about John

John did not speak. He was not toilet-trained either by day or by night. He did not eat normally. He only took liquid nourishment. He would only eat soft things and rejected hard lumps. He took a metal train to bed with him and did not use 'cuddly' toys. He was flat and unresponsive.

If father took him to the park he did not play with the other children. He seemed more interested in what made the roundabout work. He would stoop down and look underneath to see the mechanism. He also seemed to like pushing it around for the other children to have a ride rather than having a ride himself.

He loved mechanical things and would sit for hours spinning the wheels of a toy car round and round. He was very sensitive to textures and tapped smooth surfaces.

If he was taught one movement he would do it to everything in an obsessively rigid way. For example, with great labour father had taught him to throw a ball up and down. After that he threw every object he was given up and down.

He was very interested in eyes. He would close and touch his own eyes. He would examine his mother's and father's eyes. He had scratched the eyes of his younger sister. He poked at dolls' eyes. If his mother drew a face he put long lines down from the eyes. He seemed to confuse his own mouth with his mother's.

Although he didn't talk he seemed interested in the mechanisms of speech and would go and put his hands against the face of a person who was talking as though he were feeling the muscles which were being used.

He always used someone else's hand to open doors.

Early history

He was born in hospital and mother was very unhappy there. The baby was a lazy sucker. She wanted very much to breast-feed him but couldn't get it established although she had a lot of milk. She said with irritation that the nurses fed the baby with a bottle at night and so he wasn't hungry during the day. She said that he never opened his eyes for a fortnight and this was so different from his sister who was born two years later.

After the hospital she went to the house of her mother-in-law, where there were a great many interfering relatives so that she found it difficult to get together with her baby.

Mother described how she had spent hours with John trying to get him to hold a pencil. She put it in his fingers and put her hand round his hand and moved his hand over the paper.

I suggested an observation period to see whether I felt I could do something.

First interview

John is three years eight months. He is like mother. He has grey eyes but they are dead and look like dull stones. He has fair hair and delicate skin. He looks ethereal and moves with lightness and delicacy.

He left his mother without a backward glance, but stared intently at the lights as we went downstairs.

As soon as we reached the therapy-room door something happened that surprised me. His limp, seemingly inert little body momentarily came to life. I didn't say anything at the door, but, as soon as we had gone through the open door, as though he had known beforehand the position of the toys, his gaze was riveted on them and he went straight to them as if drawn by a magnet. The rest of the room might have been in darkness. He didn't seem to see it. It was as if the toys were lit up by a spotlight so that he spotted them immediately and made a bee-line straight towards them. I was surprised then, and I am surprised now as I record this, at the sudden change from deadness and inertness to momentary aliveness and purpose. It had something in common with the way he had looked at the lights as we went downstairs. I saw this as a hopeful sign. (There is usually some chink in the autistic encapsulation. It is rarely absolutely total.)

First of all he took the doll out of the cradle (this was not the top thing). Then he took the bus and turned the wheels round. After doing this for a short time, he took out the humming-top. He used this quite correctly although he couldn't get it to spin because he pressed it on to the soft couch. He played with this for a long time. He was half-averted from me and did not turn to look at me. He would lift it from the couch and tap it so that it spun round and then press it on the couch so that it went round just a little bit, but would not spin properly.

After a time he rocked the doll's cradle and then touched the doll's eyes.

He then took out the plastic figure of a man that is fixed on to a plastic car. He looked at the man and tapped him.

He then rocked the doll's cot and then played again with the humming-top.

He then gently ran the bus along the couch and looked inside at the mechanism. He took out the tractor with the large red wheels and spun the wheels round and round. He then turned back to the humming-top and seemed to look at the patterns on the top. He then tapped it and made it spin without its point being on the couch. He then put it point downwards on to the couch and made it turn a little that way.

After this, he again turned his attention to the plastic car from which he had detached the man figure. He ran this along and looked underneath as if to see what made it run. Then to my great surprise, he tried to put the man back by pushing the plastic points into the holes. I was surprised because some time had elapsed since he had taken the man out, and his activities had seemed to be an aimless going from one thing to another, to which I felt the word 'play' could not be applied. However, I now began to feel that it was not as aimless to him as it seemed to me and that, just as he had walked towards the toys with purpose, so there had been a purposeful and connected theme in his use of the toys. [At the time I couldn't see it, but later a specific set of meanings became attached to each toy; these became like concretised words with which he 'talked' to me, offsetting his lack of speech until this developed.]

He did not manage to get the man back correctly in that he was put into the car facing the wrong way, but he did manage to push the plastic pins on the figure of the man through the holes in the seat of the car. Having done this, he turned to the tiny soft panda which had been on the top of the case. He tapped the eyes and then tapped the hard round squeaker in the middle of the stomach. I was surprised at this, because the hard round squeaker button wasn't obvious.

He then turned to the paper I had put on the table and drew some lines. Momentarily, he turned back to the humming-top and used it as before. He then turned back and tapped the table top with his fingers. After this, he drew some circles.

He then turned back to the tiny baby doll and rocked the cradle.

After this, he half pulled my hand towards the humming-top as if asking me to spin it. I complied, picked it up and made it spin on the floor. He watched it with a fascinated look. As it fell down, he looked quickly at the electric fire. A stiff little smile came as he turned to look at me for the first time. It was a funny smile. Each corner of his mouth went up but the middle part of his mouth stayed stiff and unsmiling. He then lowered his eyes and turned back to the paper on the table. He drew some more strokes on the paper and then quickly turned to the tractor with the large red wheels and ran it twice back and forth across his chest.

He now picked up the humming-top from the floor. He tapped it as though trying to look inside it. I felt it was to see where the humming noise had come from when I spun it on the floor.

When I said, 'It's time to go to mummy now', he did not show that he had heard but, as I rose to my feet, he left the toys and came with me without a backward look.

[I now remember something else (which, significantly, I had forgotten until I had finished recording the session). At one point in the session, as it was warm, I took off his windcheater. He was quite limp, and neither helped nor hindered me in taking it off. However, in taking it off, the cuff of one sleeve of his woollen cardigan flopped over his hand. He pulled it further over his hand and looked at it there, and then made a slight movement as if to pull it back, but then did not do so. After this, he held the toys in this hand by stretching out his arm from underneath the sleeve. This was a somewhat awkward gesture which made me want to turn back the cuff of his sleeve. I did not do so because I had the impression that he had left it down so that I would turn it back, that is, in order to manoeuvre me so that I seemed to be part of his body and under his control.

I should also say that, although his movements were limp, as I guided him down the twisting stairs which led to the therapy room, his body felt quite hard and muscular.]

My reactions to this session were recorded as follows: 'John seemed like a blind man feeling his way around an unfamiliar room, constructing his own scheme of understanding which was very different from my own.'

After this first interview I decided to take John for psychotherapy four times a week. He came to see me for four years and has done very well. In an unobtrusive way, I have kept in touch with his progress. He was successful at a well-known public school to which, at the appropriate time, he went as a day-boy. His relationship to his parents is a good one and he has friends. His academic progress has been in keeping with his good intelligence and he is now at university. He seems likely to marry and to have a normal life. He had never needed to return to psychotherapy. His great interest is classical music and he is a talented violinist.

The experienced worker will already have discerned the features in the assessment interview which decided me to take John for psychotherapy. He showed evidence of a latent capacity for play. He showed intentional behaviour. There seemed a good possibility for the development of a medium for communication between us. Also, he was almost identical to other autistic children I had seen who had benefited from individual psychotherapy. In my experience, these shell-type children are as alike as peas in a pod in their appearance, the kind of parents they have and their early developmental history. Whether children such as John will recover from the early 'set-back' to their psychological development depends, to some extent on the width of the chink in their autistic armour, as also on the degree of co-operation of the parents, and on the therapist's capacity for insight and therapeutic skill.

John's 'play' in the therapeutic sessions which followed the preliminary interview was also characteristic of these children. He wrapped himself in the soft travelling rug which I have always provided since I found that, *faute de mieux*, such children wrapped themselves in the rugs on the floor. He crouched under tables and chairs with the rug draped over him, as if in a self-made 'den'. To him, this was not going 'inside' the object, for these children are two-dimensional. The operative state for him was that of being covered up and protected from the strange 'not-me'. We must beware of interpreting these children's experiences in our own three-dimensional terms.

A similar child in an educational day unit for psychotic children used to creep into boxes and tunnels which he closed at one end with pieces of wood. In short, these children make their own encasements out of objects in the outside world, which are experienced as if they are part of their bodies.

John's manoeuvres with the cuff of his sleeve give us a hint of the tricks such children use to get other people to do things for them, in order to maintain the delusion that the 'not-me' world is part of their body and under their control. Their passivity and lack of development of their capacities is also part of these 'tactics'. Careful and detailed investigation reveals that the parents of these children are certainly not cold and neglectful. They are usually sensitive people who, in their concern to be good parents to their children, can be manoeuvred into doing too much for them and acting as if they are part of their body. Thus, they support the delusion that bodily separateness from the strange 'not-me' has not occurred and that everything is the familiar and controllable 'me'.

PSYCHODYNAMIC FEATURES OF SHELL-TYPE CHILDREN

Since his first traumatic experience of bodily separateness, the child has had virtually no sense of bodily separateness. It is only as treatment helps him to bear the fact of his bodily separateness from the outside world that he also shows that he feels he is separated from it by a barrier and indicates that he feels enclosed in a shell. For most of the time the child behaves as if fused with the outside world, and outside objects are experienced as a prolongation of his bodily sensations or movements. In his state of imitative fusion, everything is experienced as 'me', although, paradoxically, he has no sense of 'me' and 'not-me' except in fleeting moments of awareness as he begins to respond to treatment. When these moments occur, the 'not-me' is quickly made into 'me', by feeling that it is part of his body and under his control.

Such a child lives mostly in terms of the outlines of shapes and the sensations aroused by touching, or seeming to touch, surface contours. Touch seems to be the predominant mode of experience, and seeing, hearing and even smelling are felt to be tactile experiences. In 'seeing', his eyes are felt to sweep around the contours of objects. These then become fused with bodily parts whose shape is felt to be analogous. Hearing is also a tactile experience. The shapes of sounds seem to touch the child, who then tries to block them. 'Looking' and 'hearing' are felt to make things exist. 'Not-looking' and 'not-hearing' are felt to 'black out' their existence – to make them not exist.

Such a child makes no distinction between animate and inanimate. People are treated as things which are an extension of his own bodily 'things'. He may not draw on paper, but he makes shapes with his faeces in his anus or the tongue in his mouth. These shapes are felt to be made on surfaces. The child has no sense of their being inside, for he has only two-dimensional awareness. He has virtually no fantasies or thoughts. His experience is on a concrete, physical, tactile surface level.

In outward expression, such children are predominantly asymbolic, although not completely so. Their psychological functioning has been halted at a very rudimentary level by awareness of bodily separateness which they experienced as traumatic. It had been a catastrophe when they realised that the sensation-giving mother was not part of their body. This occurred at a time when they could not bear the realisation, because their internal structures were not sufficiently organised to stand the strain.

As a reaction to this unbearable disturbance, they cultivate the illusion of being fused with hard objects. They turn their hard back to protect their soft front. The encapsulation mechanisms protect their vulnerable softness.

This well-nigh total encapsulation to form the delusion of a protective shell is characteristic of global, undifferentiated states and is a primary pathological protective manoeuvre. This shell-type protection can be disturbed, either by investigatory or remedial procedures, or by physical illness, in which the child feels that insult has been added to injury. In these cases, the child reacts with a further kind of encapsulation. In this further pathological reaction, segments of 'not-self' objects are encapsulated. [This has been described by Meltzer, *et al.* (1975).] This reaction diminishes awareness of painful and terrifying 'not-me' experiences, although it does not shut them out as thoroughly as does shell-type reaction. Both types of encapsulation prevent or interfere with the sensuous integrations which normally take place in early development and which will be discussed in detail in Part II.

ENCAPSULATION OF SEGMENTS

Another type of autistic child has been described by Meltzer and his co-workers (1975). These children also use encapsulation as a pathological autistic device, but it is not total as in the shell-type children. Segments of functioning are encapsulated; for example, the child's own perceptions become segmented and are encapsulated. This compartmentalises his perception of objects in the outside world. Certain experiences have made me suspect that such children were shell-type children in the beginning, but that further disturbances of their pathological autism caused them to react by segmentation processes.

Like the shell-type children, the segmentation children have well-formed limbs and intelligent faces. They often walk on their toes. They spin objects obsessively and have bizarre hand movements. They are nimble and deft in their movements. However, unlike the shell-type children, the segmentation children are not mute as a general rule, although they are often echolalic and use pronoun reversal. When seen for assessment, the difference between the segmentation and the shell-type children becomes apparent.

A striking example of the way in which threatening 'not-self' objects are broken into segments until they can be brought together in familiar 'me' terms is provided by the drawings of a psychotic child which are reproduced as Figures 5.1–5.8. The series of drawings, which were done rapidly one after the other, were provoked by the child's fear of the therapist's mouth. Turning from this, he first drew the mouth as he perceived it, that is, with sharp teeth. This drawing was thrown away by the child, to be retrieved by the therapist later. In the next series of pictures he proceeded to break it up into segments until, in the final picture, he brought the segments together in a more bearable way, notably with rounded teeth instead of pointed ones. In considering these drawings, it needs to be realised that the child feels that by drawing the mouth he actually traps the object on the paper and then can do what he likes with it. Used in this omnipotent way, drawing is a controlling rather than a representational activity. The child is not communicating with the therapist: he is controlling a dangerous thing. This aspect of the drawings of psychotic children will be discussed further in Chapter 12, 'The asymbolic nature of auto-sensuous states', and in the clinical study of Sam (Chapter 16).

These segmentation children also enclose their drawings in a thick black pencilled frame, or they write words and numbers which are encapsulated from each other by enclosing each one in thick black pencilled oblongs. They often say this is 'to keep them safe'.

Hoxter, in *Explorations in Autism* (Meltzer, *et al.*, 1975, p. 167), describes another aspect of segmentation when she writes that autistic children reduce objects 'to small simplified proportions, usually according to segments of sensory experience.' She continues: 'For example, the autistic child may have one maternal object which has a taste, another which has a smell, a sight, a sound and so on. Similarly, he will have a tasting self, a seeing self, a hearing self, etc.' Thus, he has many 'mothers' and many 'selves' and the impact of the full range of sense impressions is minimised.

A SEGMENTATION CHILD (SECONDARY ENCAPSULATION)

An assessment session which I had with a segmentation child will now be given. At age three, this child, whom I will call Leslie, had had a one-year period of investigation away from home. Work with this child, beginning when he was age five, gave me good reason to think that prior to the separation he was a shell-type child.

> Mother and Leslie, aged five years, were seen together. At first, Leslie went from one object to another in a somewhat aimless way, avoiding looking at me or his mother. At a certain stage, I suggested that mother might leave the room. Leslie did not watch her leave, or show any obvious emotion at her departure. However, he immediately went over to a cardboard cylinder about nine inches in length which had a pointed red lid. He smelt the lid and then pulled it off from the cylinder without looking at it. Then, with a vicious look on his face, he kicked the dismantled object around the room in an uncaring way, smelling at it every now and again but avoiding looking at it. After

Figure 5.1 'Dismantled mouth': drawing one

Figure 5.2 'Dismantled mouth': drawing two

Figure 5.3 'Dismantled mouth': drawing three

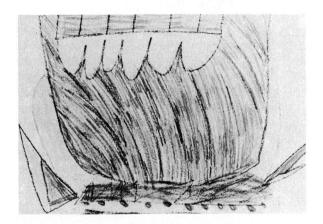

Figure 5.4 'Dismantled mouth': drawing four

Figure 5.5 'Dismantled mouth': drawing five

Figure 5.6 'Dismantled mouth': drawing six

Figure 5.7 'Dismantled mouth': drawing seven

Figure 5.8 'Dismantled mouth': drawing eight

the first touching of the object to take off the lid, he avoided touching the lid with his hands. It seemed to be a 'smell' object. Later, in treatment, he drew pictures which he said were of a 'cry' or a 'cough' or a 'laugh', which were surrounded by a thick black pencilled frame.

The fact that these children can speak makes them appear to be an easier treatment proposition than the mute 'shell-type' child. However, this is not my own experience. I have found shell-type children more responsive to psychotherapy. The primary auto-sensuousness of the shell-type child has not been disturbed, and then intensified by the development of a secondary, more intractable form of autistic reaction, such as is characteristic of the segmentation children.

THE BINARY SPLIT IN THE SENSATION-EGO

Work with encapsulated children, both shell-type and segmented, reveals a binary split in their emergent 'body-self'. The encapsulation reactions have prevented this from deteriorating into the disintegration and confusion characteristic of the confusional children.

David, who came to me aged ten years, was a striking example of a child with a binary split in his 'body-self', i.e. a child whose first disturbance had split him into two halves with encapsulation reactions which had held him together. The two halves of his face were noticeably different. The right half had clear, smooth skin and well-formed bones; the left half had muddy skin, hollow cheeks and the bones seemed hardly to have been formed. This side of his face was contorted. David himself talked of his left side as if it were the 'sinister' side, although, of course, he did not use this term. The encapsulation was shown by his enveloping a soft ball and a hard upright tin with soft malleable Plasticine to make a 'monster'. Later, from cardboard wheedled out of me as a soft therapist, he made a hard suit of armour to encase his soft body.

This child had little or no notion of 'insides' and 'outsides'. The operative delusion was the covering of surfaces with substances, the surfaces of which adhered to the surface of the thing being covered. In making the suit of armour, David 'picked' features from his father (ears, hair, etc.) to incorporate into his protective hard armour. These features then became indistinguishable from David's body stuff. It was a predatory taking over without acknowledgement to the donor. Many psychotic children who seem to have achieved a certain amount of development have grown up in this way. They have not identified in the normal way, in which the separate identity of the other person is acknowledged. They have treated other people as if they had no life and identity of their own, and have taken grown-up external features from them without any feeling of gratitude or indebtedness. This produces pseudo-development which has no depth or stability, and the child feels constantly at risk lest the 'stolen' features will be stolen back again.

CONCLUSION

In this chapter, the attempt has been made to provide a means of sorting out *young* children on the basis of findings from deep investigations into the pathological auto-sensuous procedures by which shared reality has been excluded or obscured to such a massive degree that the child became psychotic. The next chapter will deal with the auto-sensuousness of confusional states.

NOTE

As yet, there is no commonly agreed scheme of classification for autistic children. However, since Kanner went to a great deal of trouble to delineate Early Infantile Autism so precisely, I have felt it sensible to restrict the use of the term 'autistic' to those children who fitted Leo Kanner's description fairly closely. These are the ones I have called *encapsulated*. I have supervised psychotherapists who have struggled for years with a child who made very little progress and who had, in my opinion, erroneously been assessed as 'autistic', but was not of the clear-cut type to whom I would apply the term.

Chapter 6

Confusional entanglement

Throughout this book the term 'confusional entanglement' will be used for a group of young psychotic children, some of whom have features in common with adult schizophrenics. They are clearly a different group of children from the encapsulators, and it is important to distinguish between them for they have different treatment needs and prospects.

When working at deep levels with both types of child, the same traumatic sensation of bodily loss is encountered for which I prefer to use Winnicott's term 'psychotic depression'. The childhood autistics use encapsulation of various kinds to protect them from this hole-type depression, and the confusional children use confusion and entanglement with outside objects. (Their protection often seems more like a 'veil' than a 'shell'.)

The treatment situation with regard to confusionals is more difficult than with the encapsulated childhood autistic because it is complicated by this pathological entanglement with the 'not-self', and because fragments of the 'self' are felt to be dispersed and scattered, so that 'self', and 'not-self' are inextricably confused. The working over of the elemental sensations of loss is impeded by entanglement with the mother, and often by the mother's and father's entanglement with each other. Thus, the treatment of a confusional type of child usually takes much longer and, in most cases, it is of vital importance that the parents should have treatment as well as the child.

It will be seen that the confusional children are much more of a 'mixed bag' than the encapsulated children. The crucial distinction between the two is the mother-and-child situation. In the encapsulated child a 'controlling' situation predominates, and in the confusional child an 'engulfing' and 'entangling' one predominates. In order to assist differential diagnosis, other outstanding characteristics of confusional children which distinguish them from encapsulated children will now be indicated.

DIFFERENCES BETWEEN CONFUSIONAL AND ENCAPSULATED CHILDREN

1 Appearance and body movements

Many confusional children are clumsy and uncoordinated in their bodily movements, in contradistinction to the encapsulated children whose bodies are well-formed and whose movements are deft and nimble. Confusional children often look muddled and confused. This is particularly the case with the older ones. Some of the younger ones are attractive and quick-moving, so clumsiness alone cannot be a determining characteristic. Nor are all encapsulated children deft and nimble, but they usually become so as treatment progresses.

2 Muscle tone

The softness and flaccidity of their muscle tone in contrast to the hard muscular bodies of the encapsulated children is usually a determining characteristic, but I have encountered confusional children in whom this was not so marked as in others.

3 Eye-to-eye contact

The encapsulated children avert their gaze and the confusional children never do this. They look at other people, but in the older child the eyes may be bleary and unfocused.

4 Body-moulding

The confusional children 'body-mould' in a soft and yielding way when picked up, which is in great contrast to the unyielding bodies of most encapsulated children. Confusional children seem to 'sink into' a person's arms or into their cots. Occasionally, they may alternate between being rigid and melting. They often nuzzle up to people like a pet animal. They do not exhibit the excessive shyness and withdrawal of the encapsulated children. Indeed, they are often responsive to people in an undiscriminating way. To the undiscerning observer this has seemed a hopeful sign.

5 Physiological constitution

In contrast to the encapsulated children, who have a good physiological constitution, many of the confusional children have illnesses arising from physical causes such as respiratory, circulatory, metabolic and digestive difficulties. Psychotherapeutic treatment is punctuated by absences due to physical illnesses. For this reason alone, medical support and co-operation is essential in the treatment of these children. However, some of the younger children of this type are in good health, so that this alone cannot be taken as a determining factor. In contradistinction to the poor health of some of the confusional children, it is a progress in psycho-therapy when the encapsulated child begins to have the ordinary child-hood illnesses to which, in his auto-generated insulation, he had not been prone. (This surprising feature is confirmed by many workers who have cared for these children.)

6 Activity and passivity

Some of the confusional children are hyperactive, which is in great contrast to the encapsulated child, who often appears to be quiet and gentle. This quietness and gentleness is different from the limpness and flaccidity of some of the confusional children. It has a reflective, mournful quality about it. However, these seemingly quiet children can exercise a profoundly disruptive influence on the family.

7 Onset of the psychotic illness

The disordered behaviour of confusional children often follows an initial period of what looks like normal development, but, in my experience, this development is not as normal as it seems. Psychotic features, particu-larly the devastating sense of loss associated with psychotic depression, have been masked by the entanglement with the mother. In contrast, the encapsulated children are usually reported as being withdrawn from birth or just after birth. In some of these children, there may be a history of screaming or even of fits, which I have found to be a hopeful prognos-tic sign in that the child was experiencing and responding to frustration.

8 Referral features

Both types of child may be assessed by the referring authorities as being mentally handicapped, but there has not been the query about deafness in the referrals of confusional children which is so common in those of the encapsulated children.

9 Preservation of sameness

Both encapsulators and confusionals manifest this.

10 Hallucinations

At assessment interviews, hallucinations may be reported as characteristic of confusional children. These are not reported of encapsulated children, but it is my experience that, as an encapsulated child makes progress in psychotherapeutic treatment, hallucinations may occur and are a phase in the development of the child's capacity to hold pictures in his mind.

11 Unusual talents

The unusual memory, musical and mechanical performances which are reported of encapsulated children are not characteristic of confusional children.

12 Mental illness in the family background

Rimland (1964), who studied the records of psychotic children from many parts of the world, tells us that there is a strikingly low incidence of mental illness in the antecedents of childhood autistics (encapsulated children). Any mental illness reported is of a depressive and not a schizophrenic nature, but even this is extremely uncommon. On the contrary, the ancestral backgrounds of the schizophrenic-type children show a high incidence of schizophrenic-type illnesses. This confirms my own experience drawn from a much smaller sample. Dr Stroh and Dr Tischler also confirmed this from their larger sample at High Wick Hospital, London (personal communication).

The above gives a summary of the more obvious differences between encapsulated children and confusional children. When psychotherapeutic treatment is in progress, differences of a deeper kind can be discerned.

DIFFERENCES DISCERNED IN PSYCHOTHERAPY

1 Protective manoeuvres

The autistic 'armour' of the confusional child does not have the homogeneous quality of that of the encapsulated child. The latter's 'shell' is formed in terms of 'me', the 'not-me' being experienced as 'me'. For most of the time, such children have no sense of 'me' and 'not-me'. By contrast, as the result of their greater awareness of both 'me' and 'not-me', the predominant delusion of the confusional children is that they engulf and entangle the 'not-me' and draw it into the 'me-ness' of 'me'. The segmenting encapsulated child may have isolated moments of sharp awareness of 'me' and 'not-me'. These are distressing moments of icy clarity which are sometimes described by such patients when they can talk. By segmenting the 'me' and the 'not-me', the predominant delusion of the encapsulated child is that he is in powerful control of the outside world, whereas for most of the time, the confusional child feels confused with it, although there are times when he feels in control. To speak in a picturesque way, the confusional child is a Don Quixote who, clad in an ill-fitting suit of armour made from miscellaneous bits and pieces insecurely fastened together, tilts at windmills under the delusion that they are giants. The encapsulated child's armour is much more intact, for he has a stronger drive to integration and organisation. He is scarcely aware of the outside world and its 'windmills'.

2 Traumatic damage

Both types of child use the image of a 'hole' to express traumatic awareness of the bodily separateness which has precipitated their psychosis. But confusional children are teetering on the verge of becoming aware that they are flesh and blood, and they occasionally experience and express this experience as a 'wound'. They are moving to the level of primary narcissism, but of a pathological kind. This is not the case with the encapsulated children, who make no differentiation between animate and inanimate. For them, objects and people are all 'things'. 'Things' have 'holes', not 'wounds'. It is only flesh and blood that is capable of having a 'wound'. Again, the confusional child is like the adult schizophrenic who also speaks of 'wounds'. As the morbid pathology increases, the hole becomes a *black* hole, and the 'wound' becomes a festering sore. Autistic objects are felt to block the 'hole'; the soft objects of the confusionals are felt to staunch the bleeding and mop up the pus. When they become aware of bodily separateness, both types of child live in an extreme world of 'haves' and 'have-nots', which the child experiences as 'fullness' and 'emptiness'.

3 Chaos and undifferentiated potential

Another difference between these two types of psychotic child which emerges in psychotherapy is that in confusional children we come upon *chaos*, whereas in encapsulated children we come upon *undifferentiated potential*. The confusional child has made little spurts of growth which then deteriorate into chaos. The encapsulated child's in-built potentialities have been preserved by lying dormant, waiting for propitious conditions for their development. The segmented child makes spurts of progress which then come to a standstill and are encapsulated.

4 Play and fantasy life

The encapsulated children do not play. The confusional child often plays in a way which draws in the people around him. However, the discerning person has an uneasy sense that this is not healthy involvement and participation, but that it engulfs and entangles him. It is an error to see this 'play' as being like that of the normal or neurotic child, or of showing evidence of a rich fantasy life. These children have not sufficient tolerance of bodily separateness for this to be the case. They have more fantasy life than the encapsulated children, in whom it is virtually non-existent, but their fantasies are crude, having very little psychological content and being closely associated with bodily sensations from which they are scarcely differentiated. For example, a brown gorilla can be equated with a pile of faeces. As well as being illuminating with regard to encapsulated children, Hanna Segal's (1957) paper on the symbolic equations encountered in adult schizophrenics is enlightening in relation to confusional children. Objects in the outside world are not allowed to keep their quality of separateness and clear distinctiveness. The strangeness of the 'not-me' is diminished by drawing it into their 'me-ness', and then it becomes less threatening. The excessive degree to which this takes place means that awareness of the 'not-me' is very minimal and thus the confusional child's contact with reality is tenuous and flickering. That of the encapsulated child is virtually non-existent. With them, the 'not-me' has been segmented and reconstructed in 'me' terms (as in the drawings of the mouth discussed earlier).

5 Talking

Most of the confusional children talk, although some of the younger ones may not. The encapsulated children rarely talk. If they do, they are usually echolalic and use pronoun reversal. They do not have a conversation. The confusional children are rarely echolalic but some of them may use pronoun reversal. The talking of many confusional children is characterised by being garbled and verbose. They speak in an incomprehensible stream of words in which important words may be left out. Their talk seems to engulf the listener and has the effect that he ceases to attend to the meaning of what is being said. He feels drowned in a flood of sound and his capacity for initiative is sapped.

6 Drawing

Shell-type encapsulators do not draw in the early stages before psychotherapy has begun to take effect. The segmentors may do so. Confusional children usually draw from the beginning of treatment. However, it is a mistake to see these drawings as being representational or symbolic. (This will be discussed in Chapter 11.) They are part of the enveloping and entangling activities of the confusional children by which they draw into themselves the 'not-me', in order to confuse and blur it so that it seems less threatening. As with their crude fantasy play, it is a mistake to interpret these drawings as communications to the therapist. To do so means that we fall into the trap of colluding with the child's pathology. We become enmeshed when we should be helping to disentangle him. These activities need to be seen as attempts to diminish the impact of the 'not-me' outside world by drawing it into themselves. These pathological activities may be necessary until the child has developed a genuine transitional area in which 'me' and 'not-me' interact with each other in reciprocal and creative ways. Psychotic children lack the 'transitional' area described by Dr Winnicott (1958). They live in an 'all-or-nothing' world in which, in devastating moments of awareness of bodily separateness, 'me' and 'not-me' are so sharply delineated that they seem to come into headlong collision with each other. All their pathological autistic manoeuvres are to avoid this catastrophe. As such, these manoeuvres need to be treated with respect and caution. However, to allow oneself to be engulfed or entangled by them is to court disaster. If their entanglement activities are not resisted, they become corrupting and demoralising for both child and worker. The regression which occurs in such a collusive situation is not of the kind which provides a breathing space for a forward jump to be made, but an intensification of the pathological processes of engulfment and entanglement.

Some psychotherapeutic procedures encourage this and should be avoided, not only because of their deleterious effects upon the child, but also because they have deleterious effects upon the therapist, who is drawn into a pathological collusion which corrupts his moral and emotional functioning and distorts his capacity to observe clearly. However, if this pathology is grappled with in a forthright way, both child and therapist establish an inner core of clarity and stability.

7 Dimensionality

Confusional children are teetering on the edge of becoming aware of three-dimensionality and of outsides and insides. They are preoccupied with burrowing inside other bodies and with seeming to put parts of themselves into other bodies. Meltzer and colleagues (1975) have called it 'intrusive identification' and see it as an aspect of *projective identification* as described by Melanie Klein (1963). The encapsulated child lives in a two-dimensional world. He is preoccupied with surfaces, textures and shapes. If he gets inside an object, for him it is not the getting *inside* which is significant – he is not aware of that as such – it is the sensation of being covered up, of being sheltered and protected, which matters. He is forever seeking analogies and identities in terms of shapes. Things which seem dissimilar to us are equated by him on the basis of their sharing some characteristic which is important to the child. Straight lines and circles seem to be important patterns, reaction to which is in-built, and he is very reactive to these. Confusional children are also reactive to these elemental patterns but they do not dominate their activities as they do those of the encapsulated children. Pushing into objects in order to engulf them or to be engulfed by them seems to be their prime concern.

8 Distinguishing characteristics

Encapsulated children are like mechanical automatons; confusional children are like human sleep-walkers. The bewilderment of a confusional child when he begins to wake up from his grandiose delusions about himself and his powers was expressed in the following poem dictated to me by an eleven-year-old schizophrenic boy I had in treatment:

> Why am I so wonderful?
> Why does the rain fall to the ground?
> To the ground? To the ground?
> And why? why? why? WHY?
> Does the rain make us sad?
> And why should we be so sad?
> And why are we so sad, sad, SAD?
> And why don't we take the sun?
> And be happy all over again?

9 Parental reactions to psychotherapy

If the child is showing improvements in his condition, the parents of the encapsulated child support the treatment by bringing the child regularly, and they co-operate with any suggestions made to them. However, once the child is functioning normally, they are glad to finish. They want to forget the whole experience. On the other hand, the parents of confusional children, particularly the mother, 'bend over backwards' to support the child's treatment and are very appreciative of the psychotherapy, so long as it does not threaten their entanglement with the child. When the separation of the child as an individual entity in his own right threatens to occur, they tend to break off treatment, although overwhelmed by feelings of guilt at doing so. Thus, the need for such parents to have treatment alongside that of the child cannot be overemphasised. Even then, however good this treatment may be, the disentangling of mother and child, and father and mother from each other, is an extremely difficult task and, in spite of all our skill, may be impossible. Margaret Mahler's technique of seeing mother and child together seems to have much to commend it, in that the mother and the child can be kept in step with each other.

Finally, in approaching these parents and children, we need to remember Dr Tischler's wise warning that the mother–child situation which the clinician sees in the consulting room is not likely to be the same as the one which was in operation when the psychosis first started. It is likely to be much worse. As stated earlier, pathological autism is self-perpetuating and becomes more intensified as the years go by. There is nothing more hurting than to feel useless and not needed, and this is how psychotic children make their parents feel. Trying to relate to an unresponsive child can be very depressing, baffling and enraging. No wonder that, when we see them, these parents may harbour murderous feelings towards their disappointing offspring. It does not mean that these feelings were present in early infancy when the psychotic rift occurred between them. We need to help them to revalue each other in the light of a realistic assessment of their potentialities as allies in the business of 'growing up properly' (as one psychotic child expressed it to me). With all psychotic children it is important to start treatment as early as possible, and to remember that 'I am because you are' applies to both children and parents, as well as to their therapist. However, this book is concentrating on understanding the children. A detailed investigation of the mother–child situations in childhood psychosis must be left to others.

Examples of primary and secondary confusional children will now be given.

AN EXAMPLE OF A PRIMARY CONFUSIONAL CHILD

This four-year-old child, Adam, used engulfment tactics of a global kind in order to confuse himself with the 'not-me' outside world and so diminish its impact. When he was first seen, he ran around the room in a clumsy, heavy-footed fashion. He seemed distraught and unreachable. His speech was mumbled and indistinct, although at times there were great outpourings of it which were similar to his enveloping activities with his mucus, faeces and spit.

In the early days his only activity at home consisted in plastering the walls and furniture with his bodily substances. Gradually, as treatment proceeded, this changed to enveloping them with Plasticine, which was much more tolerable!

The child had a disturbed but caring mother. It seemed that a large part of Adam's engulfment procedures were directed towards fending off the chaos in the home and the derangement in his mother. The fact that, in spite of her mental disorder, the mother had Adam's welfare at heart probably explains why this child was treatable. However, it was notable that his treatment was impeded by his facility for drawing people into his confusions and for becoming entangled with them.

This child had considerable artistic talent. His drawings demonstrated his engulfing mode of reacting to the 'not-me' outside world. They were over-inclusive, being full of people and objects. These were drawn with great economy of line. In an impressionistic way, they were very like the actual people and things he had wanted to 'draw' on to the paper. It will be noticed that, in the foregoing description, I have avoided any words which would indicate that these drawings were representational. Such an undifferentiated child has not sufficiently tolerated the experience of bodily separateness to be able to use symbolic representations. (Drawing as a symbolic activity will be discussed further in Chapter 12.)

A child whose global confusional state had been disturbed, but who was not a schizophrenic child in the usual sense of the term, will now be described.

AN EXAMPLE OF A SECONDARY CONFUSIONAL CHILD

I am indebted for the following description to Dr Robert Salo, when he was acting Psychiatrist-in-Charge at High Wick Hospital for Psychotic Children, London.

Luke

Luke was admitted to High Wick Hospital when he was seven years old. He is a slim boy, with brown curly hair, and a cheerful but facile expression. He has protruding teeth and, because he breathes through his mouth, his mouth is always open. Everything about him is rather awkward: the way he stands and moves and speaks. When I first saw him he walked on his toes so that his whole body was arched backwards and his arms moved sinuously as if slightly out of control. He is curiously unperturbed at meeting new people and, on this first visit, bombarded me with a series of questions: 'What colour your car is?', 'Is it outside?', 'Has it got a lock?', 'Is it dangerous?', 'What is a steering wheel?'. He had numerous mannerisms, grimacing, suddenly laughing, rising up on the balls of his feet, raising his arms above his head, gripping one hand in the other tightly, with a writhing movement, tensing his whole body, grinding his teeth, and snorting through his nose.

He was a full-term baby, and has two elder sisters. His mother is

English and his father is of Mediterranean extraction. Luke's mother described her pregnancy as odd, but could not name her specific disquiet. She was very unsure about when Luke was expected. His birth was easy and straightforward and he was of average weight. The parents felt that they were happy together at this time. The early relationship seemed quite comfortable and he fed at the breast until about six weeks, when a bad cold developed into bronchitis and he was admitted to hospital. He spent three weeks in hospital, some of the time in an oxygen tent and being drip-fed. Anxiously, his mother visited him every day, but her milk dried up and she had to bottle-feed from then on. At about this time the family moved house, so that when he was discharged from hospital he went to a new home. He crawled at eight months and although he did not walk until about eighteen months he was an active toddler and adventurous, and would sometimes wander off. By the age of two years he had several words and short phrases. They did not notice anything strikingly unusual about his development.

When Luke was twenty-six months old they went to live abroad, against his mother's wishes. They lived in a country area and his mother felt very isolated, but the rest of the family appeared to be happy so she decided to stick it out. Luke began to be fussy about his food, which he had never been previously. He gradually became shy and rather withdrawn, and his mother felt that he was lonely for his sisters, who were at school. Luke had tiptoed ever since he could walk and, initially, no one had taken much notice of this. However, by the time he was two and half years old this gave rise to anxiety. They were referred to an orthopaedic surgeon. Spasticity was diagnosed and he was referred to a specialist centre where he was given Voiter treatment. In this he was curled up in the foetal position and squeezed. Mother felt that his facial expression was resigned and miserable and he appeared to feel that he was being punished. He stopped sleeping at night and began wandering around the house, turning on taps and getting up to all sorts of mischief so that she could not leave him. Referral to another specialist brought a milder version of the Voiter treatment. Subsequent investigation showed an atypical EEG and as a result of this he was prescribed anticonvulsants.

Since the beginning of his Voiter treatment Luke had become unsettled, throwing his dinner around the room, turning taps on and off, was fractious, walking on tiptoe, becoming very destructive and not sleeping; on three different anticonvulsant drugs he could not stand without falling. His balance was bad and his co-ordination extremely poor. He was unable to manipulate things that he had previously been able to do and appeared extremely anxious and agitated. He withdrew to such an extent that the family could get very little reaction from

him. In fact, as far as he was able to, he would do the opposite of
what was requested. The family strain at this time was intense. All
sorts of difficulties emerged between the parents, and there was great
bitterness in their relationship. Each blamed the other's country of
origin for the problems. It resulted eventually in Luke's mother returning to England when her son was four and a half years old. It was,
in fact, a separation.

After six months, however, Luke's father rejoined the family. In
England Luke was referred to Great Ormond Street Hospital for Sick
Children, where they could find no evidence of brain damage or of
spasticity, nor evidence of epilepsy, so that his medication was stopped.
This had a marked beneficial effect on him and he was less withdrawn,
although clearly very disturbed, with perhaps an increase in the energy
with which he continued his bizarre behaviour.

One of his marked difficulties was with his relationships to others.
Children he ignored, but with adults he was insinuating, insistent and
demanding, flooding them with seemingly irrelevant comments and
questions, crawling over them, pinching them and grabbing them round
the neck. He had three main preoccupations: cutting spirals out of
paper, swinging objects and throwing things out of windows. Most of
the time he appeared very confused and disorientated. He was very
mixed up as to who people were and where he was, and he showed
little ability for symbolic play. His language was restricted, with pro-
nominal confusion and stilted constructions. He appeared to be suffering from a confusional psychosis of the type Tustin describes.

In view of this confusion it was felt that a psychotherapeutic
approach might help with differentiation and clarification for him of
the differences between himself and others. Initial sessions were full
of chaotic anxieties, expressed by throwing things, attempting to break
lights. Subsequently he settled down to hours of repetitive and
obsessional exclusions of the therapist's presence by his continual play
with rushing torrents of water which came out of the tap into the
bowl, out of the bowl into the sink, out of the sink down the plug-
hole, in an endless stream: a perpetual flood of noise and bubbles
which obliterated any possible contact. All attempts to get in touch
with him were obstructed.

After six months he began to take an interest in a teddy bear. At
first the teddy bear was hung up by one ear and swung, rather like a
lot of things which were hung on hooks or projections in the room
and swung backwards and forwards in a hypnotic self-stimulating auto-
erotic activity. [At this stage, he used the teddy bear as a confusional
object. F.T.] Subsequent sessions intensified his anxieties, partly as a
result of my exerting a structure and boundaries both to himself and
to the time, as well as a continuous demonstration that his activities

were different from mine. There followed many sessions when, on entering the room, he would dispense with me altogether, put the large teddy bear on the table by the window, place the teddy bear's legs between his, stick his thumb in his mouth and peer out of a half-closed eye over the teddy bear's nose, out of the window. With the other hand, he would line up distant images, and open and close his thumb and forefinger as if squashing an image like a beetle. His immersion in the teddy bear was total. He would hide behind it and peer out at me. He clearly wanted to feel the soft protective cover of the teddy bear all around him and to peer out as if through a small hole. Inside he would be warm and safe and he would not have to face the cold hard world. Masturbatory activity filled him with intense 'bumpy' feelings in his tummy and bottom that would make him laugh and forget all about the nasty hard things that I presented him with.

I would describe to him as simply as I could how he wanted to climb inside the teddy and how he wanted the soft teddy to keep hard, sharp things away, and how he wanted soft warm things to keep away the cold nasty ones. He wanted to feel that he could squash out images and that he could tell them when they could come and when they could go by opening and shutting his fingers, just like opening and shutting his eyes. In the same way he could make me come and go. I prevented excessive masturbation because the excitement made him quite inaccessible and brought him to unbearable levels of excitement. He resented this and began using the teddy bear as a buffer between us; for example, he would hold the teddy in front of him and bump into the walls and cupboards and eventually into me. I was the nasty hard experience that he was frightened of and could not control and I refused to let him sink inside me. Explaining to him his fear of me, but my willingness to help him, led to two things. One was his turning himself upside down and allowing me to help him right himself, and the second was to get teddy to look for him. Luke would hide in some corner of the room (hide rather like a very young child who, ostrich-like, hides by covering his face with his hands), whilst I would take teddy on a tour of the room looking in all sorts of places to find him. He seemed to be interposing teddy between us, as if my firm and distinct presence were too hard and unpleasant to be experienced directly.

Lately, he has become stronger and much more of a person, resisting me directly and expressing anger towards me, as well as wishing to experience me as a separate person. The last holiday demonstrated a wish for me to be with him on holiday. He wanted to know where I lived and if he could visit me. He hid in the place where teddy stays in my room and arranged that I, through teddy, should look for him. We played this several times, I was careful to make clear to him the place where teddy lived, where my home was, and also his home, and how they were different. When I said that he could not visit me, he wrapped up his teddy, clumsily, in a large piece of white paper and gave him to me to take to my home. [The teddy bear is becoming a transitional object. F.T.]

SUMMARY

Primary and secondary confusional states have been described, and illustrative case studies have been given.

Chapter 7

Auto-sensuousness as a basis for classification of psychogenic childhood psychosis

SITUATIONS PREDISPOSING TO PSYCHOGENIC CHILDHOOD PSYCHOSIS

In many psychotic children in whom psychogenic factors seem most operative, the bodily hurt they try to avoid is delusory. As we have seen, awareness of bodily separateness, in a situation in which mother and child were so close as to feel part of each other, can be experienced as the loss of part of the body, which leaves a 'hole' or a 'wound'. This is a delusion because most children have had no actual bodily damage.

However, there are a few psychotic children who have experienced actual damage to their bodies at a very early age. Such children have been described by the late Dr George Stroh, Psychiatrist-in-Charge of High Wick Hospital for Psychotic Children (1974). From birth onwards, these children have experienced violent assaults on their body from their parents and have also observed violence taking place between their parents. As Dr Stroh has shown, they are a worrying proposition in residential care in that they are liable to sudden and unpredictable outbursts of violence towards other children in the hospital.

There are other children whose 'nameless dread' of violent bodily hurt has been actualised. These are children who have had painful medical treatments in earliest infancy. For example, David, whose binary splitting was referred to earlier, had the experience of painful manipulations to straighten a slightly twisted spine. His case is a confused one because he was breast-fed for six months and then sent to a baby hotel where, on the advice of the physiotherapist, he was not visited by his parents, and from which he was taken for daily, hair-raising manipulations. During the first six months when she was breast-feeding him, the mother knew that he was to go away, so that her thoughts about David would be likely to be sad and disturbed. After that, he was separated from her in addition to having painful manipulations.

A less complicated example is a case which has been discussed with me from time to time. This is a child, being treated by Dr Salles, who was born with a deficiency of calcium absorption for which he had to have painful injections. At three and a half years this child was brought for treatment because he was massively out of touch with reality and did not speak. Of course, constitutional factors in the child and the quality of maternal care play an important part in the outcome.

From the foregoing, it might be thought that actual geographical separation from the mother at an early age would inevitably predispose the infant to psychosis. However, Mahler has not found this to be the case. She writes that, in the cases studied at the Master's Center in New York, 'actual object loss was not an etiological factor in their psychotic break with reality'.

She instances children who had spent their first years of life in concentration camps where their mothers had been taken away from them very brutally. She tells us that 'whilst these experiences left their traces on the children's object relationships, the children developed strong ties to each other and none of them suffered from a childhood psychosis' (Mahler, 1968, p. 50).

Mahler also refers to William Goldfarb's studies of infants who had been placed in foster homes and who were moved about with great frequency. She writes, 'Although they may have paid the price for this object loss with neurotic disorders, character distortions, or psychopathic difficulties later in life, they *never* severed their ties with reality' (Mahler, 1968, p. 51).

Mahler does not state the age at which separation of mother and infant occurred. This seems to me to be crucial. However, Spitz tells us of infants who were separated from their mothers from birth onwards. Their experience of separation was complicated by the fact that they had virtually no stimulation from their caretakers, being placed in cots in separate cubicles. Apart from being regularly bottle-fed, they had no other stimulating contact with the outside world. Spitz (1949) writes of their 'anaclitic depression', and tells us that all the children left in this situation died before they were two years old. But if an infant was fortunate enough to be reunited with its mother before too much time had elapsed, the infant recovered. Obviously, the quality of mothering would be important in such a situation, as also the temperament of the baby. Successful adoption situations in which infants are taken from the care of their natural mothers at an early age and given into the care of adoptive mothers also indicate that geographical separation, if well-managed, need not be catastrophic. The adaptability of the human species seems to be on our side.

My own work indicates that the early infantile situations which may predispose an infant to psychosis are ones in which basic co-operative experiences with the mother a) do not get established, or b) only get established in an insecure way.

Some such situations are as follows: for example, the mother may be physically or mentally ill, or depressed after the birth of the baby; there may be interfering relatives; the father may be away from home; the baby may have difficulties in breast-feeding; there may be worrying or depressing outside events such as moving house or the death of a close and emotionally important relative; there may be cultural or religious conflicts in a mixed marriage; for some reason, the infant may be difficult for the mother to empathise with; the mother may not have been emotionally ready for the birth of this particular baby, for example with twins or after a difficult birth. Such factors, and probably many others not mentioned, intertwine with each other and *with factors in the child* to produce a situation in which the child cannot develop the normal attitudes to reality. Instead he develops excessive auto-sensuous activities which prevent him from focusing his attention on the mother and thus co-operating with her. It is a tragic situation for both mother and child. The mother has to live with a child who is constantly undermining her confidence and enjoyment in being a mother. This is especially hurting when motherhood has been conceived in unduly idealised terms, as has the child.

A poem by Ruth Silcock expresses the agony of a mother who experienced bodily separateness when she was not sufficiently differentiated from her child, since the baby within had seemed to plug the hole of her privation and vulnerability.

Mother and Child

You see that mother
Without a heart
A black hole in her side
Where the blood runs out.

She had a baby shut within,
Snug, warm, locked up tight
She planned to stay a mother forever
Hug, cuddle, fondle out of sight

But the child broke out
Burst the bandage, the bag and her heart
The child ran away wet in the morning
And the mother's blood runs out.

(unpublished)

However, this book will mainly concentrate on the experience of the *child*, and his protective manoeuvres against the agony of bodily separateness for which he was not ready. The type of protective manoeuvre which predominates will be used as a basis for the classification of psychotic children, particularly those of under seven years of age. It is hoped that insight into such children's predominant protective manoeuvre will enable a treatment programme to be set up that may be able to modify the pathological autism which is giving rise to the psychosis. In short, it is an attempt to find the 'method in their madness'.

USE OF THE TABLE

The classification in Table 1 is not an attempt to pin the children like butterflies to a board, i.e. to place them in a diagnostic category and then to leave them without treatment. The essential aim is to facilitate their being given treatment which is appropriate to their particular needs. At first sight, each psychotic child seems to be different from the next, as though they have nothing in common. However, deeper investigation brings to light that certain children have needs in common which are different from those of another group of children. For example, the encapsulated children and their mothers need to be freed from their paralysing controlling of each other; the confusional children and their parents need to be freed from their crippling entanglement with each other. Both types of psychotic child need to be helped to develop normal relationships with people, in which bodily separateness and the consequent sense of individual identity is borne and recognised, and co-operative interactions can be set in train.

The following classification is suitable for young children under five or six years of age. It is mainly for the use of psychotherapists.

Table 1 Auto-sensuous manoeuvres leading to psychosis

Ways of dealing with the 'not-me' that is felt to be inimical because it brings unbearably painful awareness of bodily separateness.

	Autogenerated encapsulation	*Confusional entanglement*
Psychological development	Psychological development *arrested*	Psychological development grossly *disorganised*
Type of integration	Relatively unintegrated	Disintegrated
State of awareness	Two-dimensional awareness	Teetering on edge of three-dimensional awareness of a confused kind
Sensation-body-self	Binary split in the sensation-ego	Excessive splitting and fragmentation and dispersal of the sensation-body-self
Operative delusion	Autogenerated encapsulation of 'me' with body sensations and body stuff ('not-me' being shut out)	Confusion of 'me' with 'not-me' which is drawn into the 'me' and entangled with it by means of exciting body sensations

	Autogenerated encapsulation	Confusional entanglement
Use of objects	Child uses hard autistic objects predominantly (see Chapter 10).	Child uses soft confusional objects predominantly (see Chapter 11).
Picturesque comparison	Child is like a snail, whose shell is made out of its own hardened body substances.	Child is like a caddis-worm, whose case is made out of a heterogeneous collection of objects from the bottom of the pond. Before they get these 'patchy' cases, they are like amoebas. Bion's term 'bizarre object' applies to them.
Colloquial description	These children are 'shutters-out'.	These children are 'drawers-in'.
Situation between mother and child	Since there is felt to be no space between mother and infant, *adhesive equation* describes their stuck-together situation. They feel fused.	Since there is felt to be *some* space between mother and infant, *adhesive identification* describes their situation. They feel confused.
Comparison with adult psychotic patients	These children are not like adult psychotic patients because development has virtually stopped at an early stage.	These children have features in common with adult schizophrenic patients.
General effect	Feelings of anguish, terror and rage associated with the unbearable pain of bodily separateness are almost completely avoided. 'Me' seems fused with 'not-me'.	Feelings of anguish, terror and rage associated with unbearable pain of bodily separateness are minimised. 'Not-me' is confused with 'me' and entangled with it.
Experience of animate and inanimate	Child lives in a predominantly inanimate world. His body is an inanimate 'thing', not living flesh and blood. He is like a mechanical automaton.	Child confuses animate and inanimate. Body is sometimes a 'thing' and sometimes flesh and blood. He is like a human sleep-walker.
Experience of bodily separateness	On rare distressing occasions when child becomes aware of bodily separateness, he experiences it as a *hole* (in an inanimate thing). (Autistic hole)	Child is aware of bodily separateness more than encapsulated child and experiences it both as a *hole* and as a *wound* (in flesh and blood). (Autistic hole and narcissistic wound)

	Autogenerated encapsulation	*Confusional entanglement*
Basic primary relationship	Basic primary relationship with mothering person not established	Basic primary relationship with mothering person established in a very insecure way
Relationships	No relationships because no primary attachment	Non-authentic relationships because of insecure primary attachment to mother figure

Please note that in my previous book, *Autism and Childhood Psychosis*, a type of child was described who had never had a traumatic experience of bodily separateness, as has been the case with encapsulators and confusionals. These children are like vegetables and, in my experience, their possibilities for treatment by psychotherapy are not very hopeful. I now think of them as *psychological marasmics*. They have not developed any protective structures as have the encapsulators and the confusional entanglers. They are sometimes erroneously assessed as autistic. Any therapist who takes them on for treatment is faced with a lifetime's work.

Categorisation always seems to do violence to the flow of experience which is being studied, but, in the field of childhood psychosis, it has become necessary if the various kinds of children are not to be lumped together indiscriminately so that insight into their treatment needs and their possible future development is obscured. It is hoped that the categories will not be taken as tablets of stone and used rigidly and inappropriately. For example, encapsulation and confusion are both protective modes of reaction used at elemental levels. *It is not suggested that either mode is always present on its own and in pure culture.* The basis for the classification is *the paramount mode being used*; features from the other mode are likely to be present in a subsidiary and less marked way. For example, as we have seen, the encapsulated child who predominantly employs hard objects for his protection may have an occasional soft object in his collection. Vice versa, the confusional child who predominantly uses soft objects may have an occasional hard one.

It must also be made clear that this scheme of classification will be most useful to those workers who have had a good deal of intensive experience with psychotic children. For example, on superficial observation, encapsulated children of a segmented kind can seem like confusional children when they are behaving in a disjointed way and saying disconnected things. Significant differential features to look for are the following:

(a)   A confusional child is confused and entangled in a pathological way with the mother and she with him, *the father being shut out by both of them*. They have each some sense of bodily separateness from the other, but they feel in an inextricable knot. Their entanglement is obvious. Later on, this is sometimes represented as a confused tangle of threads or as a knot. The encapsulated child often has an apparently good contact with the father, but seems to shut out the mother, although on a deeper level there is an underground connection going on between them, based on imitation and on fringe cues such as muscle 'sets' and tones of voice. However, their fusion is not obvious. As they are responding to treatment, this secret web of controlling activities is often represented by the children as an orderly 'cobweb', in contradistinction to the disorderly tangle of threads or clumsy knot of the confusional child's representation.

(b)   The encapsulated child is in a state of adhesive equation with a mothering person experienced as a 'thing'. Confusional children's movements and speech are often clumsy and hampered. They have a flickering, blurred sense of awareness of separateness from the outside world. In Kleinian terms, they are in a state of excessive projective identification with the mother; in Mahler's terms, it is a pathological symbiosis.

(c)   One or both parents of confusional children are almost invariably deranged and chaotic (some of them have had a schizophrenic breakdown), whereas the parents of encapsulated children, although they are often somewhat obsessional and controlling, are usually able to live their lives in an orderly fashion (sometimes too orderly!).

(d)   The encapsulated child is obsessed with hard objects predominantly, whereas for the confusional child soft ones are most important and most used.

The table is mainly applicable to children under six or seven years of age. In psychotherapy with these young children, it is usually clear that the binary split in the sensation-ego occurred in terms of primary sensuous contraries such as hard and soft, rough and smooth, light and dark, etc. In the encapsulated children these contraries are not felt to be connected with each other and cannot be experienced together. Thus, experiences are sharply separated from each other and become segmented into discrete entities which are not connected with each other. Such compartmentalising replaces normal differentiation, and prevents the bringing together of contraries so that they can modify each other. Encapsulated children live in a state of acute extremes; for example, they feel they have a hard back and a soft front, and a hard head and a soft bottom, and that there is nothing inside which links these two extremes together. They are kept apart and controlled by the encapsulation. The child is trapped in a two-dimensional state of awareness. In rare states of occasional awareness of bodily separateness there is a soft 'me' and a hard 'not-me', which threatens to hurt their soft vulnerability. In order to shut out this hard 'not-me', 'me' and 'not-me' are partitioned off from each other and kept rigidly apart.

Recovering autistic children feel that there is a nice 'me' and a nasty 'not-me'. Some older recovering autistics feel they are two people; for example, Ellen Stockdale, who has described her experience of being autistic, said she felt that there was 'Red', her autistic self, and 'Ellen', the one who conformed and helped her to 'get by' in the outside world. 'Red' was wayward, impulsive and uncontrolled. 'Ellen' was ultra-obedient, compliant and 'good-goody'. Recovery entailed bringing these clear-cut, very different aspects of herself together. (Ellen Stockdale describes her experiences in a paper to be published in a collection of papers on autism edited by Dr Grotstein.)

(The confusionals do not have the icy clarity of the encapsulators.) The distinctions between contraries are blurred and confused. In both types of child, normal differentiation does not take place, being replaced by segmenting (encapsulators) or fragmenting (confusionals).

As the psychotic child gets older, the picture becomes more complicated by impingements from outside events. For example, ten-year-old David, who was cited earlier, had the feeling that his body was split into two halves. He had a 'nice side' and a 'nasty side'. The referring psychiatrist wrote that, if left untreated, he could become a 'hebephrenic schizophrenic'. Thus, children who were originally encapsulated children, with a binary split in their 'sensation-self', in later years can manifest a schizophrenic-type illness just as confusional children can do.

Also, during treatment, some basically encapsulated children can develop what looks like a confusional state in reaction to outside impingements, such as the death of an important relative or hospitalisation. A definitive distinguishing feature is that these children do not develop scattering and dispersal on the massive scale characteristic of the basically confusional child. In working with them it becomes clear that normal primary differentiations into hard and soft, etc., have been halted and frozen into an intractable state of binary fission by a traumatic experience of bodily separateness. These two separate parts now seem incompatible with each other and destined to remain forever unmodified and apart. The confusional appearance has been superimposed upon the encapsulating mode of protection. This is often the case with older children and adults.

Breaking into pieces is characteristic of the secondary protective manoeuvres of both encapsulation and confusional children. The experiences of the encapsulated child are broken into meaningless *segments* (Meltzer, *et al.*, 1975; also Hoxter, 1972). Those of the confusional child are broken into meaningless *fragments* which are dispersed and scattered. Fragmentation and scattering are factors which make confusional children especially difficult to treat. Both primary and secondary encapsulators present a picture of *unintegration*, whereas both primary and secondary confusionals are at the mercy of *disintegration* which is liable to become worse as time goes by. Encapsulation prevents disintegration and fragmentation, but it suspends the processes of differentiation and integration, and thus results in relative unintegration. These children have much in common with the older children described as 'frozen' by Docker-Drysdale (1972).

Edward Fitzgerald, in a verse of his well-known translation of *The Rubáiyát* of Omar Khayyám, describes a process of 'breaking into pieces', which has features in common with what happens in childhood psychosis. He writes:

Ah, Love! could thou and I with Fate conspire
To grasp this sorry Scheme of Things entire,
Would not we shatter it to bits – and then
Re-mould it nearer to the Heart's Desire.

(Fitzgerald, 1958 emphasis added)

Here we see a normal process arising from disillusionment, which in psychotic children has become pathological. As soon as we can make contact with the reactions of these children in terms of an exaggerated version of one we recognise in ourselves, they seem less bizarre and strange. Thus, we begin to be able to make contact with them and to help them. Metaphorically speaking, we can begin to help them to 'digest' the gargantuan mouthful of their unduly magnified experiences. The next section will be concerned with attempts to do this for ourselves.

Part II

Psychodynamics and treatment of autistic states

Chapter 8

The pathological operation of auto-sensuousness

Psychotherapeutic ways of modifying the pathology of auto-sensuousness will be discussed in the succeeding chapters. But, first of all, it is important to understand some of the preliminary steps to these important developments.

My experience indicates that, in normal development, interactive activities are based upon sensuous differentiations and integrations, particularly between hard and soft sensations. The sensuous integrations provide an infrastructure for the nascent self and enable the transposition of sensory experiences from one modality to another. (This latter point will be discussed in Chapter 12.) As the child comes to tolerate the fact that hard, uncomfortable 'not-me' experiences are part of the 'me-ness' of 'me', the toughness and resilience to tolerate the 'not-me' is developed. This is an important first step, which the psychotic child has been unable to make.

For the child without this basic infrastructure and unbuffered by interactive activities, awareness of the 'not-self' mother impinges in a way which does violence to the bodily experienced self. The mother, who has been experienced as an inanimate part of the child's body, seems suddenly to break away. Patients have described this as being like a chunk of stone breaking away from the rock face. This shows us that in this situation they had little or no awareness of being flesh and blood and of being alive. In this state of feeling inanimate, the encapsulated psychotic child experiences bodily separateness from the mother as being left with a hole. The confusional psychotic child, who is teetering on the edge of becoming aware that he is flesh and blood, experiences it both as a hole and a wound. As the pathological autism becomes more morbid due to evacuations of inimical 'not-me' substances, the 'hole' becomes a 'black hole' (as John in *Autism and Childhood Psychosis* (Tustin, 1972) described it), and the 'wound' becomes a suppurating, dirty mess.

Instead of developing transitional objects and transitional activities, psychotic children have developed hard *autistic objects* or soft *confusional objects*. These will be discussed in Chapters 10 and 11. The delusion is that the hard objects block up the 'hole' to prevent inimical substances from entering or getting out. They are also something to be grasped in moments of danger. The confusional objects seem to staunch the bleeding from the wound or to mop up the seepage. They also seem to engulf the child to keep him safe. For psychotic children these pathological objects have survival value in that they seem to keep the threat of 'death' at bay, and to compensate them for the limb they feel they have lost. Unduly used, they are an obstacle to psychological development. However, their importance to the child needs to be respected until their power to hold him in thrall can be diminished.

This experience of bodily separateness (as loss of the mother as a part of the body) exposes the child to a peculiar sense of loss which needs to be understood if it is to be modified. To some workers, it seems inconceivable that a child who has little capacity for relationships and who often seems empty should show evidence of distressing feelings of loss. To understand this, we need to realise that the psychotic child's sense of loss is very different from our own emotional experiences of loss. He has experienced loss at a time when *sensation* was all. He felt, for instance, that his mouth lost an exciting cluster of sensations for which, ever afterwards, he was destined to grieve. A sensuous impression which he had taken for granted as being 'there' was suddenly 'not there'. To relate this to the everyday experiences of normal people, we might say that it had something in common with our feeling of something being missing when we have forgotten to put our watch onto our wrist. A customary sensuous impression was suddenly not there. For us, this would be mildly disturbing, but for the hypersensitised infant who later becomes psychotic this sensation of missing has been magnified many times and has been catastrophic. It could also be similar to the experience quoted by K. H. Pribram (1969, p. 73): 'After the elevated railway which ran through New York's Bowery was dismantled, people often woke in the night at the time when a train should have passed and telephoned the police, saying that something funny had happened.' (There had been a breakdown of regularities and expectations.)

This was a somewhat extreme reaction on the part of normal people to something which was relatively trivial. A sensuous impression they had unconsciously taken for granted as being 'there' had gone. But for the psychotic child the loss of this sensuous impression was also associated with the advent of the strange 'not-me' which shocked and seemed to damage him and, as such, was felt as a looming inimical presence. The tragedy for him is that, until he can find someone who can understand his sensation-dominated sense of loss, the psychotic child feels helpless to explain the psychotic sense of 'goneness' which lies at the root of his being. In my experience this is the crux of his handicapped condition. Until he can be supported in tolerating this magnified delusory loss, he will never experience an authentic sense of *need* which will cause him to turn to his parents, who are usually ready and willing to satisfy his realistic needs, or to accept a therapist, who can help both child and parents to bear the gap between their expectations and realistic possibilities. In order to do this we need to understand the magnification which comes from the state of global, relatively undifferentiated, awareness constituting the autism. In order to modify its stranglehold, we need to be able to facilitate elemental differentiations and integrations. In so doing, we give the child a medium through which experience can be filtered.

Thus, as compared with the psychotic child's excruciating sense of loss of a sublime sensuous perfection, the ordinary everyday examples given above are inadequate. They were given to help us to empathise with his sensation-dominated loss. Perhaps poets and artists can best put us in touch with the 'let-down' which comes from the cracking of the glaze of autism, whose function has been the avoidance of the disillusionment, annihilation, mutilation, loneliness, emptiness and cold despair associated with awareness of bodily separateness and individuation.

D. H. Lawrence (1960, p. 156), who was overly close to his mother, wrote vividly of the sinking sense of loss when unrealistic expectations are disappointed:

> The more you reach after the fatal flower of happiness which trembles so blue and lovely in the crevice just beyond your grasp, the more fearfully you become aware of the ghastly and awful gulf of the precipice below you into which you will inevitably plunge, as to the bottomless pit, if you reach any further. You pluck flower after flower – and it is never *the* flower. The flower itself – its calyx is a horrible gulf, it is the bottomless pit.

He wrote further:

> But the end of the rainbow is a bottomless gulf down which you can fall forever without arriving, and the blue distance is a void pit which can swallow you and all your efforts into its emptiness and still be no emptier. You and all your efforts.

Living in terms of the 'crock of gold' at the end of the rainbow inevitably leads to the 'void pit'. The quest for a thornless rose-garden of unblemished happiness and perfection leads to disaster. In everyday life, illusions of perfection need to give way to the acceptance of that which is 'good enough'. The desire for perfection becomes part of the appreciation of beauty and enjoyment of imaginative creations. The psychotic child is stuck in an 'all or nothing' world from which he cannot escape. His ecstasies and his tantrums become threatening to him because they have no outlet and no medium for communication and expression. Autistic and confusional objects block this and take the place of imaginative expression and thinking. Such children feel no need for fairy stories, for myths and legends. Indeed, if these are read to them they confirm the extreme world in which they live. Such stories are not for these a-symbolic children until their autism has been modified.

Agatha Christie, that prolific writer of murder stories, knew well these depths of human personality where romance and glamour go hand in hand with murder and suicide. In *The Hollow* she wrote:

> Yes, she thought, that was what despair was. A cold thing – a thing of infinite coldness and loneliness. She'd never understood until now that despair was a cold thing. She had thought of it as something hot and passionate, something violent, a hot-blooded desperation. But that was not so. This was despair – this utter outer darkness of coldness and loneliness. And the sin of despair, that the priests talked of, was a cold sin, the sin of cutting oneself off from all warm and living human contacts.

But losing one's individuality in the social group does not lead to 'warm and living human contacts'. It can be used to avoid the pains of separateness and the accompanying loneliness and disillusionment. In our day and age, we have seen how whole nations can be drawn into a group psychosis of ideological extremes in which murder, torture and terror are perpetuated. Thus, the need to understand these depths is becoming more and more apparent. Birth from the group when it has been unduly used as a pathological autistic protection can be a devastating affair. Following a leader, however deranged, is much easier. Psychological birth is a long and difficult process to be repeated many times at critical points in life. It is not a sudden and magical experience of being 'born again'. Such 'instant' methods are to avoid the pains and struggles of the slow process of psychological birth. They perpetuate an undue sense of omnipotence.

In normal development, some sense of catastrophic damage and amputation is probably associated with all experiences of individuation and bodily separateness. At these levels, such activities as embraces, caresses and kisses or other soothing delights and reassurances help to heal the feeling of mutilation which is often at the root of feelings of unworth. A damaged body image leads to a lack of a secure sense of personal identity. In later life, kindness, sympathy, compassion, forgiveness, tolerance and acceptance of an unsentimental kind help to facilitate psychological birth.

D. W. Winnicott understood the psychotic child's grievous sense of amputation and loss, and uses the term *psychotic depression* to conceptualise it. He also uses the word *privation* to describe this sense of being bereft of something whose everlasting sublime 'thereness' had been taken for granted. Of this experience of *privation*, which he distinguishes from *deprivation* (actual and not delusory loss), he wrote as follows:

> . . . the loss might be of certain aspects of the mouth which disappear from the infant's point of view along with the mother and the breast when there is separation at a date earlier than that at which the infant had reached a stage of emotional development which could provide the equipment for dealing with loss. The same loss of the mother a few months later would be a loss of object without this added element of loss of part of the subject.
>
> (Winnicott, 1958, p. 222)

Not knowing Winnicott's work in the early days of my work with psychotic children, I was surprised when child patients demonstrated in no uncertain terms that separation from the mother meant loss of part of the body, usually connected with the mouth (Tustin, 1972). Such an experience of 'loss' is not loss as understood by differentiated human beings who are capable of emotions such as love and hate. It is pre-verbal and pre-conceptual. It is the loss of comforting *sensations*, which in the concretised mode of functioning at these elemental levels is felt as the loss of a sensuous *object*. This loss is dealt with by the pathological use of autistic and confusional objects, about which more will be said later. From a short-term point of view, these give the delusion of perfect satisfaction and completeness. They are at the root of idealism and romanticism. Some degree of idealism and romanticism helps to balance our disillusionments. We all experience a 'salting' of disillusionment, but the psychotic child has had a 'Dead Sea' of such experiences. Thus, he goes to extremes to counteract them. The perseverative use of autistic and confusional objects by which they attempt to counteract these experiences are not life-enhancing. They are anti-life and anti-beauty. They lead to deterioration and demoralisation. This will be discussed further in the chapters concerning these objects. In our generation, the need to understand these from the point of view of both the individual and the group is becoming a pressing issue.

It is important to remember that the sense of loss is *post factum*; it only occurred when a possibility which had been taken for granted became distressingly unavailable. As stated earlier, the psychotic child depicts this loss as a 'hole' or as a 'wound'. It is the place where a comforting and relieving agency had been. To put it in another way, the illusion of a sensuous bodily flow between mother and infant seems to have been broken in a catastrophic way. The fact that this occurs in a state in which infantile hypersensitivity has been little tempered by reality means that it brings to the infant a sense of 'flop', of 'falling apart', of 'falling endlessly'. All these phrases have been bequeathed to us by Winnicott (1958), who was well in touch with such states. Like Humpty-

Dumpty or Rock-a-bye-baby in its cradle, the child's 'fall' is a cata-strophe.

Enshrined in myth and nursery rhyme, these experiences are universal, but for the psychotic child they have been unbearable and have led to his developing protective reactions. In delusion, the encapsulated child feels that he has plugged the hole with hard autistic objects to protect his soft body, but hardness and softness are kept rigidly apart and do not modify each other. These extremes are his sole experience of the world. Thus, he feels he can neither take things in nor send them out. He also feels that his survival is dependent on being fixated to these hard objects and, in this fixation, his eyes as well as his hands are felt to be grasping objects. Lacking internal sensuous conjunctions, he feels that this fixation onto objects holds him together. The confusional child feels that he has melted into confusional objects and that they have melted into him. Thus, hard outside reality is blurred and softened. In contrast to the encapsulated child, who feels rigidly bounded, the con-fusional child feels dispersed and scattered like soft snow. Both types of psychotic child feel forever dependent on auto-sensuous objects for their safety and never develop tough and resilient inner resources arising from trust in, and effortful co-operation with, lively responsive parents who are gradually experienced as being separate and different from the child's own body. Sensuous expectations are developed far beyond the capacities of human beings to satisfy; thus the child is always in a state of discontent which is blotted out by more autistic activities. It is an escalating spiral.

These insights concerning sensations of loss, culled from work with elemental depths encountered in psychotic children, suggest an integrat-ive hypothesis in relation to the origins of primal envy and penis envy. At these levels loss of the physical presence of the mother seems like an amputation. The child feels that he has lost an all-powerful, magical bodily part. Its loss results in the feelings of helplessness which Edward Bibring (1953) described as being at the root of primal depression. It provokes the savage, predatory envy of 'sticking out bits' (to put it in terms used by the children) on other bodies which are felt to be the same as the bodily bit which has been lost. Amongst other functions, these 'sticking out bits' are seen as plugging the 'holes' resulting from separation experiences, which lead to sensations of helplessness, hope-lessness and extreme vulnerability. At this level, having the 'sticking out bits' means being all-powerful and in control, and this is felt to ensure survival. This is one aspect of envy of the breast, particularly the nipple of the breast, of the later penis envy, and envy of the 'baby' within the mother's body. Putting the electric light switch on and off, which, in the early days of treatment, is a much repeated activity of most psychotic children, almost invariably has the connotation of having the bit that bequeaths control. Work with the therapist gradually brings home to the child that effortful co-operative work to develop skills, not control by magical powers, will counter the feelings of helplessness and hopelessness.

Confirmation of this elemental experience of loss comes from other mental health workers. Michael Balint (1968) termed it 'the basic fault'. Edward Bibring (1953) called it 'primal depression'. Margaret Mahler, from her long experience of psychotic children, wrote of it as loss of the 'symbiotic love object'. Of this, she wrote as follows: 'What we seldom see, and what is rarely described in the literature, is the period of grief and mourning which I believe inevitably precedes and ushers in the complete psychotic break with reality' (Mahler, 1961). The questions now arise, 'Why should there be such a break?' 'How does it come about?'

I suggest that something like the following course of events occurs. For the young baby, the mother is experienced mainly in a sensuous way as a relief-giving agency. In moments of bodily discomfort such as hunger, coldness, skin irritation or bodily pain, the infant encounters the fact that he is helplessly at the mercy of bodily discomfort. In these moments, the 'mother', who has been taken for granted as a relief-giving part of his body, with little or no differentiation being made between his body and hers, seems to be 'gone'. To put it in another way, a relief-giving and exciting part of his body seems to be missing. He is exposed to terrible 'not-me' discomfort. In this early state, discomfort is hardness and roughness, comfort is smoothness and softness. Hard, rough discomfort is evacuated and is 'not-me' (evacuation being the forerunner of projection). Thus, the child experiences a soft, smooth 'me' and a hard, rough 'not-me'. The way in which he deals with this situation is crucial. If these sensuous contraries of hard and soft, rough and smooth etc. are rigidly polarised, or are confused and muddled, then trouble is in store. The clinical studies in Part III will illuminate and illustrate this.

In normal development, without being aware of it, the infant comes to tolerate the fact that hardness and softness are both 'me' experiences and that both can emanate from the same source outside the body. In short, his body has hard bones and soft flesh and is capable of experiencing both hard and soft sensations; he realises that his hard back is *connected* to his soft front, as is his hard head to his soft bottom. His actual body image becomes established, which leads on to a sense of his own identity. He also becomes aware that there is a mother who can be both hard and soft. In these early sensuous realisations, it seems that we see the detailed steps by which the conflict between the reality principle and the pleasure principle as described by Freud (1911) takes place. Hard reality impinges upon soft, smooth, sensuous pleasure. The child has to come to terms with the black despair and disillusionment arising from this. Dealing with this disillusionment, at a *sensation* level, prepares him for the depressive position described by Klein (1937), in which the child comes to terms with his *emotions* about the 'bad' disappointing mother, who is the same as the 'good' satisfying mother.

In the psychotic child the situation is different. The confusional psychotic child has a blurred sense of 'me' and 'not-me'; the soft 'me' is threatened by the hard 'not-me', which he tries to soften by becoming *confused* with it. In these procedures, seductive behaviour is much in evidence. On the other hand, the encapsulated psychotic child feels *fused* with the hard 'not-me' to make a shell to protect his vulnerable softness.

Within this 'shell' he feels impenetrable. The encapsulating child uses moulding of hard outside objects to have control over them and to make them part of his body. They are the Peer Gynt 'button-moulders' of this world. The confusional child uses melting and 'sucking-up-to', to soften hard outside objects into the 'me-ness' of 'me'. Both types of psychotic child have encountered the reality of hardness in a situation, and at a time in development, when they could not cope with it. They could not integrate the experience of hardness with the experience of pleasurable softness, in order that new sensations could be born, those of resilience, suppleness and toughness. These are states in which adaptability and adjustment can come into operation. Instead, the feelings of loss and despairing disillusionment were so overwhelming that paralysed or crippling recoil was inevitable. In this state, either the child is frozen into what seems to him to be a situation of incompatible and unmodifiable extremes, or he melts into engulfing softness. On this primary sensuous level of experience, the child's own constitution, as well as the type of nurturing he receives, affect his capacity to integrate the hard and soft aspects of experience, and thus to develop the inner strength to tolerate the 'not-self'.

As well as the 'not-self' being threatening because it is full of uncomfortable sensuous evacuations, it is also threatening because it becomes imbued with pre-conceptual atavistic elements from our animal past which have not been humanised and civilised within the post-natal shelter. I have had constantly recurring evidence that these children feel threatened by rivalrous predators who are savage in their attacks and intentions. Thus, it is not surprising that psychotic children have many features in common with those reported cases of wild children, who were often reputed to have been brought up by wolves. Such a boy was found wandering in the woods of southern France in 1800 and was treated by Dr Itard (Itard and Malson, 1972).

In therapy, the children have made clear to me their fear that a very exciting bit of their bodies will be snatched away by 'not-me' predators. Their impulse is to hide either themselves or the exciting object which gives them such entrancing sensations. The enthralling thing which is hidden can either be felt as the tongue in the mouth, or faeces in the

anus, or food in the stomach, or, as we shall see in the chapter concerned
with autistic objects, it can be the sensation made by a Dinky car hidden
in the hollow of the hand. In their immature state, and in reaction to
these threats, some of which also come from their own evacuations,
auto-sensuousness becomes over-used in a compulsive and rigid way.
These pathological auto-sensuous procedures prevent the child from using
the nurturing which is almost invariably available, although in varying
degrees. Our job is to help parents and child to come together again so
that normal development can begin to take place.

In this work, an understanding of what several psychotic children have
called 'the black hole' or 'the deep pit' is of crucial importance. This is
a later way of depicting the unknown 'not-me', which came with the
traumatic infantile experience of bodily separateness from the mother.
In these terms, the encapsulators have been *shutting out* the 'not-me'
'black hole'. They are averted from being aware of it. The danger when
working with these children is that we may have a blind spot to this
'black hole' (both in them and in ourselves) and may collude with their
attempts to shut it out. The confusionals are enmeshed with the 'black
hole'. It is all around them, hampering them and making them feel
perplexed and bewildered. They often express this at a certain stage in
their psychotherapy as being at the bottom of a deep well or in a dark
pit out of which they cannot climb. The danger with these children is
that the therapist will be drawn into the vortex of the 'black hole', or
engulfed in the deep pit, and become as bewildered and hampered as
they are.

Another complication in treatment is that, as it begins to work, the
encapsulated child will become aware of the 'black hole', awareness of
which has been shut out. At this stage, he may become bewildered by
it and may appear to be a confusional child. However, the encapsulators
are usually stronger children, in that they have been able to develop a
hard construction (the encapsulation) to keep the threatening 'not-me'
'black hole' at bay, so the confusional state is likely to be of short
duration. But it is often succeeded by a phobic one, in which the threatening 'black hole' with all its Hieronymus Bosch-type terrors is encapsulated in the phobic object or situation. This is often difficult to deal with,
as the black despair is very intense. The confusional child is also full of
terrors but these are diffused and dispersed throughout all his activities
and are not encapsulated in one specific object or place as a phobia. In
both types of child, encountering the 'black hole' of bodily separateness,
and being helped to tolerate it, is a prelude to the journey down the
dark tunnel to achieve a *psychological birth* which, as a result of their
pathology, is protracted and difficult. This will be discussed in the next
chapter.

Chapter 9

Psychological birth and psychological catastrophe

INTRODUCTION

This chapter is based on psychoanalytic therapy with psychotic children and with the psychotic residues in neurotic children. It will suggest that the situation described by Dr Bion as a 'psychological catastrophe' is associated with a traumatic 'psychological birth'. In normal development, psychological birth coincides with physical birth, but in psychotic children psychological birth has been experienced as a catastrophe. This causes the cognitive inhibition and dysfunctioning which are outstanding features of psychotic states.

PSYCHOLOGICAL CATASTROPHE

From his work with adult patients, Bion has likened the situation which confronts a psychoanalyst, when working at depth with a psychotic patient, to that of an archaeologist who comes upon a ruined city and finds in the course of its excavation that, because of the collapse and movement of rock strata, sherds and other objects from earlier stages are jumbled together with pottery and artefacts from later stages (Bion, 1962b). The appropriate nicety of this metaphor is well borne out by work with children. Clinical work at depth inevitably takes us back to the early stages of infancy. When working with psychotic states we find that, in infancy, developmental phases have telescoped. Later stages have been experienced precociously and out of phase, alongside current and earlier stages, in a confused and disordered fashion.

Evidence of this comes from many writers. In their paper on borderline children, Rosenfeld and Sprince (1963) describe such children's precocious phallic developments. When analysing these children they found 'pseudo-phallic' elements inextricably intermingled with oral elements. This implies that the child's responses to the breast have been over-eroticised. Meltzer and his co-workers confirm that this has been the case (Meltzer, *et al.*, 1975). Winnicott has described the pseudo-maturity of patients who have developed what he terms a 'false self' (Winnicott, 1971). Helene Deutsch described the fragments of precocity found in 'as if' patients (Deutsch, 1942). Other workers have been impressed by the precocious development of certain ego functions such as musical or mathematical ability (albeit of a stereotyped kind), whilst other faculties remain in the psychological doldrums. Other writers have written of the 'precocious ego development' (James, 1960).

In this chapter it will be suggested that the telescoping and jumbling of developmental phases, some of which develop precociously, are due to a traumatic 'psychological birth', or perhaps more accurately, to the cumulative trauma of such a catastrophe since, due to repetition-compulsion, the disastrous situation is repeated over and over again in an attempt to come to terms with it.

PSYCHOLOGICAL BIRTH

I had begun to use the metaphor of psychological birth before meeting Anni Bergman at a psychoanalytical conference in London, where she gave me the book written by Margaret Mahler, Fred Pine and herself called *The Psychological Birth of the Human Infant* (Mahler, *et al.*, 1975). This is a monumental work based on long experience with psychotic children and on meticulous observation of normal infants and children as part of a carefully planned research project. It is a classic in the field.

Applying Bion's (1962a) work on 'thinking' to psychotherapy with psychotic children had led me to invest the notion of psychological birth with slightly different connotations from those used by Mahler and her associates, although their book has added to my understanding of it. Bion has drawn attention to the mother's capacity for empathic reflection, for which he uses the apt term 'reverie'. Through his writings, we have come to realise that, in normal development, the newborn infant is sheltered in what might be termed the 'womb' of the mother's mind just as much as, prior to his physical birth, he was sheltered within the womb of her body.

There is another possibility which seems to contribute to the womb-like state of early infancy. It is tenable that, in spite of the caesura of birth, there is not an absolutely abrupt transition from the sensations associated with being inside the womb to being outside it. Tactile sensations of being in the 'watery medium' (Bion's term) appear to linger on and to be carried over into the child's earliest experience of the outside world. In using the term 'oceanic feeling' for these early states, Rolland seems to have had something like this in mind (Rolland, 1930; Freud, 1930).

The poet Tagore wrote, 'On the seashore of endless worlds children play.' This line, quoted by Winnicott in *Playing and Reality* (1971), is evocative of the unbounded timelessness of womb-like oceanic states. In the early weeks of life, sensations of being in the watery medium of the womb appear to linger on and to be carried over into the child's earliest experience of the outside world. This means that the child's earliest illusions are imbued with womb experiences. As C. Day Lewis (1943) expresses it:

> Faintly they hear, through the womb's lingering haze,
> A rumour of that sea from which they are born. . . .

> For infants time is like humming shell,
> Heard between sleep and sleep

> (From *Oh dreams, Oh destinations*)

These poetic intuitions are confirmed by the recent work of certain paediatricians and obstetricians. Records of sounds from within the womb, such as the mother's heartbeat and underwater noises, have been found to have a marked soothing effect on a crying infant in the early weeks of life. If, for any of a large number of possible interacting circumstances, the infant is 'catapulted' too soon or too harshly from this essential womb-like state, then trouble is in store. Or, for some of many reasons, there may be an inconsistent nurturing situation in which the child feels at one time engulfed in an unduly soft womb-like state and at other times abruptly ejected.

As to why in certain circumstances psychosis is the result and in others it is not, is difficult to fathom. My own intuitions lead me to think that in many cases there is a constitutional vulnerability or a genetic trait within the child; in situations such as have been described, these lead to the development of massive autistic obstructions to painful realities, which have been experienced before the infant's neuro-mental apparatus was ready to stand the strain. Detailed accounts of regular observations of infants who later show autistic features will help us to get deeper insights into this problem. Even at this stage of the work with autistic children such detailed observations have done much to correct the hurtful global generalisations of earlier years when the mothers were held to be 'to blame' for their child's tragic disorder. We know now that there are a wide variety of factors which, in their interaction with each other, can result in the infant's rejection of a reality which he can share with others in his culture. We are also beginning to realise that a quite small deviation in early infancy can become progressively worse until normal processes either do not take place, or are considerably distorted.

Dr Derek Ricks's research on the language development of autistic children demonstrated that such children had not the lalling and babbling sounds which seemed to be universal in the control groups of normal infants he studied, whether they were English-speaking or from countries such as Egypt or Spain (Ricks, 1975). It seemed that the autistic children had not 'played' with the sounds which arise 'naturally' from in-built predispositions. Instead they made sounds which were idiosyncratic to each individual autistic child and which they seemed to have concocted for themselves in the way that a normal infant will do later on when 'play' with 'natural' sounds is on the wane. This is in keeping with the artificiality of autistic children, and with the impression that they have missed an early 'natural' stage of development. My thesis is that this is due to a catastrophic 'psychological birth' and the excruciating intense feelings associated with this.

MISMANAGED OR PREMATURE PSYCHOLOGICAL BIRTH

This chapter is dealing with elemental states which are normally deeply buried and not investigated. Individuals whose early infantile events were normal were relatively unconscious of them at the time they occurred and seem unlikely to have conscious memories of them later. A traumatic psychological birth is also covered over, and the individual only becomes affected by it if it disturbs his behaviour to such an extent that he has to seek psychiatric help. Other individuals with special talents may work over their psychological birth, whether traumatic or otherwise, through the medium of art, literature, music or religious rituals.

Psychological study of such states is difficult, for they are pre-verbal and pre-conceptual. Communication about them has to be by means of metaphor and analogy and these inevitably distort the original experience. The skill here is in finding the metaphor which is most apt. 'Psychological catastrophe' and 'psychological birth' have seemed to me to be apt metaphors. (Formulations about these levels seem best described as metaphors rather than concepts.)

In writing about such states we are making conscious processes which are normally left unconscious and expressed through empathy and intuition. The mother of a newborn infant has a period of heightened awareness when, through cradling him in her 'reveries', she can respond to elemental states in her child but, like the intense emotional experience of giving birth, these heightened states of responsiveness gradually fade to become dim and forgotten. However, communications about very early infancy seem likely to find an echo in the experience of earthy maternal women, in those men with marked feminine characteristics, or in men and women who follow one of the professions which develop deep maternal qualities. For others, communications about these states will not seem meaningful for they are deeply buried and should probably remain so.

In order to help ourselves and our patients, some of us are drawn into becoming aware of, and communicating about these deep levels.

Unfortunately this is an area of human experience about which vague, over-simplistic generalisations tend to be presented as precise facts. This is to be regretted, for these are states which need particularly cautious analysis and statement, plus an aptitude for evocative and apt description. It has seemed to me that, in concentrating on physical birth and pre-birth, some workers in the field of psychosis are describing states which can often more feasibly be attributed to the womb-like state of early infancy. Such workers often seem to be concretising, as bodily events, elementary psychological events which should be described as such. 'Physical birth' may prove a helpful metaphor to patients for working over a difficult 'psychological birth' but, in attempting to theorise about such states, we need to be more cautious and specific. Of course, if the physical birth has been a difficult one, then the psychological birth may be difficult, but this is not inevitable. It will depend upon the consti-tutional endowment of the infant, the events of early infancy and the quality of maternal sheltering he receives. Certainly, clinical material from deep levels seems to indicate that traversing the birth canal is not only a preparation for life itself, but is also a rehearsal for the 'valley of the shadow of death'. The parental attitudes during birth and the sort of sheltering he receives or, as the result of constitutional factors, he is able to use will affect whether he will 'fear no evil', i.e. whether he will develop 'basic trust' and thus be able to bear the mistrust which is essential to survival.

Within the sane and healthy sheltering, but not entangling, of the post-natal womb, psychological integrations take place, just as bodily integrations took place within the physical womb of the mother's body. These are processes which are normally taken for granted, for they go on at relatively unconscious levels. They can only be studied if the postnatal womb seems to have been split open before these primal pro-cesses have become integrated. If this occurs, the processes are laid bare. In psychotic states this is the case and we become aware of processes and intense states of feeling which are not normally available to study.

PRIMARY INTEGRATIONS

Work with unintegrated and disintegrated states in children has led me to think that one of the earliest integrations which needs to take place is between 'hard' and 'soft' sensations. In the sensation-dominated state of early infancy the infant's primary distinctions are between 'comfort' and 'discomfort' – 'pleasure' and 'unpleasure'. 'Soft' sensations are pleasurable and comfortable. 'Hard' sensations are unpleasurable and uncomfortable.

Gradually, 'soft' sensations become associated with 'taking-in', with receptivity. 'Hard' sensations become associated with 'entering' and 'thrusting'. At some point, these become associated with the infant's bisexuality. 'Hard' thrusting becomes 'male', and 'soft' receptivity becomes 'female'. When, on the basis of a co-operative suckling experience, the 'hard' entering nipple and tongue are experienced as working together with the 'soft' receptive mouth and breast, then a 'marriage' between 'male' and 'female' elements takes place. Out of this union of 'hard' and 'soft' sensations, a new way of functioning is born, that of firm, adaptable resilience and toughness. This means that reality can begin to be processed, and sensation-dominated delusions will wither away. The world will begin to 'make sense'. And in this 'making sense' of the outside world, the parents play a very important part. (The rudimentary psychological integrations which have just been described will, of course, be paralleled by neurophysiological integrations taking place in the child's brain and nervous system. These are not within my competence or my province to describe, but I think they should be mentioned.)

In this account of basic integrations, we might say that 'nipple–tongue' is 'hardness', and 'mouth–breast' is 'softness.' In a satisfactory suckling experience sensations of 'softness' and 'hardness' work together to produce a state of 'well-being'. 'Well-being' is a psychological as well as a bodily experience. Thus, bodily sensations have been transformed into *psychological* experience through reciprocal and rhythmical activity between mother and infant. The stage is set for percept and concept formation. But this is a mysterious process and in this chapter we can only hope to touch the fringes of it.

The foregoing is a bare outline of the processes of primary differentiation and integration as I have come to understand them. This understanding has mainly been obtained from a study of those children in whom the processes have been disturbed. Such children demonstrate for us the hazards which may have to be encountered before a salutary outcome is reached. Some of these will now be discussed.

CRITICAL SITUATIONS FOR PRIMARY INTEGRATIONS

Clinical material from unintegrated and disintegrated children indicates that critical situations in primary integration are those occasions when the infant becomes aware that 'hard' and 'soft' are both 'me' sensations, and that both can emanate from the same source outside himself. It is at this stage that processes of projection are stimulated and get under way.

In *Beyond the Pleasure Principle*, Freud (1920) alerted us to the process of *projection* by which uncomfortable states are felt to be outside the body. 'Comfort' is 'me', 'discomfort' is 'not-me'. 'Softness' is 'me', 'hardness' is 'not-me'. This is well illustrated by a commonly reported feature of psychotic children, many of whom will only eat soft foods and reject hard lumps. With this dichotomy between the 'soft me' and the 'hard not-me', 'twoness' comes into being. But, in this early phase of 'twoness', the 'soft me' is excessively vulnerable. This constitutes a critical situation. If the maternal sheltering is disturbed at this time, the infant feels exposed to 'nameless dreads' (to use a telling phrase of Dr Bion's).

The following extract of clinical material illustrates this situation as the child works over it in the protected situation of the psychoanalytic setting. The child seems to be trying to tell the psychiatrist about a time when his tender naked body felt unprotected from a hostile outside world. Just as we have to use metaphors for the description of these wordless states of awareness, so children have to use picture language. This child's representation was moving and vivid.

CLINICAL MATERIAL

Graham was twelve years old at the time when he worked over some of the elemental terrors to be demonstrated by the clinical presentation. He had been a 'school ditherer' (i.e. he was not an 'out and out' school phobic). He found it difficult to go back to school on Mondays. He was seen once a week for psychoanalytic therapy by Dr Alicia Etchegoyan, who discussed the material with me in a weekly supervision time. (I am indebted to Dr Etchegoyan for permission to use this material.)

22 *October*   Graham had an accident to his dental plate and so did not come to his session.

29 *October*   Graham came and there was material about damage to his mouth, which was related to infantile situations when he felt he lost the nipple of the breast which he had taken for granted as being part of his mouth, and then felt that his mouth was 'broken' or 'damaged'.

5 *November*   Graham brought material about having precious things to protect but his special protection for these things gets 'crashed'. He then went on to describe an underwater situation with great vividness. He said he had seen this situation when on holiday in Devon (i.e. when he was apart from his therapist). He described a little baby crab whose mother was not there to protect it. Its shell had not hardened as yet and it was pink and tender. It could easily have been attacked and eaten by the sea creatures which were around. In order to avoid this, it scuttled into an empty snail shell which was in the sea and there it was safe. Dr Etchegoyan then talked to Graham about how he turned his hard back to protect his soft front. (This was an interpretation we had discussed together previously.) Graham replied, 'No, I protect my soft front with the

hard buckle of my belt.' He showed Dr Etchegoyan a very large buckle that was on the leather belt which encircled his waist. He also said that he had hurt his left ear twice, once yesterday and once today. Dr Etchegoyan talked to him about his need to protect all the holes in his body because they were places where dangerous things could enter and where he could easily be hurt.

12 November   Graham walked to the therapy room in a 'somewhat disjointed fashion'. He sat down and looked at the set of individual cupboards in which his own and the other children's toys are kept. (Each child has his own individual cupboard with his own key which will not open any other child's cupboard.) At first, as he looked, he touched his nails and put one nail inside the other as if extracting dirt. He then put his thumb in his mouth. Then, still looking at the cupboards, he fingered the buckle on his belt. He started to count the cupboards. Dr Etchegoyan suggested that he was counting the cupboards to take his mind off his troubles, but she did not take up his fear of the other children as creatures who would attack his soft, pink, tender body which had so many open holes where he could be hurt and where dangerous things could enter, although she realised this later. (It seems to me that excessive vulnerability is one of the root causes of the massive use of obsessional mechanisms and that it is only by helping the patient with this vulnerability that obsessionality can be mitigated.) Graham, still looking at the cupboards, fingered the hard buckle on his belt. Then he joined and separated his hands by interlacing his fingers. Then, to Dr Etchegoyan's consternation, he got up from his chair and rushed out of the room. He ran round the clinic building in a state of panic before returning to the shelter of his mother in the waiting-room.

After this, there were several sessions when he refused to come to the clinic, but Dr Etchegoyan kept in touch with Graham's mother by telephone. On one occasion, the mother told Dr Etchegoyan with some embarrassment and bewilderment that Graham had said that he was afraid that 'monsters would come out of the little cupboards'. Dr Etchegoyan replied that she had realised something like this had been worrying Graham and she hoped he would come so that they could talk about it. The mother seemed very relieved that what she had reported had not sounded too peculiar and went on to report, with some amusement, that she had told Graham that he must know that monsters did not exist because he had never seen one. To which he had replied, 'Why shouldn't there be monsters? Nobody has seen God but you say he exists!' After this discussion, Graham came to his next session.

DISCUSSION OF THE CLINICAL MATERIAL

Dr Etchegoyan, Graham's psychiatrist, is about to embark on a study of the elemental depths encountered in child treatment. It was very instructive to her, as also to myself, to have such a striking illustration of their power to affect a child's functioning. (We often learn more when we have failed to understand a child's communications quickly enough than when the therapeutic process flows smoothly and easily.)

This piece of material is a good illustration of the residues of unintegration which are encountered in the psychoanalytic treatment of neurotic children. It is also a good illustration of the importance of concentrating on psychic events rather than outside circumstances when dealing with 'as if' levels of personality. Patients at these levels use outside events as a kind of psycho-drama. Their internal psychic life is negligible. Bettelheim's metaphor of an 'empty fortress' is a very apt description of them (Bettelheim, 1967).

It has been my experience that children often use underwater situations to express the oceanic feeling. The little pink naked crab who has lost his mother is a telling picture of vulnerability. This excessive vulnerability makes Graham feel exposed to creatures who threaten him. This is the crux of his fear at school. The other children are not just children, they are 'monsters' – all-powerful things from the primitive depths which threaten him with death. Kind reassurance and rational reasoning offer no permanent relief. It is only by working over these elemental terrors through the infantile transference of the psychotherapeutic setting that the child can come to terms with them. Otherwise, he feels forever at risk. The psychotherapeutic setting seems to be a kind of incubator in which the psychological 'prem' can achieve those basic integrations which he did not make in infancy. Without these, a sense of primal attachment and basic trust are not possible.

As the supervisor of this material, I learned something I had not previously known so clearly. I had become aware of such children's preoccupation with having an 'extra bit' to their bodies. This always has to be a 'hard' bit. The hard metal buckle was such an extra hard bit for Graham, and this made me aware of the ultra-protective nature of this hard extra bit. For me, this threw light on the commonly reported feature of some psychotic children who take hard things like metal trains to bed with them rather than soft 'cuddly' toys as the normal child will do.

The underwater material shows another way of getting protection. The vulnerable Graham-crab enters the 'hardness' of another creature. In this protective manoeuvre we see 'intrusive identification' (Meltzer's term) in action. This results in the 'false self' described by Winnicott; and the 'as if' condition described by Deutsch (1942). In later life, these patients live their lives through other people to an excessive and pathological degree. (They are the Strindbergs of this world.)

Encased in this 'shell', such children are impenetrable to nurturing influences and their development is halted. Important basic integrations do not take place. It is one of the most difficult situations to deal with in psychotherapy. Removal of the protective manoeuvre brings the threat of a repetition of the 'psychological catastrophe' from which the child has retreated.

This is the crux of the problem of non-integration or disintegration. Let me now summarise why this seems to be so. As was stated earlier, the child has experienced 'twoness' too harshly, too suddenly *for him*. In early infancy, comfortable 'softness' is the prime consideration. To preserve this, the hard 'not-me' is felt to be outside. But then this hard 'not-me' is threatening. This seems to be the forerunner of the 'stranger anxiety' described by Spitz (1960) for later stages of development. It seems possible that these 'not-me' threats combine with the atavistic fear of predators from our animal ancestry to which ethologists have drawn our attention. Certainly, these 'nameless dreads' often become focused upon 'creatures'.

In his paper on imitation, Eugenio Gaddini (1969) tried to clear our minds about the psychoanalytic use of terms for early developmental situations and also to clarify for us the order in which early processes occur. Based on his own psychoanalytic work with adult patients and that of his wife Renata Gaddini with infants and children, he sees primitive rivalry as being even earlier than the primary envy described by both Klein (1957) and Jacobson (1964). This confirms my own experience. Children who have experienced traumatic 'set-backs' to their ongoing psychological development seem to have been faced by death-dealing 'rivals' who could never have existed in reality, and whose threats were of worse than death. Even 'annihilation anxiety' seems too mild a term to describe the state of terror which either paralyses these children or causes them to behave in an impulsively irrational way, like dashing out of the consulting-room or refusing to go to school. The threat is of a cataclysmic catastrophe which they feel they have already experienced, a repetition of which must be avoided at all costs. (This needs detailed clinical material to make it meaningful to workers who have not experienced these elemental states.)

This dichotomy between the hypervulnerable soft 'me' and the calloused-over, impenetrable protection seems to be the basic situation in some forms of criminality. In his studies of murderousness, from psychoanalytic work with seven murderers in Wormwood Scrubs Prison, Dr Hyatt Williams (1960) has told us of the excessively tender feelings which such patients had beneath their callous exteriors. It would also seem to be a basic situation in some phobic patients.

So far, we have discussed states of unintegration, i.e. 'hard' and 'soft' sensations have not been integrated. But in some psychopathologies we come upon disintegration, i.e. 'hard' and 'soft' sensations have been insecurely integrated, to break down under strain. Critical situations would seem to arise when the attempt is made to integrate these basic states of sensation. When 'hardness' penetrates 'softness', excitement is produced. The prototype of this is when the hard nipple enters the soft mouth. If the excitement can be tolerated, it is pleasurable and a sublime state of 'oneness' occurs. But the excitement can mount until a state of ecstasy is reached.

ECSTASY

States of ecstasy result from a sublime sense of 'oneness' experienced by mother and infant. In-built predispostions seem to find exact coincidence in the outside world. But whether this ecstasy can be borne will depend upon the maternal capacity to experience and bear such states of ecstasy within herself. If, for a variety of reasons, which may be part of a temporary passing phase, the mother's capacity to bear such extreme states is muted, then the infant is left to bear such states alone. In normal development, for much of the time, the mother will seem to 'hold' (Winnicott, 1958) her infant together so that he does not disintegrate under the discharge of intense excitement. She also seems to contain (Bion, 1962b) the discharges which are beyond the infant's capacity to bear and to process. These are psychological as well as physiological. If the mother cannot hold her infant together in these intense states of excitement and cannot seem to bear the 'overflow', and process it by empathy and understanding, the infant experiences a devastating sense of 'twoness', which seems fraught with disaster. Instead of experiencing ecstasy as a peak of sublime oneness which helps him to feel 'rooted' in a nurturant situation, the infant feels cut off from it. He feels adrift and alone. The insecurity of this distressing sense of 'twoness' leads to pathological manoeuvres to reinstate the sense of oneness. In confusional psychotic children, these are entangling in nature. They result in confusion with the body of the maternal object used as a protective shell (the snail shell of Graham's vulnerable baby crab). From this, it is difficult to achieve normal separation in an appropriate and progressive way. The encapsulated children have the delusion of making their own protective shell out of their own autogenerated sensual activities.

PRECOCIOUS 'TWONESS'

Such hypersensitive children are aware of too much, too soon, too harshly, too suddenly *for them*. They experience an agony of consciousness which is beyond their capacity to tolerate or to pattern. Various protective autistic manoeuvres are used to deaden their awareness in order to avoid suffering. These result in their being out of touch with reality. Awareness of the outside world is inhibited or grossly distorted. Psychological integrations do not take place; behaviour becomes idiosyncratic. In extreme instances the child becomes psychotic.

The fact that the infant experiences 'twoness' in a state of hypersensitivity and omnipotence is also important.

In this state the infant operates in terms of bodily sensations, rhythms and in-built predispositions. For the newly born these have not been modified by reciprocal interplay with the outside world. The infant feels that his movements and urges make things occur, for example, that his crying results in 'nipple-in-mouth', which seems to be the prototype for sensual completeness. However, precocious awareness of bodily separateness and 'twoness' brings the knowledge that the nipple is not part of his mouth and that his movements do not always make for completeness and do not produce benign hallucinations. His unsatisfied crying mouth can then seem like a 'black hole with a nasty prick' (as one child vividly described the situation of the breast which was absent from his mouth). This is a malign hallucination. Also, the frustration of the absent breast, of the uncompleted gestalt, is experienced as a tangible irritant, as a hard and painful friction – as roughness. Irritating friction produces rage and panic. When this reaches a peak of intensity it results in a *tantrum* – a *fit* of temper as we often term it.

TANTRUM

On referral, autistic children often have a history of a passing phase of 'fits' which do not seem to have been strictly epileptic in nature. Other children have a history of 'tantrums' in infancy. I have found this to be a hopeful prognostic sign since it indicates that they have made some attempt to integrate the 'hard' and 'soft' facets of early experience. (Those psychotic children who have a history of having been 'exceptionally good babies' would seem to have remained in a state in which there was little attempt to integrate these basic aspects of sensation and, thus, little friction and disturbance.)

The tantrum, like the ecstasy, needs nurturing which is capable of holding the child together through intense bodily-cum-psychological states. At these levels, ecstasy and tantrum seem to be on the bodily model of a puckering of the muscles, as in the frown, the smile, the quiver, the shiver or the spasm (Darwin, 1892). The mother also needs to seem to 'contain' the bodily-cum-psychological discharges, expressed in such reactions as urination, defecation and spitting, associated with the rage and panic of the tantrum. If these are not 'contained' by the mother, the delusion will be that they spread around in an uncontrolled and explosive fashion to bring about a catastrophe.

Unbearable bodily tension which is not understood, empathised and relieved by the mother quickly enough is experienced as a disturbing 'overflow'. Unbearable bodily tension is uncomfortable. It feels turgid and hard. It is projected as 'not-me'. Thus, the sense of 'oneness' is disturbed and 'twoness' results, but in a way that is unduly painful and sudden and causes a precipitate coming together of a 'self' which is not genuine – a 'false self' as Winnicott (1958) has termed it.

Work with psychotic children has brought home to me the importance of this 'overflow' – this 'spill-over' of psychological and physiological tension. The child experiences it as tangible body stuff which overflows out of his control. He cannot process it. He recoils from this dangerous stuff in the 'not-me' outside world. Or he may feel possessed by it and be unmanageably hyperactive. In early infancy, the mother's disciplined attitudes and behaviour seem to control, channel and render harmless this overflow which is beyond the child's control. She acts as both ana-lyser and synthesiser, just as, if things go wrong, the psychoanalyst has to do in a more artificial way later on.

OVERFLOW

There are many ways in which the mother can give the child the impression that she is giving way under the impact of the 'overflow'. She may be absent in mind or in body. She may avert herself from noticing it and act as if it did not exist. She may be too permissive. She may be too strict or too teasing and thus provoke too much frustration and too much 'overflow'. The worst situation seems to be one of gross inconsist-ency, of swaying between over-strictness and over-permissiveness in a way which is inappropriate to the particular child and the particular circumstances. The situation that becomes very clear in working with psychotic states is that unbearable awareness of bodily separateness from the mother has occurred too suddenly and too harshly *for that particular infant*. This has resulted in a catastrophic feeling of being wounded and mutilated.

PRE-ANIMATE STATES

Bion's term 'container' seems very apt for the concretised functioning in terms of the inanimate objects which are under discussion. The early states of differentiation between 'hardness' and 'softness' take place before the important distinctions between 'animate' and 'inanimate' (to which Spitz has drawn our attention) are made or before they have become securely established. These early differentiations are the bedrock of human personality before the 'humanness' of psychological functioning has emerged. They are physiological integrations with incipient psychological overtones which are extremely important in giving the personality its basic 'set'.

The psychotic child who, when taken to an educational psychologist for psychological testing, would only draw a ruined house, and would do nothing else, was obviously communicating about a psychological catastrophe which he felt to be at the root of his being. This had seemed to happen to an inanimate 'thing' and not to a person. This child had been suddenly weaned at four months of age and then separated from his mother. But other children who manifest states of unintegration or disintegration have not necessarily had a geographical separation from the mother. Through no fault of their own, or of their mother, the maternal sheltering has seemed to be shattered. As Bergman and Escalona have shown, for some children the 'maternal shield' has not been adequate (Bergman and Escalona, 1949). In another situation, a mother may find it difficult to 'take to' and to empathise with her newborn child. In some cases, the mother was not emotionally 'ready' for the birth of this baby. In other situations, the mother may find it difficult to empathise with the child who is very different from herself. A marked example of this is when a baby is born with a handicap such as deafness, blindness or spasticity. It requires a great effort of imagination to sense such a child's responses. In other situations, the mother may be depressed, or the father may be away from home, or the mother and father may be having a phase when they do not 'get on' together.

These, and other situations which Dr S. Tischler (1979) has described very feelingly, interconnect with each other to produce what seems to the child to be a 'psychological catastrophe' at the root of his being. This has happened to a 'body-self' – a 'felt-self' – in a traumatic way. His self-representation is thus on a false basis and his sensation-ego is defective. Such traumatic bodily separateness from the mother is experienced by the infant as the loss of a bodily part. This means that instead of normally timed differentiation and integration, explosive disintegration or paralysed unintegration is the order of the day. In later life, such a child feels 'cursed' rather than 'blessed', for these situations are associated with hypersensitised states of omnipotence which result in feelings that are larger than life. This catastrophe has to be re-experienced and worked over if psychotherapy is to modify the pathological processes of autism.

CONCLUSION

The essence of the thesis developed in this chapter is that the young infant needs parental support in bearing the ecstasy of 'oneness' and the tantrum of 'twoness', if necessary primal differentiations and integrations are to take place. The therapeutic setting acts as a kind of incubator in which the psychological 'prem' can achieve those basic integrations he did not make in infancy. These extreme states are usually worked over within the privacy of parental sheltering. It seems somewhat indecent to lay them bare. Perhaps this is *one* of the reasons why psychosis seems so shocking and disturbing to normal individuals. Something is being made public which should be kept private. Analysing such states seems rather like trying to put a dream or a nightmare under a microscope. It just cannot be done. It is a paradox that these crude states need extreme delicacy and subtlety in their delineation. To write about them often seems brash and clumsy, but not to do so seems a professional dereliction. The ways in which psychological birth is impeded by the use of autistic and confusional objects will be discussed in the next two chapters.

NOTE

This chapter is based on a paper written for a Festschrift in honour of Dr Bion's eightieth birthday. It was presented in the Rome Institute of Psychoanalysis and the Institute of Neuropsychiatry of Rome University.

Chapter 10

Autistic objects

This chapter seeks to bring further understandings concerning autistic objects, which were first described in *Autism and Childhood Psychosis* (Tustin, 1972). Autistic objects are objects which are peculiar to each individual child. They are used obsessively in idiosyncratic ways which handicap mental development. They are mainly used by encapsulated autistic children, although not all autistic children use them. Two clinical illustrations will now be given which exemplify the nature and function of autistic objects. These objects were illustrated in Helen High's observational study of autistic children in Chapter 1.

CLINICAL ILLUSTRATION

At the beginning of treatment an autistic ten-year-old boy called David used to bring a Dinky car to every session. This car was clasped so tightly in the hollow of his hand that it left a deep impression when he took it out. In working with him, it became clear that the Dinky car was felt to have magical properties to protect him from danger. As such, it was like a talisman or amulet. The difference between David's car and a talisman was that he felt that by pressing it hard into the hollow of his hand, it became a hard extra bit to his body. Even if he placed it on the table, the deeply imprinted sensation remained, so that it was as if the car were still a part of his body to keep him safe.

Another autistic child called Peter, who was six years old at the beginning of treatment, used to bring to his sessions a large key-ring with over fifty keys on it. It became clear that he felt that this was a hard extra bit to his body.

However, during the period when these children felt protected by their autistic objects, they were impenetrable to my attempts to help them. Thus, it seemed important to understand the nature of these objects and the possible origin of their use.

THE NATURE OF AUTISTIC OBJECTS

An outstanding characteristic of autistic objects is that they are not used in terms of the function for which they were intended. Instead, they are used in ways which are idiosyncratic to each child. For example, David did not push his Dinky car along the table or play with it on the floor as a normal or neurotic child would have done. Peter did not use the keys to open cupboards or doors; he just carried them around. From a realistic point of view they were used in a way which was useless and meaningless; from the child's point of view, they were absolutely essential.

The hard metal trains and cars which some autistic children take to bed with them to put under their pillows are similarly not used in terms of their intended function as playthings. Nor can it be said that they are used for fantasy purposes. There is a 'let's pretend' quality in fantasy play and a realisation of bodily separateness from the object, which is lacking in the psychotic child's use of his autistic objects. They have a bizarre and ritualistic quality and the child has a rigidly intense preoccupation with them, which is not a feature of fantasy play. The objects which some psychotic children spin obsessively have a similar quality.

This brings me to another characteristic feature of autistic objects as used by autistic children. They may have no fantasy whatsoever associated with them, or they may be associated with extremely crude fantasies which are very close to bodily sensations. Childhood autism is a sensation-dominated state, and autistic objects are sensation-dominated objects. As a result of the paucity of fantasy associated with them, they are used in an extremely canalised and repetitive fashion. They are static and do not have the open-ended qualities which would lead to the development of new networks of association. They are the result of, and result in, vicious circles of activity which become entrenched. It is inevitable that writing about them should become imbued with this circularity to some extent.

Another typical feature of autistic objects is the lack of normal discrimination between them. The key-ring that Peter carried around with him had many keys on it. If one were lost, there was always another to replace it. David did not bring the same Dinky car each time. At the beginning of his treatment, it was the hard sensation in the hollow of his hand which was important to him. Many Dinky cars could give him the same sensation. Thus, it did not matter which one he used. If one Dinky car were not to be found, another one would do. Some psychotic children have one autistic object which is used for a time in a stereotyped and ritualised way. It is then discarded, to be replaced by another which is used similarly. Over a period of time, there may be a succession of objects which have been used in turn, with an intensity which shuts out awareness of anything else. They are used, discarded and replaced by another one. If an autistic object is gone, the child is distressed as if he had lost a part of his body, but the object is soon replaced by another one which is experienced as being the same. (The encapsulated psychotic children are relatively undiscriminating. The confusional children have bizarre modes of discrimination. Apropos of this lack of discrimination of encapsulated children Sandra Stone comments, 'Towards the end of treatment, Sam [the child whose clinical material is given in Chapter 16] confessed that he could not tell who familiar people were if he saw them moving or wearing different clothes.')

However, it is important to realise that the psychotic child's inability to tolerate the fact of loss comes from his having experienced excruciating distress described by Mahler as 'grief' about the seeming loss of an instinctually significant part of the nursing mother which had been felt to be part of his body (Winnicott, 1958; Mahler, 1961; Tustin, 1972). *This loss was experienced as a loss of part of his body and not as the loss of the mother and her breast.* It is this situation which has led to the obsessive use of objects which are experienced as if they are bodily parts.

The foregoing discussion hints at another characteristic feature of autistic objects. The sensation-dominated state of the autistic child means that such children live in a globally apprehended world. This is very different from ours. We distinguish objects from each other by more than the mere sensation of their shape. We use other clues. Autistic children do not. Their responses are solely on the basis of contour and outline: meaning and function are not taken into account. Thus, at one time, Peter thought that the word 'boiler' was 'boy' with an extra bit to his body. This was not a bit of fun. He was very serious about what, to us, is an amusing misconception. Hanna Segal (1957) describes an adult schizophrenic patient who was also operating on this basis of meaningless 'clang' similarities. To this patient, the piece of furniture called a 'stool' and his faecal 'stool' were equated because the same word was used for both. (Such adult patients have many features in common with confusional psychotic children. Psychoanalysts who deal exclusively with adult patients do not encounter the *unintegration* which is characteristic of the encapsulated psychotic child.)

Another factor which comes into this discussion is that in autistic children the sensory modalities are not always clearly differentiated from each other. Thus, seeing and hearing are often experienced by the child in a tactile way as being *touched* by the object. Written words which have roughly the same shape are *felt* to be the same. This applies also to objects, pictures and sounds. This leads to what the observer designates as the *concrete* nature of the autistic child's experience.

As his treatment proceeded David brought evidence of misconceptions which arose from this imprecise, tactile apprehension of the shapes of words. For example, an *Aston Martin* Dinky car was felt to have in it the essence of the village where he lived, which was called *Martin*. An *Austin* car was felt to have in it the essence of *Tustin*. To those people who have not worked with autistic children, this might seem to be an example of rhyming or punning. But these are developed forms of expression, used when the individual has a sense of his bodily separateness from other objects and has a normal perception of them. As he emerged from his autism, David was able to tell me that he had felt that the words 'Tustin' and 'Austin' must be the same because they were the same shape when they 'touched' his ears or eyes. (This is a good illustration of the way in which these children can learn to read and write, but solely on a mechanical autistic basis.)

In working with David, it was necessary to help him to realise that bringing the Aston Martin Dinky car did not mean that he brought a bit of his village with him. Nor did bringing and taking home the Austin car mean that he could carry Tustin around with him. A neurotic child would have used these cars to *represent* his feelings about his village and about himself. For David they did not *represent* his feelings. He felt them to be actual bits of Martin and of Tustin. This realisation means that in the psychoanalytic situation we deal with such material very differently from the way we would approach it with a neurotic patient. Gradually, as David developed more sense of his bodily separateness from the outside world, it was possible to talk to him about his homesickness for Martin (he was in a small boarding school for psychotic children) and his craving to have me always with him (quite literally in his pocket). To have talked to him about this in the early days would have been meaningless to him because the Dinky cars were autistic objects which shut out any sense of missing Martin or myself.

An important part of modifying such children's pathological use of their autistic objects seems to be the realisation on the part of people caring for the child that these objects are not experienced by him as *substitutes* for longed-for people. For him, they *are* that person because they give him the sensations he desires, the sensation of an object being of pre-eminent importance to him. Also the desired *sensation* is not localised in any specific part of his body. For example, if the car gave him nice feelings in the hollow of his hand, it was the same as if it were in his mouth. However, even to use the word 'desire' in this context makes the communication inexact. Autistic children cannot become aware of needs, wants or desires because they have little or no psychological equipment to help them to bear the frustration these feelings entail. Instead they use autistic objects by which they avoid the suspense of waiting. The way in which these children provoke others in their environment to be as concerned as they are to have an autistic object readily available is a striking illustration of their power to keep the autism going and to get others to collude with it.

The use of autistic objects is directed towards bodily survival. They bring almost instant satisfaction and prevent the delay between anticipation and realisation which, so long as the suspense can be tolerated, leads on to such symbolic activities as fantasies, memories and thoughts. Thus, the autistic child continues to live in a bodily way but his mental development is massively restricted. This is why many of these children function as mentally handicapped when first seen for clinical assessment. The pathological use of certain objects perpetuates the child's lack of basic trust because it prevents him from having experiences of his needs being met by people whom he recognises as being outside himself. It is only when insightful caring gets through to him that he is able to begin to give them up.

'Hardness' is a characteristic feature of most autistic objects. This gives the child the feeling that they keep him safe. Anne Alvarez (personal communication) has told me of an interesting example of an autistic object which was communicated to her by a twenty-five-year-old man who seemed to be a 'recovered' autistic child. He was talking about his childhood and said that he used to take a cannon-ball to bed with him. When asked what was important to him in this object, he said, 'It kept me safe.' He then went on to say that what he valued was its 'hardness' and its 'smoothness'. Autistic children, because they lack experience of civilising relationships with other human beings, feel constantly threatened with being attacked and hurt. They feel that their helpless bodies are a target for savage and brutal attacks. They particularly feel that the projecting parts of their bodies will be bitten off in very barbarous ways. The castration anxiety of neurotic children is mild as compared with the perils that autistic children feel they have to face. The main purpose of autistic objects (that is, objects used as part of the body to give reassuring and diverting sensations) is to shut out menaces which threaten bodily attack and ultimate annihilation. *Hardness* helps the soft and vulnerable child to feel safe in a world which seems fraught with unspeakable dangers, and about which he feels unutterable terror. These objects help to prevent the realisation of bodily separateness and to promote the delusion that impingements from the outside world are obstructed. One of the ways in which they do this is by focusing attention on familiar bodily sensations rather than the strange 'not-me' outside world.

But this is the sophisticated view of the observer and, in order to bring clarity to a discussion of undifferentiated states through the differentiated medium of words, it is necessary to distinguish the experience of the observer from the very different experience of the relatively undifferentiated child. For the *child*, an autistic object is primarily a *sensation*. But the *observer* is aware of the object which provokes the sensation. However, for the child who is functioning on these undifferentiated, elemental levels, a *sensation* is experienced in a concrete way, as an *object*. But the *sensation-object* of the autistic child is not the same as the objects which are seen by the observer. The observer distinguishes differences in objects which all seem to be the same to the child, who only distinguishes them in terms of the sensations they give him as they seem to touch his body.

The pseudo-protection of autistic objects (or sensation-objects) prevents the child from using and developing more genuine means of protection. In particular, it prevents him from getting in touch with the caring human beings around him who would help to modify his terrors. It keeps him trapped in a bereft state, beset with fantastic terrors and with no authentic means for these to be alleviated and modified.

Because of the autistic child's lack of differentiated perception, almost any object which gives a sufficiently definite and repeatable sensation can be used. This means that an odd assortment of objects are used by different children. This was well illustrated by Helen High's observations of autistic children presented in Chapter 1.

THE ORIGINS OF AUTISTIC OBJECTS

Clinical work indicates that these pathological autistic objects have their origin in hidden auto-sensuous activities which began in earliest infancy, or even within the womb itself. Psychotic children often suck their compressed tongue. Or they suck the bunched-up pads of their cheeks. Or they wriggle their bottoms to feel the faeces in their anus. All these observations have been culled from the psychoanalytic situation in which children demonstrate to the therapist what they are doing or, when they can talk, tell her. The children may do other things to which I have not been alerted. As a rule, the caring adults are relatively unaware of these activities because they do not see them. This means that these auto-sensuous activities become more and more deviant and perverse – outside agencies cannot modify them because they are unobserved. The infants who practise such activities become increasingly odd and eccentric. The autistic objects which such children use later on, as if they are part of their bodies, seem to arise from this earlier pathology. This accounts for the idiosyncratic and compulsive nature of autistic objects.

Such objects divert the infant from turning to the suckling mother. A depressed or under-confident mother would not be able to muster sufficient firmness and resilience to attract her infant away from the delusory delights of autogenerated objects, to the real enjoyment of her breast, which for much of the time the normal child experiences as separate from his body.

The need to shut out the outside world to the massive degree character-istic of the autistic child arises from a wide variety of situations, all of which seem to occur in infancy. According to my observations, a very common precipitating infantile situation for psychogenic childhood autism is one in which a particularly vulnerable child experiences a series of shocks at a time when his neuro-mental apparatus is not sufficiently developed to stand the strain. These occur in a nurturing situation which, at that particular time and for some particular reason, cannot help him to handle it, or cannot handle it for him. Tischler (1979) has deepened our understanding of the parent's difficulties in this situation. A sad situation, which often seems to be the starting place for autistic behaviour, is that of a mother and baby who, for some reason, have been unduly close to each other, and who suddenly experience bodily separateness from each other as being torn violently apart and wounded (Bick, 1968). Rosenfeld's term 'psychic bleeding' seems apposite for this tragic situation (Rosenfeld, 1965). (At these elemental levels where psyche and soma are scarcely differentiated, physiological images are apt.) Autistic objects seem to staunch the 'bleeding' by blocking the wound. They also seem to plug the gap between the couple so that awareness of bodily separateness is occluded. Unhappily, these delusions prevent a healing, reciprocal relationship between the couple from developing.

The response to the suckling mother and her breast has been grossly disturbed, with a consequent distortion of sensuous development. These infants have turned to the instant satisfaction of autistic objects which were over-used in a pathological way. This accounts for the eccentric and unregulated behaviour of the autistic child.

For these children disillusionment occurred in a way that could not be tolerated. They have had to cope with the fact of bodily separateness from the breast before their neuro-mental organisation was sufficiently integrated to cope with this ordeal. The gap between instinctual in-built expectations and actual happenings was intolerable for them. These gaps had to be closed immediately by the over-use of bodily sensations through which they felt that they had a perfect mother always with them who gave them ecstatic and instant sensual satisfaction. This also helped to offset the devastating loneliness which bodily separateness and the ensu-ing movement towards individuation and self-identity brought in their wake. The use of autistic objects meant that they had sensation-dominated artefacts which impeded their approach to the outside world instead of gradually developing a differentiated and differentiating medium for communication and interpretation which would have amelior-ated their loneliness in a more realistic and healing way than the autistic objects can do.

THE EFFECT OF THE USE OF PATHOLOGICAL AUTISTIC OBJECTS

Such a child has missed the 'practising' stage of normal infancy which takes place during the mother's absences. For example, when studying the language development of autistic children, Dr Derek Ricks (1975) found that many of them had missed the lalling and babbling stage of normal infancy. My own observations have shown that many of them have missed the normal sucking and mouthing stage when the child creates a working simulation of the breast. This simulation enables them to develop a more skilful and efficient use of the actual breast when it comes. In short, they have missed the early learning experiences associated with play. Such a child expects to do everything at the first attempt without any practice away from the actual situation. When he fails to do this, he desists from effort. This seems to be an important component in the passivity and lack of confidence of autistic children. They have missed the creative work of adjusting illusions and developing fantasies which Winnicott's work on the transitional object and transitional phenomena has shown are a *bridge* to reality (Winnicott, 1958). Instead, they use pathological autistic objects which are a *barrier* to it. They block the apprehension of a reality which can be shared with other human beings in their culture. Nothing can get in but, more important still, nothing can get out.

Autistic objects are the result of primary creativity having gone wrong. Such children's traumatic disillusionment means that they have had insufficient opportunities for imaginative anticipation. Felt needs which are tolerable provoke anticipatory pictures which prepare the infant for what is to come. This is the beginning of hope. Instead of creating a valid working simulation of the breast which enables them to use it when it comes, they develop fake artefacts which *replace* the breast and for which they do not have to wait. (In neurotic development, a rubber 'comforter', if over-used in an obsessive way, long past the time when it is usually given up, can become such a pathological autistic object.)

Winnicott (1958) writes, 'The mother places the actual breast just where the infant is ready to create, and at the right moment.' However, as Winnicott well realises, the 'good-enough mother' inevitably fails in this feat of adaptation to her infant. For the child who is developing normally, these 'failures' on the part of the mother are his opportunity for 'creating' anticipatory pictures and new responses to the mother. As in her absences, so in the times when she does not perfectly understand and meet his needs, he has opportunities for adjusting his anticipatory pictures and adapting to his changing perceptions of her. He learns to wait. He learns to control his impulsivity. He begins to create ideas which are a *substitute* for the mother, but which do not obliterate his

need for her, or inhibit his instinctual responses to her. He begins to
relate and respond to people and situations when they are not actually
present in the physical sense. Thus, imagining and thinking develop.

The frustration of unbearable disappointment means that instead of
the creation of healthy illusions and hallucinations which lead on to
dreams, fantasies and ideas, the infant begins to manipulate autistic
objects in an excessive way. These, being tangible, sensation-dominated
and ever-present, keep the child stuck at a primitive level of over-
concretised mental functioning. Material objects become unduly important because they stimulate entrancing bodily sensations. Thus, autistic
objects come to be used to deal with unbearable frustration, but they
prevent the development of thoughts, memories and imaginations which,
in normal development, compensate in some measure for the inevitable
lack of complete satisfaction which being a human being entails. Another
result is that the children themselves are vulnerable to being manipulated
as autistic objects instead of being treated as human beings. The *echo-
praxia* of some autistic children is an extreme example of this.

When sensuality becomes directed towards inanimate autistic objects
instead of towards human beings recognised as being alive and separate,
it does not become humanised, regulated and adaptable. Instead, it
becomes impulse-ridden, uncontrolled, stereotyped and excessive. If, as
therapists, we unduly collude with the child's autistic use of objects, we
leave him in the grip of his pathology with no possibility for developing
genuine relationships characterised by effort and co-operation. Pathological autistic objects are anti-life but, paradoxically, they are used to fend
off a delusory 'death' ('nothingness', 'annihilation').

If mother and child become autistic objects for each other, they live
in a sensation-dominated cocoon in which they seem to fit each other
predictably and perfectly. They become each other's ecstasy. Some psychotic children come into treatment with a history of such an idyllic
infancy. But the benefits from such an infancy are spurious. A beneficial
feature of the bearable lack of fit of the 'good-enough mother' is that it
provides a space in which chance happenings can occur. Such chance
happenings are agents of transformation and change. The mother and
child who become entrancing autistic objects for each other, so that they
fit each other perfectly, prevent the possibility of such a space. This
means that the child's development is massively stunted and goes awry
because agents of change are shut out.

In my experience the father in the family has an important part to
play in supporting the mother and infant through the pains and tribu-
lations aroused by the lack of perfect fit with each other and the realisation that they cannot absolutely control each other. Children in such
families have never learned to 'put up' with the world as it is, and to
adjust to it. It is only by such adjustment that psychological changes can

take place which enable them to become agents of change in the outside world.

The autistic child (or the autistic child in all of us) is always trying to rubber-stamp the world in terms of rigid systems which seem to be 'me'. In doing this, an endless succession of autistic objects are manipulated which hamper genuine change and growth. Thus, it is obvious that the study of autistic objects has implications far beyond the study of the serious mental illnesses of childhood which bring such tragedy to the families in which they occur. The over-use of autistic objects also brings tragedy to the societies in which we live. However, these wider implications, such as the part played in bigotry and fanaticism, cannot be developed in this book, which is concerned with the development of autistic pathology in children.

THE INADEQUACIES OF AUTISTIC OBJECTS

Our understanding of the development of autistic objects is helped if we realise that, at first, it is not the milk which is significant to the nursing infant, but the cluster of sensations experienced as 'mouth-encircled-nipple'. (It seems that 'mouth-encircled-nipple' is the nucleus of the child's responses to the mother's body experienced in auto-sensual terms.) Nature baits the hook, as it were, and ensures that a life-giving instinctual activity is also pleasurable. But things can go wrong here for many and varied reasons, which can be in different constellations in each bonding couple. The infant is then driven to obtain almost instant trance-inducing ecstasy from his own body to distract his attention from the unutterable pain of the outside world.

Erikson is trying to convey the notion of the deleterious effects of deviant auto-sensuality when he writes that the infant 'will find his thumb and damn the world' (Erikson, 1950). But this notion is too narrow and not sufficiently developed. In normal development, as Winnicott (1958) has shown, finding the thumb leads to exploration and enjoyment of the world outside the child's own body. Sucking the thumb or the fingers becomes associated with rich fantasies and ideas which enable the child to wait until more appropriate and authentic satisfaction comes. This is not the case with the infant who shows signs of psychogenic autism. Clinical work with such children shows that, whereas in normal development the use of the thumb becomes associated with fantasy, with psychotic children it has become associated instead with covert sensual activities. These activities become the be-all and end-all of the autistic child's existence. He has no space for anything else. Erikson's statement would certainly apply to these children.

Such a child never experiences 'missing'. In his concretised mode of experience, absence of a needed person is experienced as a 'hole', which can be filled immediately with an autistic object. He experiences 'emptiness' and 'nothingness', which are different from *missing* a needed person. The persistent repetitiveness of some autistic children in psychotherapy may be the result of undue collusion with their use of autistic objects. Also, if the analyst is unduly passive and malleable, she can become used as an autistic object. It is a progress in the analysis of an autistic child when he begins to *miss* the analyst. Until this occurs, he has replaced the absent analyst with autistic objects which block any sense of lack and the consequent development of memories to compensate for this lack. Thus, he is 'mindless' in Meltzer's terms, and lacks the capacity for hope (Meltzer, *et al.*, 1975). Instead, he is at the mercy of what we term 'despair', which, in the concrete mode of the psychotic child's experience, was described by one such child as 'the black hole with the nasty prick' (Tustin, 1972). (Sandra Stone comments, 'A therapist may appear to be missed when, for the child, it is a set-back caused by the breaking of the autistic-object-therapist. The distress is that the hole has become unplugged.')

Autistic objects have another disadvantage: in times of extreme crisis, hard autistic objects are liable to seem to break under the strain and to let the child down. This is due to their inflexible, rigid nature which makes them brittle. It also comes from their being inanimate objects. Autistic objects have developed to deal with the stresses which have prevented the distinction between animate and inanimate from being made, or from being made normally. The encapsulated child lives in a world of non-living things. The confusional child lives in a world in which things and people are not differentiated in the normal way; for example, he will talk to his faeces as if they were alive and treat people as things. The fact that most autistic objects are inanimate has disastrous effects on the child's development because such objects are a dead-end. Alive people can grow and change and be healed. They can recover from states in which they failed the child. Inanimate, inflexible autistic objects can seem to break irreparably. Such an irreparable 'breakdown' is the source of the psychotic child's despair.

Autistic objects are 'cast' in the mould of innate dispositions and in their formation have not been 'wrought' by experience as, for example, the transitional object has been. Thus, they seem more liable to snap and break. The rigidity and hardness of some autistic objects would seem to come from their being associated with situations of extreme stress which promote hard muscular tension. Thus, a hard object seems suitable for the autistic child to grasp in moments of danger. But it can seem to break and let him down.

THERAPEUTIC IMPLICATIONS

In the therapeutic situation, this replacement of needed people by autistic objects, which help the child to feel held together and safe, leads to behaviour on the part of the child which to the outside observer appears idiotic, but which to the child seems essential. It is only by finding what such behaviour means to the child, and by entering and understanding his world, that we can help him. If we stand outside and merely describe it, we shall try to manoeuvre and manipulate him into our more normal ways of behaving. This will leave untouched and unmodified the rages and panics which give rise to this peculiar state. Also, if we ruthlessly deprive him of his autistic objects, we shall expose a hypervulnerable child to 'nameless dreads' (Bion, 1962b) for which he is not ready. To cope with this he may develop an even more entrenched form of autism or he may become phobic. Thus, the handling of the transition from the undue use of autistic objects to developing feelings of trust in the alive human beings around him needs consummate tact, patience and skill. It cannot be done in a hasty, mechanical way. We need to wait patiently for the appropriate moments when we can demonstrate to him that human beings, in spite of their unpredictability and mortality, give more long-term and effective support than these objects imbued with excessive auto-sensuality (As stated earlier, there is usually a chink in the autism through which healing understanding can enter.)

This brief survey of the origins and development of autistic objects would not be meaningful if something were not said about the rages and panics which give rise to the use of such objects. This is a large topic and can only be discussed briefly.

THE RAGES AND PANICS OF AUTISTIC CHILDREN

Perpetual recourse to autistic objects means that autistic children have remained in a raw, unnurtured state, relatively unmodified by the disciplining and humanising elements of the nursing situation. They are at the mercy of elemental in-built patterns which are stereotyped and unmodified by experience. These are unregulated and have not been co-ordinated in the normal way. They also seem to be affected by atavistic elements. Such children feel threatened by predatory mouths and creatures. They feel they can be trodden underfoot like insects. They feel they are jostling with other creatures in a desperate effort to survive. It is rivalry 'red in tooth and claw', and the hard autistic objects seem to be extensions of nails and teeth.

The constant use of autistic objects means that the autistic child has little possibility of learning to tolerate frustration and to develop a more realistic evaluation of inner and outer stimuli which are felt to be life-threatening. When frustration impinges, tantrums pound through muscle and vein and cause the child to fear total annihilation. To counteract this deadly terror he clutches a hard autistic object. He never learns to deal with bodily and mental irritation in a considered, thinking way.

This schematic survey of the elemental passions which are associated with the use of autistic objects will have to suffice. However, before concluding this chapter, some of the practical implications of the foregoing findings need to be discussed.

PRACTICAL IMPLICATIONS OF THE RECOGNITION OF AUTISTIC OBJECTS

First and foremost, the foregoing understandings concerning the nature, origins and functions of autistic objects enable us to take a compassionate but unsentimental view of psychogenic childhood autism. Those workers in the psychological and psychiatric field who propose inhumane methods for the treatment of these children may begin to realise that, behind such children's seeming lack of fear, there is a terror so great that it cannot be expressed. This needs to be put into words by the therapist, who supports the child in experiencing it. This does not mean that unbridled abreaction is the order of the day.

Those educationists who are unduly permissive in their approach to these children may change some of their attitudes. Both they and some psychoanalytic therapists may become more active and rigorous in discouraging, and even stopping, pathological activities. For example, certain objects may have to be taken away from the child so that he can be helped to develop more appropriate ways of relieving tension. Or at a certain stage, we may be more strict about whether we allow a child to take toys home with him, or to bring toys from home to the consulting-room. However, any such action on our part needs to be associated with interpretations which show that we understand the meaning of such behaviour to the child. As well as our being both more disciplined and disciplining in our technique in the consulting-room, recognition of the impeding efforts of pathological autistic objects will modify the ways in which we couch our interpretations. This should make treatment more effective. As the child begins to feel held in our awareness by our thought, care and concern for him, he begins to hold experiences in his mind as thoughts, memories and imaginations. The undue use of autistic objects begins to wane. As Dr Bion (1962b) has pointed out, the mother mediates sanity to the nurseling as well as nourishing milk. By their sensible attention and behaviour, therapists can convey such sanity also. The feeling-tone of the therapeutic setting is of especial importance to psychotic children.

Second, it has been my experience that an autistic object is often mistaken for a transitional object. These understandings concerning the nature of autistic objects should help to prevent this. Confusion between autistic objects and the transitional object leads to mismanagement in both education and psychotherapy, in that the caring person colludes with the use of objects in pathological ways, instead of patiently and gently weaning the child from using them in these inappropriate and eccentric ways. This is done by giving him more authentic means of protection. In terms of Winnicott's definition of the transitional object as 'the child's first not-me possession', it can be said that autistic objects are 'me-possessions'. They are not companionable objects as is the trans-itional object; their role is that of giving protection and escape from danger. Autistic objects are peculiar to each individual child. Transitional objects, such as teddy bears and comforting pieces of cloth, are objects the like of which many other children use. They have communality in their use (Winnicott, 1958; R. Gaddini, 1978).

Third, understanding the nature and function of autistic objects enables us to have a deeper understanding of the ways in which the development of the mental life of certain autistic children has been impeded. For example, we begin to realise that the autistic child's eccentric and impatient way of relieving himself by the persistent and pathological use of autistic objects has prevented him from learning the appropriate skills and techniques which he can share with other human beings in his culture. Thus, a valuable adjunct to psychoanalytic therapy is a setting in which, as autistic objects are given up, the child can begin to learn from experience and can be helped to make the basic distinctions and integrations which in normal development are taken for granted.

In psychotherapy we shall be more aware of such children's lack of, or shaky capacity for, symbol formation. Symbol formation is based on the capacity to use *substitutes* for actual things and situations. It is also based on the capacity to feel separate from the outside world and thus to use abstractions. The use of material objects which are felt to be part of his body and to permanently replace the real thing has prevented the psychotic child from doing this. Thus, we shall not read into his behaviour the complicated fantasies and ideas which are encountered in neurotic children, but which are not possible for him. We shall realise that the complicated and esoteric interpretations which are sometimes given to psychotic children do not convey to them the meaning they have for us, although they will probably feel 'touched' (quite physically) by our care and interest. Paradoxically, a more sophisticated understanding will sim-plify our approach to these children.

Fourth, this understanding of the nature and origin of autistic objects would seem to throw light on the perversions, and also on the develop-ment of fetishistic objects. There have been attempts to relate Winnicott's concept of the transitional object to the development of fetishism (Greenacre, 1970), but findings from work with psychotic children would seem to indicate that fetishistic objects have more in common with autistic objects than with transitional objects. The obsessive quality in the use of autistic objects also indicates that they could add to our understanding of the early beginnings of obsessional neurosis.

CONCLUSION

In this chapter, emotions such as love, hate, aggression, envy and jealousy have not been ascribed to psychotic children as being the main determinants of their behaviour. This is not because these feelings are thought to be unimportant, but clinical work with autistic children indicates that distress, panic, rage and predatory rivalry need to be talked about with the child, before interpretations about love, aggression and jealousy will be meaningful to him. There is much evidence that psychotic children have experienced an unduly traumatic agony of consciousness in early infancy when these more sophisticated feelings were experienced precociously and in a compacted way. If we interpret these feelings too soon, before the child has the primal basis to distinguish and bear them, we reinforce the precocity which led to the development of a 'false self' (Winnicott's term). Our aim is to help a sincere but tactful child to emerge from the artificial layers of pathological auto-sensuousness by which he has felt protected. To do this, we have to be in touch with basic elemental depths in ourselves.

Also, technical terms have been kept to a minimum. In certain circumstances, technical terms lose their normal usefulness. They come to be misused to plug the holes in our understanding. (As such, they become pathological autistic objects!) It has seemed better to avoid such possible impediments to communication when discussing a topic which is fraught with verbal difficulties. Furthermore, in describing the relatively unexplored levels of autistic functioning, it has seemed necessary to find terms suited to the elemental levels being described. The technical terms in current use were evolved to describe later stages of development and, as such, do not adequately describe these earlier levels. We owe a debt of gratitude to Dr Bion, who has evolved linguistic ways of expressing these 'proto-mental states' (Bion, 1963). Writing about these states involves one in a constant struggle to find evocative words for what were pre-verbal and pre-conceptual experiences.

SUMMARY

In this chapter, the nature, origin and function of autistic objects have been discussed. It has been suggested that pathological autistic objects arise from auto-sensuality which becomes excessive and takes a deviant and perverse course. The psychotic child has developed undercover activities with bodily parts and substances. These are developed to enable him to avoid the pains of frustration and disillusionment which for him have been unutterable. (Sandra Stone comments: 'It is not just the pains of frustration but the terrors of unmanageable experience. This could be a tummy-ache or sicking-up or loose bowels or perhaps too-cold experiences or noises which are too loud, etc., etc.') The muscular hypertension associated with these stressful situations means that hard objects in the outside world have seemed appropriate to enable the child to feel protected from further experience of painful impingements. These hard objects are felt to be part of his body. They are felt to be inanimate since the encapsulated child does not make a distinction between animate and inanimate, and the confusional child makes it only in a confused and bizarre way. Since the mother is experienced as an inanimate object which is part of the child's body and as such can be taken for granted, there is no space for psychological change and growth. Nor does such a child experience an *authentic* maternal object. Such a child's undifferentiated mode of apprehension also has significant effects upon the nature and development of autistic objects. The impeding effects of these objects on the child's mental development have been discussed. It has been suggested that recognition of these impeding effects has important implications both for education and psychoanalytic therapy. The need for circumspection and sensitivity in the use of these insights concerning autistic objects has been stressed. Their significance for further understanding of the perversions and fetishism has been indicated. They also promise to throw light on the beginnings of obsessional neurosis. Finally, it has seemed important to avoid importing concepts which have been evolved for the description of later levels of development since they would distort the descriptions of these much earlier levels.

As well as hard objects, psychotic children also use soft objects, which do not serve the same function as transitional objects, nor are their protective qualities the same as autistic objects. Since they are mostly associated with confusional states, they have been called 'confusional objects'. These will be discussed in the next chapter.

NOTE

This is a revised version of a paper published in the *International Review of Psycho-Analysis*, vol. 7, no. 1, February 1980.

Chapter 11

Confusional objects

In working with psychotic children, a range of objects is encountered whose nature seems to lie between that of autistic objects and that of transitional objects. Winnicott defined the transitional object as 'the child's first "not-me" possession'. In the previous chapter, autistic objects were defined as 'the child's first "me" possessions'. *Confusional objects* are a confusion of both 'me' and 'not-me' elements. From an assessment and a treatment point of view, it is important that they should be recognised and the specific character of their use and functions understood. (In Chapter 6, these objects were seen in use by Luke, the confusional child described by Dr Robert Salo. This child's use of a teddy bear also illustrates how a confusional object can develop into a transitional object, when helped to do so by an insightful therapist.)

THE NATURE OF CONFUSIONAL OBJECTS

Confusional objects are *soft* objects. Like autistic objects they are idiosyncratic to each individual child, or they may be ordinary objects the like of which other children use, but which the confusional child uses in ways which are peculiar to himself. They are not shared objects.

On investigation, it becomes clear that these soft objects are an amalgam of 'me' and 'not-me'. They are most commonly used by the confusional-type children, who are in an entanglement with the 'not-me' mother in which the boundaries between the couple have melted to become vague and confused.

Because confusional objects are an amalgam of 'me' and 'not-me', and because they are soft objects, they are often mistaken for transitional objects. This leads to misinterpretation of the child's state of being and errors in practical management. Thus, it is important to differentiate them from each other, and also from autistic objects. Both autistic and confusional objects divert the child's attention away from the tension associated with painful, 'not-me' situations. They are evasive distractions rather than aids for helping the child to pattern and manage tension, as the transitional object does.

CONFUSIONAL OBJECTS DIFFERENTIATED FROM TRANSITIONAL OBJECTS

Transitional objects are used in ways which are shared by other children; confusional objects are used in ways which are peculiar to each individual child. Confusional objects are used compulsively. They blunt the child's awareness of needing nurturing care and prevent him from recognising that it is separate from him. Children who use confusional objects are in a twilight state of awareness all the time whether they are using the confusional object or not, whereas the child who uses a transitional object may be in a transient dreamy state whilst he is using it, but at other times he will have a good grasp of reality in which 'me' and 'not-me' are becoming normally differentiated. The normal differentiations between 'me' and 'not-me' are not necessarily sharp and clear but they are not confused, as they are when the child is using a confusional object.

In normal states of awareness, there is a dynamic flow from the 'me' to the 'not-me' through transactional activities which buffer the edges of 'me' and 'not-me', to prevent them from coming into sharp collision with each other. In the first place, the mother's 'maternal preoccupation' (Winnicott) does this, and this state of 'reverie' (Bion's term) on the part of the mother facilitates the development of transitional phenomena. The mother for whom the distinction between 'me' and 'not-me' is unduly sharp and clear, such as will be described in Chapter 13, has as much difficulty in doing this for her infant as the mother who is in a state of derangement and confusion. The former type of mother feels split down the middle and in imminent danger of falling apart; the latter type of mother feels liable to disintegrate into fragments. In a reasonably normal relationship the mother has the capacity to identify with her child without seeing him as unduly representing her own unfulfilled needs or damaged and handicapped parts. This capacity to identify with her child, so that she can meet his needs as distinct from her own, buffers both of them from coming into sharp collision with each other or from becoming fused or confused with each other. Both extremes are avoided. The child in such a partnership does not need to develop the delusion of the intact armour of the encapsulated child, nor the disorderly protective bits and pieces of the confusional child. Nor does he need the massive collection of autistic or confusional objects developed by the psychotic child. He may use a transitional object, but this is not inevitable.

The above exposition needs some qualification. I am sure all infants become the focus to some extent of the parents' needs, hopes and ambitions, but in most cases these are not so pressing as to constitute a threat to the child, who is robust enough to develop well in spite of these pressures. But a child who has experienced the shock of bodily separateness very early in life is vulnerable and so cannot withstand as much as a normal infant. The situation is a complicated one. I cannot stress enough that different underlying causes can give the same presenting picture. In some cases, there *has* been undue parental pressure and insufficient healthy maternal preoccupation. In others, the child was unduly vulnerable even to normal pressures; maternal preoccupation which would have been adequate for a normal infant was not adequate for him.

The transitional object is associated with a web of ever-changing fantasies; the confusional object is predominantly associated with sensations and with sensation-dominated fantasies which are rigid and repetitive. Its main function is protection from delusory 'not-me' dangers, which are experienced concretely as material entities, and the child is too tense to fantasise in a normal and free-flowing way.

In *Autism and Childhood Psychosis* (Tustin, 1972), I brought an illustration of a transitional object which is so relevant to the present discussion that I will repeat some of it here. It concerns a child's use of a piece of cloth. The network of fantasies associated with *sucking* this piece of cloth are so rich that they throw into relief the absence of them in encapsulated or confusional children. In a similar situation, such children would be solely concerned with the sensations aroused by the piece of cloth as they felt it *with their hand*. (They would never suck it.) As Geneviève Haag has pointed out (personal communication), they would be fascinated by the creases and folds and undulations in the cloth. Their interest would be in the *sensations* on their skin; there would be little evidence of fantasy. Their interest is directed towards surfaces and the sensations aroused by them.

In the following example, a piece of cloth which was associated with much fantasy was used as a transitional object. (I am grateful to Dr Edna O'Shaughnessy for permission to use this material.)

> Philippa, aged six years, is a pale little girl who easily passes unseen in a large class of children. She will not be separated from a dirty piece of cloth which she calls her 'bibby' and her teacher said that she kept the piece of rag with her at all times.
>
> (Tustin, 1972, p. 67)

It is a long observation in which it is clear that the 'bibby' represents a complicated cluster of fantasies. It represents the peaches which Philippa wants to bite. It is associated with seeing her new baby brother being fed at the breast. The 'bibby' is also her baby whom she comforts as it comforts her. But it has other meanings, as the following dialogue indicates:

Observer: Who is Bibby?

Philippa: It is my baby.

Observer: What do you give him to eat?

Philippa: Nothing. He feeds me. But I'm going to boil him and eat him and put him into my tummy.

Observer: What will happen then?

Philippa: He will grow into a baby.

Let me now bring two examples of *confusional objects* so that the difference between them and the transitional object will become clear.

EXAMPLES OF CONFUSIONAL OBJECTS

In her study of prenatal life with the aid of ultrasound scanning, Dr Allesandra Piontelli gives us a rare and privileged glimpse of behaviour in the womb. In her 1987 paper she describes a boy foetus who throughout the mother's pregnancy

> . . . remained immobile tightly crouched in a corner of the womb, with his hands and his arms screening his eyes and his face, and with his legs so tightly folded and crossed as almost to cover his face. His immobility . . . seemed to be born out of tension, if not terror, not out of peace.

Significantly, Dr Piontelli continues: 'The umbilical cord was often seen between his arms and his legs, but it was impossible to tell whether he did something with it, other than holding on to it' (Piontelli, 1987, p. 460). This unborn baby's mother had previously experienced a still birth due to *abruptio placentae*, and was thus very anxious to retain this baby. It seems possible that in some way this tension was conveyed to the baby in her womb. This unborn baby seemed traumatised.

Dr Piontelli records that after this baby was born he was still very immobile. He also clung to the breast for hours on end. His mother said, 'He doesn't want to let go . . . he is using me as a dummy . . . he doesn't care about the rest of me . . . when he grasps it, he kills me' (Piontelli, 1987, p. 460). This mother did not attempt to dissuade the baby from this behaviour, but instead allowed it to continue. After five months the mother went back to work. She told Dr Piontelli, 'I feel as if I am breathing again . . . [H]e seems better too' (Piontelli, 1987, p. 461).

At one year of age, this child was backward in his mental development. Dr Piontelli tells us: 'He preferred to sit in a corner holding the same toy and almost never moved about.' (It would be interesting to know what toy that was.) He had no words, only sounds.

The report ends here, but this short observation encouraged Dr Piontelli to do more long-term work with other infants. This pilot study is a sad story of an infant who had become addicted to an entangling confusional object even before he was born (the umbilical cord), and then after he was born continued to use the mother's breast in the same way. The lack of clear differentiation between mother and infant, and the strain this put on both mother and child, was evident.

Although Dr Piontelli does not say anything about this child's later development, I would suspect that it was likely to be that of a schizophrenic type of child who was overly dependent.

I now want to bring another example of a soft confusional object, which was used by an infant boy observed by Rachel Pick. (Mrs Pick was a child psychotherapy trainee at the Tavistock Clinic. As part of their training, the trainees observe an infant from birth up to two years of age. Mrs Pick's observations were discussed in a seminar led by Mrs Isca Wittenberg.) Mrs Pick records as follows:

> From the age of eighteen months, the object to which he has become attached (I feel it cannot truly be called a transitional object) has been his pillow, inside whose cover he slips one of his arms. Mother herself directly compared this to the hand inside the vest or sheet of earlier months.

Mrs Pick observed this baby boy every week from birth onwards. Very early in life he showed worrying features. One of these was the fact that his tongue often got in the way of his feeding at the breast. On one occasion, when he was five months old, the observer noticed that the baby's tongue was deep purple as it protruded from his mouth. The mother said that this occurred when he gripped it with his gums. (There was no evidence of epilepsy in this child.)

As the observation proceeded it was very clear that this baby could have become an extremely disturbed child. However, it was also clear that the mother was confident and skilful. She persisted in going forward to relate to and try to understand her difficult infant. At two years, there was a marked change for the better. It cannot be ascertained why this baby was difficult from the word 'go', but it can be seen that a confident, happy mother can modify the pathological responses of a difficult early start. In this respect, it is an important and interesting observation.

Another feature distinguishing between a transitional object and confusional object is that almost invariably the psychotic child has several or even a large number of autistic and confusional objects, any one of which can replace any other one, whereas the transitional object is the child's 'first treasured possession' (Stevenson, 1954), although at times the child may treat it roughly. (Sometimes a child may have two or three transitional objects, but this is unusual.)

A child who uses a transitional object has known and used the actual mother in a need-satisfying way and has the sense of having something good inside, even though this may not be securely established. The confusional and autistic objects are not based on memories nor on thinking. Indeed, they impede these developments. They are based on elements of in-built dispositions which have not developed normally. They are not related to the souvenirs or mementoes of everyday life as are transitional objects, but to magical amulets which will ward off dangers and to totems which demand blind obedience, adoration or worship. They do not revive memories of previous good experiences as does the transitional object. They are material objects which replace the 'holding' qualities of the parents which the child has never been able to use, even though these may have been there, at least in some measure. They also increasingly prevent him from using the parents as they try to get in touch with him. (No wonder they often give up in despair.) To put it in another way, they are 'as if' objects, that is, objects which are used as permanent replacements, instead of temporary substitutes, for the 'holding' aspects of the parents. When used to the virtual exclusion of anything else, as in psychotic states, they lead to feelings of unreality and a 'false self'.

The main function of both confusional and autistic objects is that of *evasion*; they are a protection against, and an escape from, the 'not-me' outside world, whereas the main function of the transitional object is to help the child to tolerate, express and manage his feelings in relation to it. Thus, transitional objects are a *bridge* to the 'not-self' mother; they enable the child to wait until she comes; they keep her alive in his mind. Objects used in autistic and confusional ways are a *barrier* between the child and the nurturing people who want to help him. (For simplicity, the pronouns 'he' and 'him' are used to refer to children in general.) Through their use he avoids having a sense of need. He does not have to recognise that he has to wait for satisfaction, or face the fact that it is not always available. He does not have to bear suspense and delay action. He can and does act impulsively. The transitional object helps the child to bear suspense and to delay action. It not only channels his feelings but also modifies them. If the suspense does not go on for too long, it helps him to control impulsiveness. Thus, the transitional object is an agent of change and transformation. Autistic and confusional objects are not; they reinforce repetition-compulsion. As such they are anti-life; they deny life with its unpredictabilities and uncertainties but also its unknown possibilities.

Unduly protected by either his autistic or his confusional objects, the psychotic child does not feel the need to learn or to acquire skills. With patience, confidence, tact and persistence, the therapist tries to demonstrate to him that there is something better than these unreliable protections, and that this is something which must be shared with other people and is part of everyday natural experiences. However, although autistic and confusional objects serve the same function, which is that of evasion of difficulties and escape from delusory dangers, they have certain important differences. These must now be discussed.

DIFFERENTIATION OF AUTISTIC FROM CONFUSIONAL OBJECTS

Both types of object are used to help the child to deal with the elemental sense of 'loss' – the loss of soothing and fulfilling sensations which were taken for granted, but which helped him to feel held together in a safe-keeping unity with the mother. In order to counter this sense of 'loss', the hard autistic object is felt to be part of the child's body; he feels fused with it. When the sense of loss threatens, he can grasp it. In using a confusional object, the child has a hazy awareness that it is separate from his body, but it is always available to sink into in order to feel confused and hidden.

The autistic object is used in two-dimensional states of awareness, in which there is no knowledge of outsides or insides. It is a surface which can be grasped and which, in the delusion of fusion, can seem to enplate the child in a protective shell. The confusional object is associated with confused awareness of three-dimensionality and of outsides and insides. The child is aware of *entering* the soft confusional object whereas, if the encapsulated child gets inside an object, the operative sensation is of being covered over, not of entering.

Hard autistic objects completely obstruct awareness of the 'not-me': soft confusional objects obfuscate awareness of the 'not-me', but do not completely obliterate it. Hard autistic objects support the delusion of encapsulation, either global or in segments; soft confusional objects support the delusion of being enveloped in a veil, a fog or a mist. Both delusions are powerful obstacles to using the nurturing which is almost always available. The segmented encapsulated children treat people, their parents included, as autistic objects, and are very cut off from them. Thus, with discretion, autistic and confusional objects can be used as diagnostic features to indicate the type of pathological autism used by the child.

In the normal working partnership of mother–infant interaction, the infant's needs are total and the mother's needs are relative. It is very different in the confusional entanglement of child and mother. In this situation the mother's needs outweigh those of the infant – at least, the child feels that they do. He feels totally eclipsed by them. He feels not mothered but smothered. His confusional objects are soft and melting. The state of the encapsulated child is very different. He feels he lives in icy isolation. His autistic objects are hard and unyielding. He is cut off from the outside world and the people in it. His world is stark and bare and empty.

The confusional children have a very blurred awareness of the difference between 'me' and 'not-me' all the time. The awareness of the segmented encapsulated children is different. They are either acutely aware of the 'not-me' with a hypersensitised clarity or they are completely oblivious. Their awareness is stippled with 'blind spots'. Awareness of the 'not-me' goes in 'fits and starts'.

CONCLUSION

Finally, it must be made clear that it is the massive and persistent use of objects in confusional and encapsulating ways, virtually to the exclusion of using them in transitional communicative ways, which leads to the psychosis. Probably many normal or neurotic people behave in this way to some degree. It is their over-use which leads to psychosis. This over-use impedes (in encapsulated children) or hampers (in confusional children) the capacity for symbol formation. The undue use of confusional and autistic objects leads to the underfunctioning of all of these children and the seeming mental deficiency of some of them. Thus, the asymbolic nature of pathological autistic states needs to be discussed in some detail. The next chapter will be concerned with this.

Chapter 12

The asymbolic nature of auto-sensuous states

DEFINITION OF SYMBOL

A symbol is an object or activity which is used as a substitute for something else, and which is very different from that which is being symbolised. Thus, the word 'cat' can stand for a cat, and we do not need to be able to see, touch and handle an actual cat in order to communicate about it. It is also not like a cat in any way. Symbolisation is dependent upon the capacity to feel separate from the outside world and upon being motivated to communicate about what is being experienced. It is therefore dependent on the capacity to tolerate frustration to some extent.

In some psychoanalytic writings the term symbol is given the specific meaning of denoting unconscious material by something not directly connected with it. For example, in dreams a snake can stand for the penis.

PSYCHOTIC CHILDREN AND THE USE OF SYMBOLS

Psychotic children have very little repressed material and they have very little capacity to tolerate frustration. Thus, their symbolising capacities, in both the general and the psychoanalytic senses, are very rudimentary. In such children we encounter pre-symbolic material; in treatment, it is important to be aware of this and not to interpret as 'symbolic' those activities which have not reached that stage. As the child makes progress in treatment, we see the successive stages in the development of the capacity to use symbols. These seem to be as follows:

Stage 1 An 'as if' phrase leading on to:
Stage 2a Pictorial representation
and
Stage 2b Symbolic representation

Stage 1 'As if' phase

In the *as if* phase, things which are alike in certain respects are equated as if they were the same. Those features which are important to the child are attended to in great detail, and differences between the objects are ignored. Thus, two things can be equated by the child which to us seem very different. For example, cupboards and drawers and stomachs are felt to be the same. For the infant in this 'as if state' of functioning, objects which we know to be different are equated on the basis of feeling the same in the infant's mouth or in his hand or on his skin. Thus, the finger, the fist, a button, the knob of the cot, a bunched-up piece of shawl, the nipple of the breast, the teat of the feeding-bottle – are all equated with each other. Hanna Segal (1957) has given the name 'symbolic equations' to these early precursors of symbol formation.

Stage 2a Pictorial representation

In this stage, there is some sense of bodily separateness from objects in the outside world. One object can be a *substitute* for another object, but they are not *equated*. The substitute object has certain significant features which are like those of the original object, similarity of outline being paramount. I will now bring some clinical material to illustrate the movement of the psychotic child to this important stage.

Clinical material

Paul was a mute seven-year-old psychotic child of low intellectual potential. He was in treatment with Mrs Lynn Barnett, who has allowed me to use this material. At the time of the recorded sessions, Paul had been in treatment for one and a half years. Psychological tests given at this time showed that he was still asymbolic. But the reported material shows evidence that he was moving from the stage of symbolic equations to the beginnings of pictorial representation.

> *9th March 1971.* Paul was beginning to notice holiday breaks and was becoming preoccupied with holes, both in himself and in the outside world. This is the psychotic child's concrete way of expressing feelings of *lack* and *emptiness*. It is always a progress when he begins to bear being aware of this sense of *privation* [Winnicott, 1958, p. 226] because it shows that he has some awareness of bodily separateness from the outside world.

Following the evidence in the session that holes and the filling of holes were preoccupying him, the therapist interpreted Paul's putting his thumb in his mouth as his feeling that his mouth was a hole he wanted to fill. The therapist's notes continue:

> In direct response to this interpretation, Paul put his finger into the outlet hole of the sink, turning so that I could see what he was doing. After this, he came and sat on my lap. After a few minutes, he left my lap and turned on the water tap, watching the water run down the sink hole.

After another short piece of activity, the record continues:

> Paul picked up the plug and looked at it carefully. He put it to his ear, his mouth and then the plug-hole. Following some excited exclamations about the bowl which was filling with water, Paul made a circle with his forefinger and thumb and let the water from the tap run through it. He then put the tips of his fingers in his mouth, looking at me whilst he did so. He then delicately put his fingers into the circular bubbles on the surface of the water and also touched the bubbles with his tongue. He smiled when I linked the plug-hole, his mouth, and finger-circle and the bubbles with the suggestion that he wanted to fill up holes as he was trying to suck water into his mouth.

Discussion of the clinical material

There are several small signs of progress in the foregoing material. For one thing, Paul had *smiled* at the therapist, and this was a rare occurrence. He had shown that he had understood her interpretations, and also that he felt understood. Sequences of behaviour were developing which could be understood and related to each other although, of course, there was much that we did not understand. Finally, in his making of the finger-thumb circle, we saw the beginnings of *pictorial representation*. By an action, he had indicated a situation he wanted to share with the therapist. With speech some distance away, this was intentional communication and not just reactive signals such as body movements, crying, tantrums and evacuations. He was not duplicating the actions of a 'not-me' object and so feeling equated and fused with it. With finger and thumb he made an elementary pictorial representation of his empty mouth and of his need and emptiness.

The drawings of psychotic children

Of course, drawing on paper is a more developed form of pictorial representation. As such, it is associated with the development of the important capacity of being able to hold pictures or shapes in the mind. This is related to the beginnings of thinking. Psychotic children lack this capacity to hold things in the mind and to represent them on paper. However, as their pathological auto-sensuousness is modified, they may begin to draw. It is important to realise that this drawing may not necessarily be a communication to the therapist or to himself. As with other states, it can be used in the service of their pathology. For example, they often feel it to be a magical act by which they manipulate the 'not-me' outside world so that it becomes 'me'. Their drawings may show incredible powers of observation and meticulous skill in recording the observations on paper, but the driving force behind these activities is to control and dominate the 'not-me' and to make it into 'me', controlled by 'me'. Of course, normal drawing can spring in part from this motivation, but it is not the overriding consideration that it is with the psychotic child. Such a child feels that the picture has become part of him, whereas with a mature work of art there is always the feeling that it is separate from the creator, who is often surprised by what is there.

Some of the drawings of psychotic children have features in common with the cave-paintings of primitive man. In some of these, the imprint of hands can be seen as if 'catching' the animal. Psychotic children often draw pictures with hand-prints on them. This is felt to be a magical act to 'capture' (in a literal sense) the objects depicted on the paper. 'Blacking out' the objects can also seem to them to annihilate the actual objects. It is akin to the sympathetic magic in which a replica of a person is stuck with pins in order to annihilate that person.

The drawings of these children also have much in common with the drawings of primitive people. They are magical acts to draw some desired feature into themselves. Thus, Peter, the child whose sessions are reported in Chapter 17, had a phase when he drew tall towers endlessly in order to draw their tallness into himself. He felt that increased skill in drawing would make his magical acts more potent. Even his obsessive persistence was felt to be a magical activity to make desired things come true. If he tried hard and long enough it would happen.

It is no good treating such pictures as communications. As therapists in this situation, we do not interpret in terms of the *content* of the picture, but in terms of the child's *intentions*. We also need to correct some of his misconceptions, such as that the quality of 'tallness' is a material object which can be drawn from objects and people in the outside world and stuck onto himself. These children really feel that this is the way to grow up. They feel that they sneak inches from the grown-ups to stick them onto themselves. They also feel that, by doing this, they make the grown-ups smaller. This feeling of growing up at the expense of annexing grown-up appurtenances leaves them exposed to the threat of attack from the grown-ups so despoiled and mutilated. It is important to deal with both their misconceived intentions and the fears to which this makes them feel exposed. Interpretations which do not take note of this are confusing rather than clarifying to the child.

Normal pictorial representation can be seen in the pictograms or ideograms of certain languages in which the written representations are very like the objects they represent. Toys are also pictorial representations of objects in the external world and can stand for these objects in the child's play activities. Thus, the normal child plays with such things as baby dolls, doll's houses, Dinky cars and farm and zoo animals. He knows very well that these are not 'real', but he can use them in a 'let's pretend' way. This is a very important development.

This normal pictorial representation is also characteristic of one type of miming, in which the gestures go through the exact motions of some activity; for example, 'I want something to eat' is mimed as putting food to the mouth and pointing to the self. In another type of miming known as 'symbolic gestures', there does not seem to be any connection between the shape of the gesture and what it represents. This is often seen in ballet.

Stage 2b Symbolic representation

In a *symbolic representation*, the symbol is very different from the object it is representing. Thus, the word 'cat' does not depict the shape of a cat, as a pictogram would do.

Normal children use such symbols all the time and are very at home with them. For example, a normal ten-year-old boy called Solomon wanted to have a day in which everyone in the household signed a Treaty of Peace. The treaty was drawn up with great ceremony with Latin embellishments from his work at school. At the bottom of the scroll on which the treaty was written there was a cross, drawn so that the horizontal line of the cross intersected the vertical line, the two lines being of equal length. I was puzzled and asked, 'What is that?' He replied in a tone which implied that it was self-evident: 'Why, everybody kissing everybody else, of course.' This was a symbolic representation of a situation and not a pictorial one, and at first I did not understand the symbol. This brings in the important point that symbols can either be 'private' or 'public', but there need to be sufficient 'public symbols', that is, 'shared symbols', for communication to take place.

As soon as we develop symbols to stand in place of actual objects or happenings, these happenings or objects are distanced from us. The 'me' and the 'not-me' no longer collide with each other, or melt into each other; there is a bridge between them. With the development of symbols, the outside world becomes more manageable and bearable. For example, to take an extreme case, to give a name to 'death', or in the child's terms 'being gone', is more bearable than the looming sensation of a 'nameless dread'.

When the psychotic child develops symbolic capacities, he no longer needs to thrust the nasty, hard, rough, dirty things into the 'not-me' void, where they flap around in an uncontained way to threaten him, giving rise to phobias. Instead, he can begin to express them through symbolic activities in which they feel contained. These symbolic activities are such things as speaking, thinking, fantasising, imagining, dreaming, acting, playing, writing, mathematics, music, art, dance, etc.

LANGUAGE AS A SYMBOLIC ACTIVITY

Dr R. Kennedy (1980) has described how the development of language helped a borderline psychotic boy to begin to manage his feelings. At the beginning of his paper, Kennedy quotes Saussure, who 'emphasised that without language thought is vague and uncharted; that the mechanism of language is a partial correction of a system by nature chaotic; and that language limits arbitrariness (Saussure, 1972)'. Kennedy then goes on to illustrate by carefully recorded details of clinical sessions the ways in which his patient improved as he developed language. This came as the result of psychotherapy supported by education in the Daleham Gardens Day Unit for very disturbed children. Kennedy brings in a very apt quotation from Brecht:

> Lamenting by means of sounds, or better still words, is a vast liberation, because it means that the sufferer is beginning to produce something. He's already mixing his sorrow with an account of the blows he has received: he's already making something out of the utterly devastating.

The task of both therapists and teachers, when working with the psychotic child, is to help him to make 'something out of the utterly devastating'. However, to do this he needs to be held by someone who is alive to his capacity to devastate the skills he has acquired instead of using them in a progressive way. Anne Alvarez (1980) alerted me to the way in which these children can use language as autistic objects which *block* communication instead of facilitating it. She instances how, with a certain psychotic boy, words which had been full of life and meaning and used for communication with his therapist would gradually deteriorate and become 'dead', being then used to block communication. In therapy, it is important not to be misled into taking up the content of such use of language but rather to understand the purpose for which it is being used.

INTERNAL LANGUAGE

It is also important to be aware of the fact that the mute child almost certainly has internal language. For example, he will understand and carry out actions he is asked to do. Also, when such a child first speaks he often comes out with quite a long sentence. For example, one autistic child's first words were, 'Poor little baby Johnny left all alone on the island'. There is an apocryphal story of the young Lord Macaulay, who never spoke until he was four years old. At this age his nanny accidentally spilled some very hot water over his foot. There was great consternation and much activity to alleviate the pain. He is reputed to have suddenly said, 'You may now desist from your efforts. The pain has considerably abated'!

There is another apocryphal story of a child who had never spoken until, at age five, he said, 'This toast's burnt.' When asked why he had never spoken before, he replied. 'There wasn't anything to complain about.' This story amusingly makes the point that undue gratification is as great an inhibitor as extreme deprivation.

These stories concerning language indicate that latent possibilities are present in the child long before they are expressed in outward behaviour. A recent interesting piece of research with the title of 'Intermodal Matching in Human Neonates' (Meltzoff and Barton, 1979) demonstrates that this is the case with regard to pre-symbolic activities; it indicates that these are latent and present from an unbelievably early age.

LATENT PRE-SYMBOLIC ACTIVITIES

In the November 1979 issue of *Nature*, Andrew Meltzoff and Richard Barton reported on some very precise and ingenious experiments with 32 full-term infants ranging from 26 to 33 days old. Half of these infants were given a rubber comforter of the usual type and half were given one with small projecting knobs (see Figure 12.1).

The infants were not allowed to see the rubber comforters; experience of them was to be solely on the basis of the sensation in the mouth. The experiment started with a 90-second 'tactual familiarisation' period, during which the infants sucked on whichever rubber comforter they had been given. The comforter was then removed in a way which prevented the infant from seeing it, and he was then turned to look at the two types of comforter which were suspended in an illuminated black cardboard aperture. These visually apprehended comforters were considerably larger than the ones which the infants had sucked. Observers, who were not visible to the infants, then recorded the length of time the infants looked at each of the comforters.

The results were striking in that, of the 32 infants, 24 fixated on the

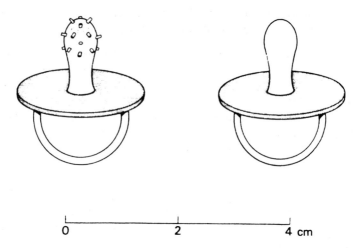

Figure 12.1 Two types of comforter

shape matching the tactile stimulus of the sensation in the mouth for a much longer length of time than on the non-matching shape. These results were significantly different from chance. There were no significant differences due to sex of the infant, or whether they had been breast- or bottle-fed, or were used to normal comforters. Neither were there significant preferences for fixating right versus left side nor for fixating the sphere without knobs versus the sphere with knobs.

When the experiment was repeated with another set of infants of comparable ages to the first set and with different observers, the results were again significantly different from chance.

DISCUSSION OF THE RESEARCH

In terms of pre-symbolic activities, this report is interesting in that it indicates the likelihood of there being a basis for symbol formation much earlier in life than might have been thought possible. It seems that, at about thirty days old, the sensuous experience of mouth sensations alone can be transposed and matched with visual experiences. If one thinks in terms of survival value this would not seem to be so surprising. Such a transformation of experience from the tactile to the visual mode of apprehension would enable the infant to begin to be able to find the nipple of the breast by *seeing* as well as by the primary mode of 'rooting' for it by 'feel'. This experiment is also important in that it indicates the basic importance of mouth–breast experiences for cognitive as well as emotional development.

The experimenters were interested in another aspect of early mental development which is relevant to the general thesis of this book, although not specifically to symbol formation. They write:

> A basic assumption of piagetian theory is that infants begin life with independent sense modalities that gradually become inter-coordinated with development. Our findings, however, show that neonates are already able to detect tactual–visual correspondences, thereby demonstrating an impressive degree of intermodal unity. Thus whatever develops in the first year of life, it is apparently not the *de novo* co-ordination of functionally independent sense modalities.

They go on to say:

> [These experiments] suggest that neonates are capable of using and storing surprisingly abstract information about objects in their world. They can abstract information sufficiently to recognise objects across changes in size and modality of perception.
>
> (Meltzoff and Barton, 1979)

This flexibility of movement from one sensory mode to another of normal infants is in striking contrast to the way in which the encapsulated child isolates and separates each sensory modality from the other. The above research suggests that this could be a fundamental cause for their seeming mental subnormality. Such blockage of the integration and co-ordination of sensory experiences can be as damaging to mental functioning as actual brain damage. Indeed, as stated in Chapter 3, it may sometimes lead to brain damage.

The fact that the etiology of psychogenic elements in childhood psychosis goes back to very early infancy makes them difficult to treat. This means that a deeper understanding of the autistic blockage to normal functioning is of great importance. One of the major themes of this book has been that support and encouragement in making the differentiations and integrations between such contraries as hard and soft, full and empty, strong and weak, big and little, light and dark, rough and smooth are an essential part of the work with a psychotic child. This is followed by the need to understand the peculiar sense of loss experienced by an infant when sensuous rhythms and regularities, which have been taken for granted and experienced as part of the body, break down. Such a catastrophic breakdown lays the child open to being in the grip of a pathological repetition-compulsion which is difficult to modify. Clinical work has convinced me that insights into pathological auto-sensuousness can be effective in modifying the repetitive behaviour of young psychotic children so that more normal on-going developments are set in train.

CONCLUSION

The psychotic child is drowned in an uncontrollable sea of waves of sensation which have not been held by adequate symbolisation. Thus, it is important to be aware of the asymbolic nature of such a child's functioning, so that our behaviour and our interpretations will be appropriate to his state of being, and so that we shall be alert to facilitate the stages in the development of symbolising capacities and to correct those situations which handicap this development. To do this we need to be in touch with the peculiar nature of his states of awareness. These will be discussed in the next chapter.

NOTE

This chapter is based on a short paper given at a Round Table in the Congrès international de psychologie de l'enfant (July 1979, Université René Descartes, Paris).

Chapter 13

Awareness in autistic states

This chapter will be concerned with elemental states which are not part of everyday conscious experience. A major difficulty in discussing such states is that rational deductive accounts do not describe them adequately. Of necessity, this account will be evocative. Indeed, at times I shall turn to the poets to help me in this task. Creative artists retain the freshness of vision of the child and often manage to give form and shape to naïve states of awareness. The difference between the creative artist and the psychotic child is that the latter has remained inflexibly trapped in these states. They are his sole states of being. This is not the case with the creative artist, who has what Plato called 'divine madness' from which he can move flexibly to more ordinary states of functioning.

In working with a psychotic child, there is the danger that, because it seems threatening to us to go back to raw states of feeling and crude thinking, we may put our sophisticated constructions on to his naïve behaviour and assumptions. In my view, constructions of this kind have prevented us from being in touch with psychotic children, and have hampered the effectiveness of our work with them. This chapter will indicate some of the educational and therapeutic implications of the attempt to get in touch with the autistic child unprotected by hasty assumptions. Inevitably, this adventure will upset some of our views on educational and therapeutic procedures.

THE AUTISTIC CHILD'S EXPERIENCE OF BODILY HOLES

Clinical experience indicates that, at the same time as the realisation dawns on the child that there is a gap between his body and that of the mother, he becomes aware that his body has holes through which substances can go in and can go out. A great variety of conditions, which have been discussed in other chapters, have meant that the autistic child in whom psychogenic factors predominate has experienced the gap between his body and that of the mother as being unbearably painful. In this situation, instead of the orifices in his body being places where fulfilling connections can be made, they are felt to be holes through which obnoxious painful things can enter. In illusion, to prevent this, he blocks these holes with autistic objects, thus shutting out experience and remaining naïve. In my view, this is the key to understanding the autistic child. In such children, development has been disturbed at an early stage when they were in a hypersensitised state, and the distinction between animate and inanimate had either been insecurely made or had been avoided. Their hypersensitivity, and the fact that such children live mostly in a world of inanimate objects, has important effects on their states of awareness. One of these effects is that the notion of growing is not possible for them.

THE NOTION OF GROWING

Time and time again, child patients in a state of pathological auto-sensuousness have demonstrated to me that their notion of how they grow is that they take bodily bits away from grown-ups or other children. These other human beings are experienced as inanimate objects from whom the bits can be plucked like apples from a tree. These 'bits' are felt to be stuck onto their bodies to make them taller or fatter or bigger or better or stronger. Thus, for example, an increase in stature is felt to be under their all-powerful control. However, beneath this illusion of being in omnipotent control, there lurks the terrible dread that these 'stuck-on' bits will be snatched away by predatory rivals in the savage and barbarous ways by which they were felt to be acquired. The children then feel that they are in a helpless state of being, a mass of holes and vulnerable to attack.

Thus, growing up is not a natural, inevitable process but a cut-throat competitive struggle to acquire extra bits to their bodies. For example, one autistic child showed me that he felt that he had a hook on the end of his tongue, which enabled him to hook the things he wanted from the stomach of his mother whom he experienced as a 'thing' – a sort of pond in which he fished with the hook on his tongue! These fished-out 'things' enabled him to shut out the menaces with which he felt surrounded. For a long time he said that I was a 'vending-machine'. As such, he felt I was under his absolute control. He would ask a question to which he well knew the answer and to which he well knew that I knew the answer. When, and if, I gave the expected answer, he felt he had got it out of me by inserting the 'coin' of his question. This was not a game but a deadly serious occupation. If I did not give the expected reply, or if he did not come to see me on the expected day, he feared that I was empty. In that state I was very threatening. So he had to refill me. On these occasions, he brought his favourite motor-cars about which he talked almost non-stop. (He was talking by this time, although when he first came to me, aged six years, he was virtually mute.) Sometimes he drew picture after picture. If he felt that he could not refill me, or mend me, he was thrown into deep despair. He could not understand that I existed and had capacities for recovery quite apart from him and his efforts. In his omnipotence he felt he brought me into existence and that I was a part of him. Therefore, he was burdened with the overwhelming responsibility of keeping me in existence because his survival and my survival were inextricably linked together.

Another younger patient, aged four years, related these notions quite directly to the breast. It was a turning-point in his psychotherapy when, having seen a friend of his mother feeding her baby at the breast, he came to his session and said in tones of wonder and surprise. 'The red button *grows* on the breast!' (John in *Autism and Childhood Psychosis*, Tustin, 1972).

Until he developed the notion of 'growing', this autistic child had felt that the 'red button on the breast' was a source of contention between the mother and himself, and between himself and the predatory rivals inside the breast who threatened to snatch the unique sensation-giving button out of his mouth. At times, he felt he gripped the hard bit between his gums and that it was his. But then he felt that he had deprived the breast-mother of her source of power and strength since there was only one such powerful object. This weak breast-mother could not help him to control the bodily excitements which, in his state of omnipotence, were felt to be so all-powerful as to overwhelm him. Thus, he oscillated between the heights of fulfilment and ecstasy and the helplessness of pits of despair. In the pits of despair he felt in the grip of a broken inanimate mother. Such a mother from whom sensation-giving bits could be snatched was not the real alive caring mother. This auto-sensual 'mother' (i.e. a 'mother' constructed almost wholly from his own undifferentiated bodily sensations) did not set human limits to his omnipotent illusions such as an alive and limited mother would do. Thus, he swung from one extreme state to another. He lived in an 'all or nothing' world. Either he had everything and was all-powerful or he had nothing and was completely helpless. He was either in the pitch-black darkness of total ignorance or he was in the blazing sunshine of knowing everything. Both states stopped him from making efforts at ordinary learning and kept him in a handicapped condition.

The musician Scriabin described this state when he said:

I am God
I am Nothing
I am a fire enveloping the Universe.

'Fire' is an image which is often used by poets to give form and shape to the states of frenzy and passion associated with unregulated omnipotence. T. S. Eliot (1909–62) tells us that when such states are experienced in adult life we are:

Whirled in a vortex that shall bring
The world to that destructive fire
Which burns before the ice-cap reigns.

As therapists, it behoves us to realise that when, and if we succeed in lifting the psychotic child's 'ice-cap' of pathological auto-sensuousness, we shall have to meet and help him to deal with the 'destructive fire' of his impulses.

For some of a wide variety of factors, either in the child or in both child and parents, the autistic child has not been able to cope with the 'destructive fire' of his stormy elemental passions other than by clamping down on them or by 'dismantling' his perceptions (Meltzer, et al., 1975). The parents could not help because the child experienced them as inanimate autistic objects. As therapists, we have to establish ourselves as alive human beings who, by establishing co-operative enterprises with the psychotic child, can help him to regulate and pattern such feelings because we are in touch with these elemental depths both in ourselves and in him. As he feels taken care of by people who can withstand his domineering, monopolising attacks, he will feel that potential rivals are similarly kept in order. As he begins to feel less open to attack, the use of autistic objects will diminish. His openings will become places where fulfilling connections can be made instead of being places which need to be blocked against the entry of inimical substances. He will begin to realise that they are places where healing influences can come in.

HEALING

Living in a world of inanimate objects means that the autistic child has the notion of things being 'broken', and possibly of being 'mended', but that he has no notion of healing. In his hypersensitised, magnified awareness, his body and other people's bodies can be *broken* in such a catastrophic way that, like Humpty-Dumpty, they cannot be put together again. The premature realisation of bodily separateness from the mother of his infancy meant that his body and that of the mother with whom he had felt fused or entangled were felt to be broken, never to be repaired. He has a terrible sense of being irreparably broken away from this mother and thus from the outside world. This is usually experienced in the mouth (Winnicott, 1958; Tustin, 1972).

His lack of capacity for being clearly aware of alive beings and their capacities means that such a child does not become aware of the natural processes of healing through which, if given time, a knitting together of damaged tissues can take place without manipulative interference on his part. The qualifying phrase 'if given time' also indicates his dilemma. He cannot wait. In his sensation-dominated state he is at the mercy of impulses which demand immediate outlet and satisfaction. Thus, things which are broken have to be mended immediately or not at all. Also, anything which cannot be controlled by handling and touching is not within his comprehension. Thus, the natural processes of healing which go on apart from his manipulations cannot be understood by him. Healing and growing are outside his control. They are beyond his understanding. They also take time. The autistic child is impatient to be grown up in order to be in control.

The understanding of the notion of healing brings a new dimension into the treatment situation for both child and therapist. A 'breakdown' may seem irreparable so long as the child feels that it has to be 'mended', and that this 'mending' is his sole responsibility. The emergence of the notion of healing takes it right out of his hands. As he becomes able to accept the fact that helpful events such as healing and growing occur apart from his efforts, new possibilities emerge. Both he and the therapist become more concerned with such human activities as forgiveness, understanding and sympathy, than with retribution and reparation for destructive attacks. These give dimensions of hope and compassion to therapeutic endeavour. Trustful co-operation with another human being becomes possible. Grandiose illusions become modified. More normal states of consciousness come into being: the child ceases to swing from states of vegetative unawareness to states of agonising hypersensitivity.

In the literature on autistic children their states of vegetative unawareness have been discussed more than have their excrutiating states of hypersensitivity. In this chapter I shall concentrate on describing their states of ultra-sharp awareness, since it is as important to understand and help the children with these as with their extreme passivity.

STATES OF HYPERSENSITIVITY

In my experience, the hypersensitive states of autistic children arise when awareness of bodily separateness cannot be avoided and bodily holes are felt to be wide open. Such a child has little capacity for the appropriate regulation of sensory experience. This regulation normally comes as perceptions are developed through interactive experience with the outside world. The controls of an autistic child are of an all-or-nothing variety. Either an autistic 'plug' is in, or it is out. He is either devoid of sensation, or he is flooded by it. Such floods of sensuous experience seem to have much in common with the states of heightened consciousness produced by hallucinogenic drugs in which the subject feels that colours and shapes are apprehended with ultra-vivid clarity and there is the sense of being actually inside a colour or a shape. Autistic children who have become articulate have shown me that they experience things in this way. For example, an autistic child called Peter, as he left the therapy room, pointed to a tall yellow daisy and said, 'I'm inside that yellow flower – it's the yellowness I'm inside.' He was at a loss to describe his experience any further. His whole body was taut with heightened responsiveness, the pupils of his eyes were dilated and his eye shone with preternatural brightness.

I talked with him about this experience, in a quiet, non-intrusive way. I said that perhaps he felt bathed in the yellowness; I said that perhaps he felt that it was a beautiful feeling and so the gap between himself and myself did not feel so sharp and frightening. Perhaps he felt that beautiful things could be around him and go in through his holes, rather than the ugly, frightening things he sometimes felt were there. I also said that perhaps he wanted to go inside me to feel safe because it was frightening to feel that there was a gap between his body and mine. As I talked, his whole body relaxed, his pupils stopped being dilated and suddenly he said, 'I'm ready to go home now.'

I do not pretend that what I said interpreted the whole of his experience, but it helped. It is a great comfort to me that much goes on in the therapeutic situation of which I am not aware. If the child had available to him only what I understood, the therapeutic situation would be a very limited one. But, on the occasion cited above, I understood enough for Peter to feel that I was in touch with him, and that he could come back to an ordinary state of awareness and find me waiting for him.

Some of the mothers of encapsulated children know well these states of icy clarity, which are sometimes extremely beautiful and sometimes extremely terrifying. Dr Salo Tischler, who has written moving papers on his work with the parents of psychotic children, quotes from the writings of one mother who shows remarkable insight about the needs from which such states arise and their dangers. She writes as follows (personal communication):

> If I were successfully withdrawn surely I would be calmer, easier to live with? All impressions, all contours seem so sharp. I take offence so easily. I listen carefully to the fine meaning of all conversations. I can accurately assess how people feel . . . I could not live closer to the children, their pains and pleasures are mine. I can hurt them by my abuses of this proximity.

As she realises, such a mother has maintained extraordinary and hypersensitised modes of communication with her children, so that both they and she do not have to bear the pains of the realisation of bodily separateness. It seems as if the state of maternal preoccupation has been carried on long past the time when it should have waned. Both she and the infant fear the natural and inevitable destruction inherent in breaking the physical connections between them so that psychological ones can begin to be established. But in *unduly* maintaining the elemental, hyper-sensitised forms of connection based on empathy and bodily vibrations, both she and the infant feel caught in a 'cobweb' from which they struggle to escape. When they find that escape is impossible, such fiery explosive violence is aroused that icy withdrawal seems to be the only answer.

By attempting to avoid the ordinary pains of life, they suffer extraordinary agonies and ecstasies, which make them feel cut off from the common experience of the human race to which they feel they do not belong. At the same time, they fear the fiery feelings from which they have retreated and which threaten to break through the 'ice-cap' of their pathological autism. This burning annihilation is experienced concretely as obnoxious bodily substances which threaten to implode and explode through all the holes in their body. As one psychotic child expressed it, they are threatened by a 'black hole'. In T. S. Eliot's terms, they are 'whirled in a vortex'. They have to be either in a keyed-up state of hypersensitive awareness or in a muted state of inanition in order to fend off these threats of their bodily survival, to their 'going-on-being' (as Winnicott, 1958, so aptly expresses it).

PSYCHOLOGICAL BIRTH FROM PATHOLOGICAL AUTO-SENSUOUSNESS

In clinical work, I have had convincing evidence that these hypersensitive states are associated with separation from an auto-sensual mother, i.e. a mother who has been experienced as an inanimate object and mainly in terms of the child's own bodily sensations. Psychological birth from such an inflexible, unadaptable delusory 'mother' is hard and protracted. Emily Brontë (1972) writes of a belated psychological birth of this kind in such a vivid way that it brings cold shivers to the spine. It will be remembered that Emily, her sisters Charlotte and Anne and their brother Bramwell for many years pretended that they lived on an imaginary island. Moreover, in their remote Yorkshire vicarage they were very cut off from outside contacts. Emily writes of her painful psychological birth as follows:

Oh dreadful is the check – intense the agony –
When the ear begins to hear, and the eye begins to see;
When the pulse begins to throb, the brain to think again;
The soul to feel the flesh, the flesh to feel the chain.

In the state of ultra-sharp awareness associated with an abnormal or precocious psychological birth, some encapsulated children observe objects with astounding accuracy. Through amazingly detailed drawings, they make phenomenal efforts to cope with the flood of sense impressions impinging upon them. Some of them even show a precocious grasp of perspective in their pictures. They will draw birds or aeroplanes getting smaller and smaller as they go into the distance. Or they will draw doors receding and becoming smaller one behind the other. Or they will draw roads going away into the distance. These drawings are always associated with impending separations from the therapist and there is always an over-strained, anguished quality about their state when they draw in this way. Such drawings remind one of the receding, converging lines which in the Rorschach Projective Test are found to be associated with depression.

THE PROCESSING OF SENSATIONS

Organic psychiatrists often mention a disability of the psychotic child which they term 'a dysfunction in the processing of sensory input'. Such a dysfunction can, of course, occur through damage to those parts of the brain concerned with such processing. However, clinical experience indicates that, as well as arising through brain damage, it can also occur through the excessive use of autistic objects or confusional objects, which block the child's use of the mother to help him to sort out sensory experiences. In psychosis, for some of a variety of reasons, the sorting-out function of the mother has not been available to the child. Therefore, an orderly setting and a therapist with a clear and orderly mind are indispensable to these children. Interpretations in the early days will be concerned with sorting out the child's sensory experiences, in which hard and soft, light and dark, full and empty, nice and nasty, rough and smooth, hot and cold, clean and dirty, loud and soft are some of the predominating ones. We shall realise that their primary modes of apprehension will be touching and smelling, and that hearing and seeing are likely to be experienced in a tactile way. We shall try to experience the world as the child experiences it in order to respond to him on his level, but this does not mean that we shall collude with the pathology of his autism. Our aim is to facilitate primary integrations so that he begins to tolerate the fact that the rough and smooth, sweet and bitter, hard and soft, the globe of light and boundless dark, nice and nasty, are both 'me' experiences. As these contraries are brought together within the 'me', he begins to tolerate the fact that these contraries come together in the 'not-me'. Precocious awareness of separateness from the mother's body means that, in an unprotected state, unbearable states of ecstasy and tantrum are experienced simultaneously, as 'hardness' and 'softness' come together. This is the excruciating situation from which they have retreated. (The implication of 'hardness' and 'softness' coming together as 'me' experiences was developed in detail in Chapter 9.) Such children also 'blow hot and cold' in a sensuous way, but have not the warmth of emotional response.

Techniques which try to stimulate the autistic child by tickling, caressing or cuddling are crude and are likely to reinforce his over-reactive auto-sensuousness. We need to help him to modify his use of pathological auto-sensuousness and the associated use of confusional and autistic objects. In this way, we shall help the child to turn to human beings, who, by caring for him through the minutiae of everyday life, will enable him to process his sensory experience in relationships with other people, by the development of expressive activities, and by percepts and concepts which enable him to live in the ordinary world. Gradually, his extreme states of beauty and terror will find form and shape through artistic and possibly religious expression. Thus, they will not prevent or distort his everyday functioning. From his therapist and the people around him, he will begin to learn the disciplines inherent in social life. He will learn to share and to co-operate with other human beings. Thus he will begin to develop a moral sense.

THE ENCAPSULATED CHILD'S MORAL SENSE

Undue reliance on an inanimate auto-sensual construct of 'mother' means that such a child's empathic sensibilities and thus his moral sense are very undeveloped. Snatching 'bits' from such a mother in order to grow up to be strong and powerful means that he does not have to acknowledge his dependence on, or gratitude towards, a mother, parents, family or social group. Also, reliance on an autistic object means that he does not have to learn to co-operate with and adjust to a person different from himself, for the autistic 'mother' is made in terms of 'me'. In some autistic children sterile cerebration seems to take the place of hidden sensual activities. These so-called *'idiots savants'* are usually emotional and moral morons. Perhaps this is at the root of the common man's distrust of those intellectuals he terms 'eggheads'!

The foregoing account indicates that a lively, active approach is needed in pyschotherapy with encapsulated children and with the encapsulated elements in neurotic children. Otherwise we therapists are liable to be treated like inanimate autistic objects. In my experience this is why some more passive forms of psychotherapy, which do not actively confront the child's pathological responses and activities, are not as effective as they might be. As the result of such psychotherapy, the once-encapsulated child may become a good, conforming pupil in school, he may learn in a stereotyped way, his responses may become more appropriate but they are stilted. He may also draw in a draughtsmanlike way. If he develops a moral sense, it is of an extremely rigid and obsessional kind. He is certainly in a better state than when he first started psychotherapy, but still the basis for his functioning is the use of autistic objects rather than a living, breathing, pulsating mother's breast, to which he has learned to adjust and with which he has learned to co-operate; these objects do not promote a sense of security. Autistic objects are an insecure, inflexible basis on which to manage intense states of feeling. They stultify movement and responsiveness. Such a child's apparent stability is liable to break down when confronted with biological strains and stresses such as puberty, sexual experiences and intense emotional involvements and conflicts. The mother's breast, with all its seeming deficiencies of mortality and temporality, is stronger than autistic objects with their seeming completeness and perfection.

On the other hand, those methods which rely exclusively on active, educational techniques are not adequate to the needs of these children either. This is particularly the case with those educational methods which are based on simplistic theoretical assumptions. Some of these techniques are even inhumane and damaging to the children. Clumsy interference is liable to result in a child who retreats to a more entrenched autistic state than he was in when he first came for treatment. It is no good trying to graft by force a whole set of normal responses upon his abnormal, immature state. If we seem to succeed and produce a little performing animal, we shall merely have imposed another kind of autism upon him which will be more difficult to remove then the one with which he came.

A skilful working together of both educationalists and psychotherapists who have developed insights into the deep needs of the encapsulated child seems to be the answer. Sadly, in England, this is in scant supply.

PSYCHOTHERAPY

Although, at the beginning of treatment, these children function in a predominantly asymbolic way, an interpretive treatment procedure is possible because they have 'internal language' and understand but do not speak. (This was discussed in Chapter 12.) However, our interpretations will be very different from those we would give to a neurotic child. Psychotherapy with a psychotic child needs a therapist who has been rigorously trained in detailed infant observation. This will make for the necessary degree of objectivity on the part of the therapist and the possibility of understanding non-verbal communications. However, an unduly subjective technique, using a predominance of intuitive insights, is liable to reinforce the autistic child's rarified modes of response and communication. This is not to dismiss the use of intuition but merely to give a warning about its over-use in a way which hampers the effort to use more objective means of understanding the child. To acquire this understanding based on following the details of the child's behaviour, a careful training in disciplined observation is an essential preliminary. It is akin to the difference between playing the piano 'by ear' and playing from the musical score.

In order to illustrate what I mean by an objective technique based on careful observation of detail, I will summarise the notes of Mrs Lynn Barnett. (This observation was quoted in Chapter 12.) At the time of the recorded sessions, her patient, whom we will call Paul, was a mute seven-year-old psychotic child. He was beginning to notice holiday breaks and was preoccupied with holes both in himself and in the outside world. Following evidence in the session that holes and the filling of holes was preoccupying him, Mrs Barnett interpreted to Paul that his putting his thumb in his mouth was due to his feeling that it was a hole he wanted to fill (see pp. 136–7).

Her response to Paul's behaviour (linking it to his desire to fill up holes) is a good example of the way in which the therapist, from a careful observation of small details of the child's activities, helps him to sort out his experiences and to represent them in a simple way. She also helps him to see the connections between these experiences in a way which is meaningful to him. She establishes contact with him at the level at which he is functioning, and develops what he is doing along meaningful lines for him. It will be obvious that exacting psychotherapeutic work of this kind is extremely taxing for the therapist and that such treatments should not be undertaken lightly. The next chapter will deal with the practical aspects of treating psychotic children by means of psychotherapy.

Chapter 14

Psychotherapy with autistic states in children

The practical suggestions given in this chapter have been culled from thirty years of working with autistic states in both psychotic and neurotic children. (It has been my experience that some neurotic children have a capsule of pathological autism which has to be worked over if therapy is to be effective. This will be discussed in Chapter 19.) An indispensable capacity for therapy with psychotic states is the ability to tolerate and understand acute terror, for which Bion's term 'nameless dread' has seemed an appropriate description.

THE TERROR ASSOCIATED WITH AUTISTIC STATES

Evidence of this terror comes not only from the psychoanalytic situation but also from the recollections of psychotic children who have made spontaneous recoveries. In an interesting paper on the life history, current states and memories of a 31-year-old man who, as a child aged four years, had been diagnosed by Kanner as suffering from Early Infantile Autism, the author Jules R. Bemperad (1979, p. 197) writes as follows:

> Jerry's recollections are extremely enlightening. The author was indeed surprised at the intensity of remembered fear and terror that was described, which seemed in direct contrast with the unperturbed and serene external appearance of autistic children he had observed. A similar pursuit of childhood memories might be attempted with other autistic individuals particularly those with good outcomes whose recollections would be less distorted, so that we can begin to reconstruct the elusive inner world of non-communicative autistic children, a task that could not but help us in our therapeutic efforts.

The trouble is that these terrors are so bizarre that when psychotherapists try to write about them they are liable to be dismissed as nonsense, which in a way they are, but to the psychotic child this 'non-sense' is crippling. Thus, an important part of work with these states is to become sufficiently in touch with them so that fantastic misconceptions can be modified and potentialities for emotional, cognitive and aesthetic functioning can be released.

This is a difficult task but over the years I have come to realise that the encapsulated child deals with elemental terrors by feeling *hard*, which means to him being strong and powerful. Either he collects hard objects which he can grasp (autistic objects), or he feels that his hard back protects his soft front, or he feels that his body is made hard and impenetrable by exciting auto-sensual activities. For these children, hardness becomes synonymous with the turgidity which comes from whipped-up sensual excitement. It is as if their body is a phallus. In this state the child feels that he is able to withstand threatening impingements. But when the inevitable collapse to this orgiastic experience comes, he feels soft in a flaccid and limp way. This sets in motion the whipping up of sensual excitement in order to feel hard and impregnable again. This is followed by the inevitable 'flop' (the 'helplessness' described by Bibring (1953) as characteristic of what he terms 'primal depression'). The relevance of this to manic-depressive states is obvious, and, as stated in Part I, these encapsulated children manifest manic-depressive states when they come out of their autism, and their mothers are usually cyclothymic characters. The confusional child sinks into soft objects and becomes confused with them as an escape from the terrors with which he feels surrounded.

The aim of psychotherapy is to help both types of psychotic child to internalise protecting and nurturing care, and to get in touch with the ordinary, everyday world which is a corrective to their outlandish notions arising from auto-sensual activities. Obviously, we shall not do this by scoffing at these activities nor by ridiculing the children. The only way in which we can help these children to achieve normal functioning is to be in touch with the states in which such a child lives and moves and has his being. One major aim of this book is to share the understandings of these states that I have gained over the past thirty years. For example, I have found the interpretation 'You are turning your hard back to protect your soft front', to be a very meaningful and mutative one. I first used this interpretation with a school-phobic child aged six years. After he had gone through the assessment procedures, he became phobic about coming to the clinic. However, his mother managed to drag him along, but when I went to fetch him from the waiting-room, he refused to come with me and knelt on a window-seat looking steadfastly out of the window. I tried many of the standard interpretations without any effect. Suddenly, remembering what I had learned from the autistic children, I addressed his unyielding back with the interpretation, 'I think you are turning your hard back to protect your soft front.' This had an immediate and surprising effect. He turned and looked at me from under his arm with a roguish smile, and went to sit astride the hard wooden hobby-horse. He made it jump up and down so that it banged against his penis in an exciting way. I now realise what I did not realise at the time, that he was giving himself feelings of hardness in this way. With this increased insight, I could have been still more in touch with him. However, my understanding had been good enough, and he came along to my consulting-room where he proceeded to draw a fort with very strong walls!

The 'flop' part of the vicious circle of whipped-up sensual excitement leads to the 'black hole' phenomenon, so often described by psychotic children, as they become able to formulate their experiences. The 'black hole with the nasty prick' (as John described it in *Autism and Childhood Psychosis*, Tustin, 1972) seems to be a psychosomatic experience. This was the best verbalisation that the child could make of a non-verbal experience which was the result of recoil from, and 'blacking out' of, the nasty 'not-me', which was experienced as an inimical presence. The parents, and later the therapist find this recoil and seeming rejection hard to bear and to understand. However, insight into the nature of the situation helps us to keep on going forward to meet him, which is an essential part of helping such a child. In this going forward to meet the child to encourage him to give up his autistic protections, we shall need to be more active than is usually the case in psychoanalytic therapy. Thus, I agree with Meltzer (Meltzer, *et al.*, 1975, p. 15) when he writes that in working with autistic children the therapist needs to allow 'a degree of permissiveness with regard to physical contact . . . that one would not easily allow in the course of child analysis ordinarily'. (This does not apply to confusional children.)

This responsiveness is not sentimental self-indulgence. It is the compassionate and disciplined response of one human being who knows what it is like to feel raw terror, and who uses all the resources at his or her command to help another human being who is going through these states. Used in this disciplined and insightful way, such responsiveness does not impede the clinical work by over-identification with the patient, but makes of it the warm, personal, active experience such children need if their frozen terror is to be thawed. On the other hand, it is important not to allow the kind of over-indulgent physical contact which perpetuates their delusion of fusion with the outside world.

Active responses may take the form of holding the child's hands when he is flapping them or using them for his idiosyncratic stereotypes. As we do this, we talk to him. For example, we might say, 'I know you're so excited – or so frightened – or so upset – that it is spilling into your hands. But I am holding them, and the upset – the overflow – is going into me. I can hold it for you. There's no need to flap – there's no need to rub your hands together [etc.]. Tustin is holding the upset.' I have found that repeating a simple phrase over and over again, such as 'Tustin is holding the upset' or 'Tustin is holding the flap' or 'Tustin is holding you together', is often very helpful to these children. Even if the child does not always understand the full import of the words we use, they seem to wrap him around with thought and care. Our words and actions provide a 'container' for the overflow, until the child can establish the necessary sensuous integrations which enable him to contain it for himself. They also establish that shared talking is one means by which such overflowing sensations and feelings can be expressed and patterned.

Such behaviour is not idle reassurance which fobs off the child and his terrors. It is genuine and caring support for a child who is overwhelmed by primitive impulsions because he has no apparatus to process them. We contain them for him. The tumult of rage, terror and excitement passes. The child feels he has not been left to bear it alone. Like the cough, the sneeze, the orgasm (and I would add, in some cases, the seeming epileptic fit), *ecstasy* and *tantrum* are patterns for the discharge of physical sensations too intense for the body to bear. Properly handled, both states can stimulate mental growth and development. If they are left to 'flap' around in an uncontained way, pathological autistic manoeuvres are exacerbated.

At each milestone in his psychological development, and at each daily crisis, the encapsulated child experiences again the terror of failure and helplessness aroused by his first disastrous encounters with the 'not-me'. With gaping mouth he gives again the gulp and gasp of horror as the 'black hole' of the unknown 'not-me' yawns before him. Psychological growth seems to mean taking a step into the unfathomable darkness down which he will fall endlessly to his doom. This experience comes into the dreams of normal and neurotic people, but the encapsulated child lacks the capacity to dream. The primordial stuff of dreams is his waking reality. In his relatively undifferentiated state, agonies and ecstasies come together like an electric shock. In a state of what should be 'pre-ruth' (Winnicott's term), oral, anal and phallic states, œdipal conflicts and depressive feelings about destructiveness come into operation prematurely and in an impacted, schematic and distorted fashion. The child cannot sort them out and deal with them in a way which facilitates psychological development because they are compacted together, and also because he has not developed the necessary apparatus to do so. Encapsulation (either total or segmented) and the engulfment and entanglement of confusional states are autistic manoeuvres which blunt the sharpness of unbearable experiences of separateness of a bodily kind. As we have seen, encapsulation puts a protective shell around the 'me'; engulfment and entanglement draw the 'not-me' into the 'me' and confuse and dim the perception of it. The child retreats from the 'not-known' 'not-me' to the familiar fastnesses of well-tried pathological autosensual manoeuvres. Thus, his psychological development is either halted as in the pathological autism of encapsulation, or it is patchy and hampered as in confusional autistic states.

Another way in which psychotherapy with encapsulated autistic states differs from the usual pattern of psychoanalytic treatment (at least as it is practised in some quarters) is the fact that practical help to the parents over caring for their child is usually necessary. The non-directive ways of working with parents which are currently in use, and which are effective for work with the parents of most neurotic children, are not suitable for these parents whose confidence has been undermined by their rejecting child. However, this help has to be given tactfully and sensitively. For example, at the beginning of treatment, collision situations between mother and child often arise. I have found that discussion of them needs to be supplemented by practical but sensitive help with management. This is not intrusive interference. Indeed, in my view, psychoanalytic interpretations which are not related to the level at which the child is functioning constitute the greatest interference with therapeutic progress. Also, during the course of treatment, we may hear that mother and child have come into collision with each other over some piece of homely activity such as bathing, hair-washing, toileting or going to bed. If this can be discussed in a practical way in terms of the management of the situation or even, if the mother requests it, a visit is made to the home (not by the therapist), to take part in the activity, the situation between mother and child can be relieved and a transitional area of compromise facilitated. In this adjustment, neither mother nor child has her or his own autistic way; a new shared way is found. This is very therapeutic in such cases. For, in infancy, encapsulated children and their mothers have had a 'head-on' collision with each other from which they have both recoiled. The alarm states of this collision go on operating and increasing as the years go by. A tactful worker going into the home can become a useful buffer between mother and child until co-operative activity has developed between them. (Professor Didier Houzel of the Hôpital de Bohors in Brest has especially trained nurses who do this. This works very well.)

In treatment, we have to help the child to develop this capacity for adjustment and adaptation. This is not achieved by esoteric interpretations, but by insistent encouragement to the child to carry out the simple actions which keep the treatment setting in working order, such as hanging up outdoor clothes on the peg provided, clearing up at the end of the session and saying 'Goodbye' before he leaves. These children try to rush in at the beginning of the session and to rush out at the end, so that the therapist is treated like a piece of furniture. To bring to the child's notice that the therapist is different from 'things' and that there are social niceties which take note of this, whilst buffering the 'not-me-ness' with familiar phrases such as 'Hello' and 'Goodbye', is very helpful to these children. I had an unconventional upbringing and I had to learn, from working with such children, the value of these simple social conventions which are not niggling but facilitating.

This brings me to an important difference between encapsulated psychotic states and neurotic ones. This is the fact that, in line with the paucity or differentiation in other areas, in encapsulated psychotic states there is very little differentiation between conscious and unconscious processes. That which in neurosis is repressed and is only expressed symbolically in encapsulated psychotic children is crude, untransformed and raw. The capacity for symbolic expression is very limited. Asymbolic states predominate. Thus, in these states, encapsulated children do not have dreams, thoughts and fantasies to a degree which can be used as they can with neurotic children and, to some degree, with confusional psychotic children. Auto-sensual activities, many of them covert and surreptitious, are their predominating expressive modes.

In normal and neurotic children, in-built dispositions which were pre-programmed to emerge at certain stages of growth in an orderly fashion are not part of conscious functioning. They go on at what we call an *unconscious* level. But in encapsulated children, the situation is different. First of all, the traumatic disturbances these children feel they have suffered (albeit this is often a delusion) mean that, as well as there being little distinction between conscious and unconscious activity, in-built dispositions have become compacted. This means that the encapsulated psychotic child needs different treatment from a neurotic child, because a first major task is to sort out the stages of growth and to help him to go through them in an orderly and normal fashion.

In working with neurotic states in children, we come upon repressed unconscious material which the patient has strong resistances to recognising. This is not the case with encapsulated psychotic states. In these states, the 'not-me' has been shut out and there is strong resistance to bringing together the 'me' with the 'not-me', the 'hard' sensations with the 'soft' sensations. This resistance is different from that encountered in neurosis, where resistances are mainly directed towards repressed conflicts concerned with emotional relationships with people.

For most of the time, autism is a relatively conflict-free state. Thus, the psychotic child (both encapsulated and confusional) has to experience firm restraints on his idiosyncratic activities to bring about the type of conflict and repression which is characteristic of normal healthy growth. This also brings about the sense of self which comes from contact of the body-self with the limitations of the world outside the body. With this comes the knowledge that there is a point where his body ends and the 'not-self' begins. It also results in the development of the constructs of time and space with their inevitable frustrations. The child also becomes aware of other people.

The need for a certain amount of appropriate restraint means that abreaction and catharsis are definitely not treatment measures to be used with psychotic states, either confusional or encapsulated. These appropriate restraints need to be coupled with ample opportunities for expressive activities such as music, art, and cognitive and physical skills. Expressive activities are not opportunities for 'letting off steam' in a 'do as you like' way, but opportunities to develop skills for the patterning and expressing of feelings which are being aroused by the realistic constraints of which the children are becoming increasingly aware.

In my experience, much individual psychotherapy with psychotic children is too permissive and too passive. For example, they are allowed to wander from room to room instead of being kept within the bounds of the consulting-room, which helps them to develop self-boundaries. They are allowed to bring toys from home to the consulting-room and to take toys home after a session. This blurs the distinction between home and the therapeutic situation. Of course, the insistence on the separation between objects used at home and those used in therapy has to be done through interpretation and, at first, some toys brought from home have to be tolerated for the time being, but they must not be colluded with as a permanent event. Also, some therapists allow the children to continue with their stereotypes and repetitive activities instead of helping them to take part in interactive activities, even if it is merely rolling objects from child to therapist. Again, this has to be done with skill and sensitivity. To stop these activities in a clumsy, insensitive way is as harmful as letting them continue, perhaps more so. The overriding aim should be to help the child to feel held in firm and understanding hands so that inner structures can begin to develop.

Restraints associated with interpretations which show the child that he is being cared for by someone who is in touch with him will enable the child to develop a more adequate simulation of the external world, which grows and changes as new experiences play upon him. At first, this comes through effortful activity with a therapist who gives evidence of sustained attentiveness and effort, motivated by genuine feelings of care and concern. The child's attention is directed towards the task on hand, which is appropriate to his physical development and to the situation in which he is. It is also appropriate to the nature of his autism and his needs. Such activities arise naturally in the course of individual psychotherapy and very often the container for the child's toys becomes the fount from which good things come. But this 'fount' is experienced autistically, that is, in terms of his own body. This is the case with such a child's first experience of the breast, which is not a breast as we know it, but is experienced in terms of the gestalt of a soft receptive mouth encircling a rounded object with a hard nipple-tongue in the middle. Children often speak of this middle sensation as the 'button'. As these children develop the sense of having 'good things inside', particularly the integrating sensation-giving 'button', they begin to feel held together. I have found that this integrative experience comes into the therapy situation in the following, somewhat surprising, way. At the point at which he is beginning to feel held together and is coming together with other people, the child will make a cross by intersecting a vertical line with a horizontal one. He may do this by drawing, or he may do it by using sticks or pencils so that they intersect. I first became aware of this in John, who is described in *Autism and Childhood Psychosis* (Tustin, 1972, p. 20). The description is as follows:

> *Friday January 25th, 1953 (Session 153)*
> (Before giving this session, I should say that in December John had seen a baby feeding at the breast and had shown great interest. I had not used the word 'breast', not knowing whether he knew it. It now came into his material.)
> He carefully arranged four coloured pencils in the form of a cross and said 'Breast!' Touching his own mouth he said, 'Button in the middle!' (I interpreted baby John's desire to make up a breast for himself out of his own body.)

Since that time, many other children have shown me the importance of the stage when they use a vertical line to intersect a horizontal one (which is the same length as the vertical one) to make a cross.

Dr Geneviève Haag, who is a psychiatrist at the Institute Claparède in Paris, brought the following observations to discuss with me. She felt that they represented an important stage in the child's recovery.

> Marguerite, aged ten years, was patting a balloon about the room. She was much more co-ordinated in doing this than previously and related to Dr Haag much more than formerly. After a while, she began to pat the balloon towards the window, taking great care that it only hit the wooden intersecting pieces of wood which hold the panes of glass together and are in the form of a cross. It was clear that Marguerite felt that these protected the fragile glass and was reassured by this. She was also interested in the wooden cross-pieces for the glass in the top part of the door.
>   Later, she rubbed her hand over the smooth solid wooden planks in the lower part of the door, and then went over to the roughcast wall and rubbed her hand over that, as if comparing the roughness of the wall with the smoothness of the door.

This confirms my own observations that, as straight lines are brought together to intersect each other, so the child begins to bring together basic sensuous contraries such as hard and soft, rough and smooth, hot and cold, light and dark, etc. So long as these are kept discrete and apart, they cannot modify each other to produce new and subtle combinations.

Marguerite went on to draw a large cross on a piece of paper, pointing out that the ends of each of the lines went over on to the table. When children do this, I have found that it usually means they are wanting a larger piece of paper than they have been given. This linked in my mind with other children who have behaved similarly when reaching this stage of making a cross. John, whose session was quoted earlier, exemplifies this very well. The session quoted previously continued in the following way:

> After my interpretation that he wanted to make a breast out of his own body, he put out more pencils in a hasty, careless fashion to make a ramshackle extension to the cross. To this he said, 'Make a bigger breast! Make a bigger breast!'
> (I interpreted baby John's desire to have a bigger breast than really existed.)
> He angrily knocked all the pencils so that they spread in a higgledy-piggledy fashion over the table. He said, 'Broken breast!'
> (I interpreted his baby rage that he could not have a breast as big as he wanted.)

Marguerite expressed this frustration with reality limits by biting the wooden cross-pieces in the window. Thus, the fragile part of the window was left unprotected. The vulnerability of these children is, in part, the result of making the outside protecting shelter (the mother) into a fragile thing with no protections. An important part of our work is to bring home to them the need to exercise restraint in their destruction of connections and to bear the frustration of reality limits. They cannot have unbounded care, attention and satisfaction. This dissatisfaction with the actual world is characteristic of such children's reactions at this stage. It brings in the possibility of conflict and the need to come to terms with it. This is a very important development.

There is much I do not understand about the significance of intersecting one vertical straight line with a horizontal one of the same length. I have found that, when encapsulated children start to put pencil to paper, they draw straight lines, as if these shapes have innate significance. I can only say that the stage at which they make a vertical straight line and a horizontal straight line of the same length to intersect in a right-angled way has always proved to be a significant stage in psychotherapy.

Also, when this occurs, the children develop the sense of being able to hold good things *inside* their body. Until this stage is reached, they have no notion of insides, but relate only to surfaces. For example, the hard back is not connected to the soft front by the inside of the body. Front and back are two separate, discrete surfaces, and hardness and softness are opposites which seem incompatible with each other. As the qualities of hardness and softness become connected with each other, more subtle combinations come into awareness. Also, as there develops the notion of insides which cannot be seen, touched or handled but which can link and hold things together, there develops the sense of having a 'mind' associated with such unseen mental events as thoughts, fantasies and memories. The processes by which this occurs in therapy seem bizarre to our sophisticated minds used to dealing with abstractions, but something like the following occurs.

The concrete mode of functioning of primitive states means that 'mind' is felt to be a material container which holds things together as in a sack, which prevents them from falling apart or into pieces. When a person is mad, we say he is 'out of his mind', as if his mind were a material object, instead of an immaterial and convenient illusion which enables us to talk about mental events as distinct from brain activities. In the early stages, encapsulated children have not developed this feeling of being able to hold things in their minds. Their so-called 'good memory' is a kind of *déjà vu* experience whenever a configuration similar to a previous one which was significant occurs, as if the situation is happening all over again. They may even repeat the words associated with that experience. In these early stages, the arrangement of bricks and other objects in straight lines on the ground or strung onto a string, with one object being separated from and unrelated to the next, can be either a precursor to or an obstacle to thinking, depending on how the therapist uses it. These objects which are placed one behind the other seem to be on the bodily model of food going down the throat or faeces down the anal passage. However, it is not experienced as a process. Each piece is separated and isolated from the next. They are not contained in anything. Also, the existence of anything which cannot be seen, touched and handled is inconceivable to children in this state. 'Thoughts' as immaterial mental events are not a possibility. This makes the psychotherapeutic treatment of children in this state very different from that of neurotic children. With encapsulated psychotic children we are helping them to develop thoughts, dreams and fantasies, which have developed to some extent in confusional psychotic states and to an even greater degree in neurotic ones. We are helping them to give up excessively concretised modes of awareness and to develop the capacity for abstraction. This can only occur as they tolerate their sense of bodily separateness from the outside world and the frustrations and conflicts which this entails.

Children in these over-concretised psychotic states may experience our words as material objects aimed at them to hurt them, and not as healing interpretations. We have to use words, both to establish with the child that this is an important medium through which human beings get in touch with each other, and also to help ourselves to think aloud in this puzzling and worrying situation. But we have to be on the alert for the fact that 'talking' will not mean to the child what it means to us. We have to be quick to talk to him about this. Fortunately, there is always a part of the child, however miniscule, which wants to grow up properly and can listen to us and use our words for the purposes of growth, and for freedom from the rigidity and artificiality of his autistic encumbrances.

An important first step in this difficult task of freeing the child from his hampering aberrations and of setting free the natural processes of growth is the provision of protective and supportive sheltering while the essential primary sensuous integrations described in earlier chapters are enabled to take place. These hold the child together, but for this to occur he needs to feel firmly held in the outside world. If these primary integrations do not take place, he is forever dependent on outside support. He has no firmly established 'sensation-self', and the 'not-me' outside world becomes unduly important because although it constitutes a threat, paradoxically it is also used as a support when it is experienced as 'me'.

As well as enabling these sensuous integrations to take place, a firm framework of support in the therapeutic situation gives the encapsulated children something more authentic than their shells of 'me-ness' to keep them safe from the threatening 'not-me' outside world. It helps the entangled child to dare to disentangle himself from the mother. This is not soft, passive, permissive protection associated with such sentimental procedures as cuddling, kissing and sweet-giving combined with empty reassurances, but firm, insightful, compassionate and disciplined care and guidance.

In the early days of work with these children it was thought to be therapeutic to give them the sensuous experiences they were supposed to have missed. This was appropriate for the deprived institution children described by Geneviève Appel in her film *Monique*. But most psychotic children are not like these children. With most of them, it is not that sensuous experiences have been missing, but that the child has been disturbed in the early situation when sensation was of predominant importance, so that basic sensuous integrations have not taken place. An important first part of work with psychotic states is to assist the awareness that the basic sensations of hardness and softness, light and dark, hot and cold, sweet and bitter, nice and nasty, rough and smooth *exist together* both in the body and in the outside world, and that there can be interplay between them.

The facilitation of this integration is work for the therapist. It is not the therapist's role to give the child sensuous experiences by cuddling, kissing, tickling or providing sweetmeats and food. This interferes with the roles of the parents. The work of the therapist is to firmly extricate himself from the mechanical constructions of the psychotic child. For example, one autistic child tried to make me behave as if I were a 'vending machine', that is, to behave in terms of his mechanical expectations of me and not as a human being who might say and do surprising things. As the therapist stands firm against being encapsulated by the child's mechanical constructions, so the encapsulated child will turn to the parents as distinct people in their own right and separate from him, who can give him sensuous love and care. As the therapist disentangles the confusional child from being entangled with him, so the parents will be treated in a less entangling way. But the parents of both encapsulated and confusional children need to be prepared to meet their changing child and to re-evaluate him. It is hard to describe these subtle processes in a way that will enable them to be understood. It is also hard to carry them out in practice. But in the course of time, with firmness, patience and discipline, a great deal can be achieved, especially when co-operative attachment processes begin to be set in train. These will be discussed in the next chapter, which is concerned with transference phenomena.

Chapter 15

Transference phenomena in autistic states

Transference in the psychoanalytic sense is a re-evocation in the present of feelings towards the parents in the past. Melanie Klein and Anna Freud take different views about the transference situation with regard to children. Anna Freud's view is that transference and transference neurosis as defined by Freud cannot develop in children in the same way as they do in adult analysis because the actual parents are still active agents in the child's life. However, both Anna Freud and Melanie Klein see transference as a major agent of change in the analytic situation with children. This is because the relationship with the therapist is used to modify the pathological elements of the child's relationship with his parents.

But the encapsulated child has not developed a relationship with his parents. This is the crux of his pathology. The confusional child has entangled relationships and develops the peculiar type of transference relationship which has been described for adult schizophrenics by writers such as Rosenfeld (1965), Searles (1965) and Kohut (1971). Since the transference relationship of the encapsulated child is different in some ways from that of a confusional child, and since it does not seem to have been described elsewhere, this chapter will concentrate on these children.

THE DEVELOPMENT OF ENCAPSULATED CHILDREN

The thesis of this book has been that the pathological auto-sensuousness of the encapsulated child is an automatic reaction to an unbearable shock or series of shocks. It seems that the shock or shocks occur very early in life. It is even possible that, in some children, they may have occurred before or during the birth process itself. This has meant that the child has never developed the primal attachment to the suckling mother which we are realising is the corner-stone of human relationships.

PRIMAL ATTACHMENTS

The work done by ethologists such as Martin Richards of Cambridge (Richards and Bernal, 1976), by paediatricians such as Marshall Klaus (Klaus and Kennell, 1976), and by psychoanalysts such as John Bowlby (1969) has added a further dimension to our understanding of how human relationships develop. A mechanical extrapolation of their concepts from animals to human beings is liable to lead to error. However, used cautiously, they throw light on elemental levels of human development. The encapsulated children have not developed primal attachment to their mothers. Thus, they have never developed the sense of having a working simulation experienced as 'something integrating inside'. In normal development, this sense of inner integration becomes a regulating element in the child's emotional life. It is the basis from which human relationships develop and it promotes the development of psychic life. For this important prototype to become established as a working construct in the child's experience, the child has to tolerate the fact that the mother is not a piece of his body which gives him sensual pleasure just when and how he wants it, but that she is separate and different from his body sensations and has links with other people. Thus, he cannot take her for granted in a passive way.

The encapsulated child has experienced bodily separateness from the mother in an unbearable way. This may have been before he was put to the breast (or bottle experienced as breast). He has certainly never experienced the need for effort with a succouring and sustaining being who is separate and different from his body. A traumatic experience of bodily separateness has caused him to recoil from this awareness and has produced massive inhibition in all spheres of development.

Thus, therapy with encapsulated autistic states is different from the psychoanalytic treatment of neurotic states and confusional ones, because the child has to develop a co-operative attachment which will form the basis for relationships with people. 'Transference', as Freud (1922) defined it, is based on the capacity for relationships. It is also a symbolic activity based on the capacity to 'recollect'. Freud wrote that the way in which the pathological elements of a past relationship to the parents were transformed was by being repeated with the therapist, so that 'repetition' could be 'transformed into recollection' (Freud, 1915). But the encapsulated psychotic child enacts with the therapist pre-verbal elemental early situations which were too painful to be borne. Such a child has to develop the capacity for recollection. (The way in which the capacity for recollection develops in therapy with such children will be indicated in Chapter 18, 'The struggles of a psychotic child to develop a mind of his own'.) Thus, the transference situation with such children is different from that in the psychoanalytic treatment of other types of emotional disturbance. The fact that their emotional life is also a raw, crude elemental one, in which the extreme emotions of rage, terror and anguish ('grief' as Mahler terms it) are the only ones experienced by the child, also makes a difference to the transference situation.

We cannot give such a child early infantile experiences in the exact forms in which he has missed them. For example, he has physically outgrown the breast. For this reason, I have found it inappropriate to provide feeding bottles for such children. It is an important and surprising finding that co-operative effortful activities with insightful people, suited to the child's capabilities, can evoke infantile experiences. Thanks to the marvellous adaptability of the human species, they can go through an important early stage in a manner which is suited to later conditions. (The so-called 'regression therapy' can lead to such inappropriate and misguided practices as older children being put into nappies and pushed around in prams.)

In psychotherapy, activities arise which can seem equivalent to early infantile experiences. For example, the container for the child's toys often becomes the fount from which good things come. In these activities the child is firmly helped to co-operate with another human being who has an orderly yet flexible mind, and who demonstrates effortful behaviour towards him and insists on the need for effort on his part. His evasive tricks and time-wasting activities are discouraged. At the same time, insights are given about how his growing up is impeded by them. It is a relief to find that, even in these very uncooperative children, there is a part of them that is waiting to be helped 'to grow up properly' and to commit themselves to an attachment to a parent figure.

In normal development, the sensuous experiences of bodily care are important in developing the co-operative attachment of mother and baby. In this, suckling experiences seem to be nuclear. Any maternity-ward nurse or midwife will confirm that to help a mother and baby to come together in a satisfactory nursing situation is not a passive affair but an active, sensitive, skilful one of alternately nudging the couple along and then supporting them and building up their confidence in each other. The same is true in the early days of psychotherapy with encapsulated children. At the same time as we are encouraging the development of the equivalents of early infantile attachments we are modifying the pathology of autism. We are also facilitating the primary sensuous differentiations and integrations which have been described from various aspects throughout this book.

Gradually, the budding self comes to comprise hardness as well as softness, roughness as well as smoothness, hotness as well as coldness, etc. These contraries are differentiated but 'compresent' (to use Bertrand Russell's useful neologism). They become part of the 'me-ness' of 'me'. Thus, they are the infant's first taste of reality. This is an important step that the encapsulated psychotic child has never been able to make. His encapsulation insulates him against the cold, hard, bitter, rough 'not-me'. In psychotherapy with such children we have to help them to do consciously that which ordinarily takes place without our being aware of what is happening.

As the primary differentiations which have become possible interact with each other, new sensations are born. For example, from hardness and softness there develops the notion of resilience and firmness. There are bitter-sweet reactions. The child learns to 'take the rough with the smooth'. I had the following discussion with Peter, some of whose sessions are presented in Chapter 18. It was two years after he had begun to talk and he was in his third and last year of treatment. He was grumbling about some nasty thing that had happened to him, so I said, 'You've got to learn to take the rough with the smooth, haven't you?' To which he replied, 'Would that mean to be reconciled to it? We had that word in spellings the other day and I thought about what we had talked about here.' It is fascinating to see the way in which our everyday idioms 'pick up' these basic experiences, which in most of us have taken place without our ever knowing that they were happening. Soft, receptive mouth and hard, thrusting nipple, pulling together in a concerted effort, create a critical situation which enables these sensuous integrations to take place. As skill develops, the child feels held together by these internal conjunctions just as he is held together by the external 'holding situation' in which mother and father seem to be pulling together to rear him.

As was shown in the tape-recording of the baby feeding at the breast, which was referred to in an earlier chapter, rhythmical consonance and skill are not achieved without effort. It has to be worked for. The hard and the soft have to work together. The child has to learn to take the rough with the smooth; the dissonance with the consonance. And the parents and the therapist have to help him with the tantrum about this. It will be obvious that the time when the hard teeth come through the soft gums is also an important time for the further conjoining of hard and soft sensuous experiences. (The early infantile situation of a normal adult was reported to me, who as an infant obstructed her sucking at the breast by putting her tongue in the way. This was very worrying to her good and concerned mother, who sought help from several quarters. However, when the teeth began to come through the gums, the obstructing tongue became a thing of the past, and feeding became normal and easy, to the great relief of the mother. We can imagine that in another nursing situation, with a less confident mother, the outcome could have been different.)

But, as instanced earlier, this preoccupation with the mouth has other origins also. It seems to be the focal point for the catastrophic sense of being disconnected from the mother, for which the term 'psychotic depression' has been used. This has to be worked over in the therapeutic situation if the child is to be able to develop satisfactory experiences which have some equivalence with those of an infant at the breast and with the network of related experiences which give him the feeling of being 'held' in reliable arms.

PSYCHOTIC DEPRESSION

One experience of this 'flop-type' depression is that the autistic child feels that his body is like a piece of rock which has broken away from a rock face. In this experience of his body as an inanimate object, he feels that his skin is an outer covering which is damaged by being broken away. The reaction is to make a second skin – a false skin – an encapsulation. In her paper, 'The Experience of the Skin in Early Object Relations', Esther Bick (1968) has described this process with meticulous illustrative observations from infants and psychotic children. This encapsulation insulates the psychotic child from the sense of elemental loss which is associated with the catastrophe of bodily disconnection from the mother, but it deadens the response to normal sensations. He feels wrapped in either the autogenerated hard sensations of the autistic objects, or the soft sensations of the confusional objects, so that his apprehension of the outside world is constricted by these delusions. The bodily disconnection from the mother is experienced as having lost a cluster of exciting and relief-giving sensations which are located in the mouth. The important thing is that the child was not aware that they were there until he had lost them. He feels he has lost an essential part of his body and experiences precocious feelings of grief and mourning. This has been described by Margaret Mahler (1961).

Infants who were traumatically shocked before or during birth would be prone to traumatic experiences of bodily separateness after birth. They would need extraordinarily good nurturing if they were to be protected from this. Lacking this, they will replace it by pathological auto-sensuality. When this breaks down, as inevitably it must, the child is exposed to a bodily sense of loss of a traumatic kind. If, before birth, the child has become attached to the pathological use of autistic objects from which he cannot be attracted by especially confident mothering, then the stage is also set for psychotic tragedy. It will be seen that different situations can lead to the same presenting appearance and to vulnerability to a psychotic sense of loss.

This 'loss' makes the child feel that he has a hole where the cluster of sensations had been. This 'hole' type of depression has to be experienced and worked over in the therapeutic setting. This will modify the pathological repetition-compulsion with which the child is ensnared. As he is released from this vicious circle, he begins to use situations in the therapeutic setting as equivalents to infantile experiences. The *infantile transference* now develops.

THE INFANTILE TRANSFERENCE

This is the most important mutative agent of change. In therapy with neurotic children, actual experiences with the breast of infancy are re-evoked, but the encapsulated psychotic child has to have these experiences at a later date and with the therapist. As these feelings become focused around the therapist, the child's relationship to the mother develops. In some ways, it is the usual transference situation in reverse. The therapist sets elemental infantile relationships in train by establishing the primal core of these relationships, and this is transferred to the home situation. The therapist works with the infantile elements in the child in the mode which is suitable to the child's physique and capabilities, and the mother establishes a relationship with the child of the present day.

I have found that premature transference interpretations, if given to the child when there is no basis for them, can get in the way of promoting the relationship with the mother. Also, premature transference expectations on the part of the therapist can seem to be pressurising and intrusive to children whose pathology has arisen from an inhibitory recoil from a 'not-me' mother, who is felt to be full of hardness, roughness, irritation, darkness, blackness and nastiness. It goes without saying that crude methods of therapy in which the therapist aims to be a 'mother-substitute', are to be avoided. The number of autistic children who do not have good parents to turn to as their withdrawal is abated is fortunately quite small. With most of these children, especially the younger ones, our aim is to help them to accept their parents, 'warts and all', and for them to feel similarly accepted.

The conclusion I have reached after thirty years of working with such children is that the transference situation cannot be established by the use of interpretation alone. Other, more active, measures need to be employed but, in doing this, we need to beware of allowing these active measures to take the place of interpretive therapy. The need to be constantly developing insights which are transmitted by interpretation must be paramount, and activity on our part needs to be combined with reflective communications to the child about why it is being done. If such communications are not possible because, on occasions, our actions are impulsive and unintentional, in later moments of reflection we need to become aware of what feelings were being stirred up in ourselves which led to these actions. This brings us to the subject of *counter-transference*.

In an interesting paper concerned with adult psychotic patients, Lea

Goldberg (1979) makes the point that clinical material from patients in psychotic states indicates that in those states transference is directed into the therapist's body. She tells of bodily sensations experienced by the therapist, such as a hot sensation in the stomach, which were related to the patient's experiences. Thus, she thinks that experiences 'which are usually called counter-transference in its broad meaning, should rather be seen as very early forms of object relationships'. In the present book, the evacuation into the therapist's body of experiences which are more than the child can organise has been seen as part of the infantile transference, in that it reproduces situations in early infancy in which the mother, by this evacuation procedure, is called upon to help her infant to manage such experiences. If an illusion of fusion prevails at that time, she does this as if she is part of the child's body. This 'containing' (as Bion calls it) of the 'overflow' is an important part of maternal nurturing, and is thus an important part of the therapist's task. Being a 'nappy mummy', as Meltzer (1967) has picturesquely termed it, plays an important part in mother–infant attachment. Thus, when working with patients functioning at these elemental levels, transference and counter-transference cannot be clearly delineated. Lea Goldberg adds the important corollary that verbal interpretation to such patients often represents an elaboration of the transference, which can also be seen as counter-transference because it is based on sensations and feelings which have been provoked in the analyst, as if they had been evacuated by the patient.

A further complication is that in encapsulated psychotic children, who have little sense of bodily separateness and little capacity for symbolic representation, repetitions of early events are not placed in space and time. They are events which seem to be going on again whenever some configuration similar to a previous significant tone happens to occur. As Eleonora Fe d'Ostiani (1979) has termed them, they are 're-presentations'. They have not the symbolic quality of the transference manifestations characteristic of the treatment of neurotic children.

With the confusional psychotic children, whose symbolising capacities are developed to a slightly greater extent than those of the encapsulators, a peculiar entangling transference situation develops, similar to that which has been described for adult schizophrenic patients (Kohut, 1971; Rosenfeld, 1965; Searles, 1965).

COUNTER-TRANSFERENCE

In the literature on work with adult psychotic patients, the need to use the counter-transference is often stressed. A few words of warning about its use are necessary in relation to psychotic children. But first we must be clear about the sense in which we are using the term 'counter-transference'.

Originally, this concept referred to the process by which the therapist transferred certain aspects of his relationship with important figures in his past onto the current relationship with the patients. Thus, his understanding of the patient could be distorted by feelings towards him as if he were a younger brother or sister. In recent years, the term has been widened to cover situations in which the therapist feels that the patient represents a part of himself, for example, a psychotic part of himself.

However, in some writings, the term has been widened still further to cover the evocation by the patient of strong feelings in the analyst. For example the analyst

(a)   may be urged to some course of action such as cuddling or comforting the patient;

(b)   may feel he has to bear certain feelings for the patient who is finding them insufferable;

(c)   may feel that the patient is trying to communicate about certain feelings by provoking them in the analyst.

These feelings are communicated to the analyst by fringe cues such as muscle tensions, small bodily gestures, facial expressions and tones of voice. They are not communicated directly. Although, obviously, we use these fringe cues in relating to people, I have come to think that we should be careful not to use them too much in working with psychotic children. These children are constantly on the alert and live in a world of fringe cues in order to fend off dangers. This means that they scarcely respond to direct communications from the people around them. They also want to feel that these people are part of their body and under their control. If we respond to these indirect communications too readily, on the basis of intuition alone, we act as if we are part of their body, and collude with the delusion that we are under their magical control. We also collude with the child in letting him continue to live in a hypersensitised, rarefied world of sensuous rather than verbal communication. In working with these children, our capacity for empathy is called into play, but this should be used with circumspection and caution.

An undue use of hypersensitised modes of functioning can be very exhausting and can even result in physical and emotional illness in the therapist. I have come to think that the welfare of both therapist and patient can best be served by the objectivity which comes from a careful following and recording of the details of the patient's behaviour (and even of those details which do not fit into our scheme of understanding. Lack of fit is the important point where learning takes place. We have to help the psychotic child to learn from these experiences of lack of fit, and we have to learn from them ourselves!).

This objective approach means that our attention will be focused upon the patient rather than being unduly concentrated upon our own subjective feelings and reactions so that the patient is forgotten. An essential preparation for this type of psychotherapeutic work is the systematic and detailed recording of observations of infants and children. Of course, supervision and personal analysis are the safeguards against distorting what we see in the children by our own pathology and, as such, for most people these are indispensable.

CONCLUSION

In taking the scales from our own eyes in order to help psychotic children, we begin to look at everything with fresh eyes. This has the salutary effect of cracking open some of the concepts which have hardened into clichés, and the discarding of those shibboleths which have been applied to situations for which they were not appropriate. For example, the technical terms which were evolved for the description of neurotic functioning are sometimes applied to that of psychotic children, for whom they are not appropriate. They merely mask our ignorance. The attempt to use concepts arising out of direct experience with these children and to write in a simple non-technical way which is suited to the elemental levels being described has seemed to be a salutary exercise.

Part III

Clinical studies

Chapter 16

Sam

PREAMBLE BY FRANCES TUSTIN

Sandra Stone (now Mrs Lewis), who presents here the clinical material of the child she has called Sam, worked for many years in the James Jackson Putnam Children's Center in Boston, Massachusetts which, at that time, was a research and treatment centre for psychotic children ('atypical' children as this centre called them). When she came to England, she became a child psychotherapy trainee at the Tavistock Clinic. I supervised her clinical cases, of which Sam was one. He was not a Kanner-type autistic child, but he was obviously encapsulated and was severely psychotic. Sandra Stone's exposition is focused around a number of Sam's drawings (Figures 16.1–16.12), which illustrate the course of treatment and his progress therein. This child was transformed by treatment into a relatively normal little boy from a child whose psychotic state was so crippling that it seems likely he would have remained ineducable and severely cut off from human contacts. The drawings, with Sam's and Miss Stone's comments on them, show some of the changes in his internal state which led to the rewarding outward changes.

An important point needs to be made concerning such a child's early drawings. He had obviously developed some capacity for pictorial representation, but it was used in the service of his pathology. The early drawings could not be interpreted as we would interpret those of a neurotic child. They did not depict his fantasies, his imaginations or his dreams. At times, it was as if he felt part of the drawings: he was *in* the pictures, living his day-to-day life and expressing his bewilderment about it. In short, his early drawings are a continuous stream of life as he lived it; his body and the drawings being scarcely differentiated from each other. Later this changes and he begins to communicate to his therapist through the drawings.

Such 'lived-in' material is difficult to work with, and also difficult to make meaningful to people outside the situation. At first, Sam had little sense of communicating to the therapist through his bizarre drawings and infrequent verbalisations. He was merely living in his world and feeling muddled about it. Miss Stone was on the outskirts, trying to make sense of it for herself and for him.

An important point needs to be made. Writing in retrospect, knowing that the child has come through to relatively normal functioning, means that the whole process seems more smooth, more orderly and more comprehensible than in fact it was in the day-to-day situation. There were times when both therapist and supervisor felt lost, bewildered and in despair. The whole process involved child, therapist and supervisor in a constant struggle to understand. In reading Miss Stone's presentation, it should be borne in mind that these are struggles 'reflected in tranquillity'. The actual situation was much more 'craggy' and difficult. It is a nice judgement of how far to involve the reader in these difficulties. In my view, it is the responsibility of the writer to hold them within and to present the material in such a way that, although it gives readers some feeling of the atmosphere of the sessions, it does not unduly overwhelm them. It is hoped that Miss Stone's exposition, with its detailed clinical documentation, will make this difficult and disturbing material assimilable to the reader just as she performed this process of digestion for Sam. Part of this 'digestion' has been in the selection of material so that, as far as possible, Sam's drawings and his behaviour can be left to speak for themselves, with an occasional interpolation from Miss Stone or myself. It will be seen that his drawings provide valuable insight into the problems faced by a psychotic child with marked autistic tendencies.

Sandra Stone will now take up the story.

SAM'S EARLY HISTORY

During the pregnancy and Sam's early years, his mother was under considerable strain. Adding to it was her concern that something was not quite right about Sam. For instance, it troubled her that while being breast-fed, he did not appear to notice whether the milk flowed or not. Most of the time, in fact, he failed to respond to her. He seemed distant and indifferent. However, when propped up in his baby chair, Sam kept his eyes glued to her, watching her every move. If she left the room, Sam completely collapsed. So profound was his distress when parted from her that everybody, including grandparents who lived nearby, refused to babysit. When mother walked Sam in his pram, terror of passers-by made him plug his mouth desperately with his finger, as if his life depended on it, and turn his head away to avoid looking at them.

Unfortunately, when Sam was fifteen months old his mother was hospitalised for toxaemia of pregnancy. Sam was traumatised by the six-week separation. The grandparents who took care of him found him impossible. When reunited with his mother after the birth of a baby brother,

Sam refused to look at her. From this point on, mother felt Sam completely rejected her. Yet he still demanded her constant physical presence. So much so that for the first year of playgroup, begun when he was three, mother had to remain with him because he screamed unceasingly if she left. It was striking that he never used her presence to settle in. Watching, mother became increasingly worried by the contrast between other children and Sam: he would not separate; he refused to speak to any adults besides her; he never played with other children; and he never attempted to draw people, although he drew often. At four, Sam still would not speak to adults other than his parents. But they took heart because he was finally toilet-trained. Mother described Sam's behaviour over this as particularly characteristic: 'He was determined not to co-operate and put up barriers.' When he began school at five, his withdrawn, uncooperative, bizarre behaviour prompted a referral for psychological evaluation almost immediately.

PSYCHOLOGICAL EVALUATION

During the evaluation, Sam rocked and masturbated continuously. The psychologist felt Sam was overwhelmed with anxiety about what was happening inside him: he moaned that a family of pains lived inside him all the time he was at school: the 'children pains' came from his feet and joined the 'parent pains' in his tummy: and the 'boy pains' had sharp points. The results showing above-average intelligence surprised Sam's parents and teachers, who had believed he was slow.

Severe emotional disturbance was evident from Sam's behaviour and from the projective tests. Only one of his responses to the Pickford cards was feasible, and in every instance females were omitted or denied. The picture of a mother nursing her baby with another child looking on brought the following response from Sam: 'There's a daddy, there's a little boy, they're running.' For the 'draw a person' test, Sam produced a giant with his bottom where his head should have been, and his head where his bottom should have been, and 'all pooh coming out of the top of him'. [This equation of head with bottom is very characteristic of a psychotic child.] Asked to draw a house, Sam drew one burning down. The smoke went down the chimney and into the house where it came out the windows. One hopeful note was a fireman who struggled to put out the blaze through the chimney. Intensive psychoanalytical therapy was recommended, and the parents chose to send him privately. Treatment, three sessions per week, began a month before Sam's sixth birthday and continued for three years and nine months.

Several pathological 'protective manoeuvres' became the foci of treatment. Sam was to call them 'tricks'.

(a) Sam reacted to frustration by appearing not to notice it; he withdrew and the world passed him by.

(b) Sam put up barriers to experience. Plugging the 'hole' of his mouth with his finger and averting his gaze, which he continued to do, were two such barriers. But they were merely the visible tip of an iceberg of magical devices Sam used to keep himself safe whenever anything occurred that was the least bit unfamiliar, new or unexpected.

(c) Ego skills, acquired out of phase with emotional development, were used to maintain the pathology of autism rather than contributing to normal development. Hence people believed he was slow because his good intelligence was mainly being used in the service of his delusions.

(d) Whilst overly dependent on his mother's physical presence, Sam failed to relate to her properly. Thus, he cut himself off from the help she wanted to give him.

DRAWING ONE (FIGURE 16.1): SESSION 16

[The fact that Sam was coming out of his autism sufficiently to draw provides us with useful information about that state. F. T.]

The multiple difficulties expressed in this drawing foreshadowed the work that would need to be done in the course of treatment. But here they were impacted: they poured out of Sam all at once, too many and too fast to be dealt with. The contortions of a circus acrobat seemed required of me if I were to keep up with them. We shall slow the pace down by considering the drawing in three sections:

1 the castle and the shop;
2 the castle interior;
3 the identical pairs: soldiers, witches and kittens.

The castle and the shop

This session began with Sam firing a non-stop barrage of nonsense syllables and imitation farts at me. They drowned out all my attempts to help him with his upset. Meanwhile, he was drawing the faint but massive yellow-stone castle. Struggling to draw in one continuous line, Sam laboured to complete the walls. It was as if in his mind's eye he could not see the castle. He tensely watched to see what would emerge from point to point. Sam had spent previous sessions building a 'Miss Stone' of blocks and then hiding away from me behind it. Now, since my hair is blonde and my name is Stone, I suggested over the noise that Sam had taken my 'yellowness' and my 'Stoneness' to build this castle as he

Figure 16.1 Sam: drawing one

had done before with the blocks, but this blocked him from getting help from the real me. [This material is reminiscent of the 'mouth' material cited in Part I in relation to a segmented encapsulated child. Sam dismantled the yellow Miss Stone therapist into segments and then put her together in his own way, so that she became part of him and was not unknown and strange. The actual therapist was then ignored. Carried to excess, this manoeuvre prevented him from being able to relate to her as a separate person who could help him, just as he was disconnected from the parents who could nurture him. It was the source of his 'fracture-dislocation' and his lack of 'roots' (to use the strikingly pertinent words of one of Balint's patients). F. T.] Rushing on, Sam drew a comparatively insignificant building to the left of the castle. When I asked what it was, Sam snapped at me in a belittling tone: 'It's a shop.' His manner made it clear that he considered me to be as little as the shop, and since he had taken what he wanted, of no further use to him. I said he seemed to feel he could take my bigness from me to make himself into a big castle and make me small. Ignoring this, Sam continued drawing the guards on the castle turret and fortifying the entrance and exits of the castle. The noisy offensive continued. It seemed he feared a counter-attack from me to get back my 'yellowness', 'Stoneness' and 'bigness'.

The castle interior

In contrast to the grand superstructure of the castle, conditions inside were primitive. Over-sized washbasins had inflow pipes, but waste water simply dropped out of the holes underneath. A tiny king and queen stretched out their arms to the basins. When I said these people had a serious problem – they were far too small to reach the taps – Sam stopped making noises and listened. His manner shifted to overly close and intimate instead of remote as usual. Sam drew two unidentifiable overlapping circles under the floorboards. Moving near me he murmured in hushed tones and unintelligible whispers. We seemed to overlap as the circles did, as if we were one person instead of two. I gently began to explore what Sam agreed was 'the muddle underneath'. But with my first question Sam became more remote than ever, and hurriedly turned his attention to drawing a little man running towards the castle exit. He seemed wary of letting me learn more about the muddle. Throughout his treatment I would need to be constantly on the alert for this overlapping or fusion of the two of us, because it tended to occur 'underneath' what seemed to be more interesting material, or as an 'undercurrent' in our interaction. When it surfaced Sam avoided discussing it, perhaps because it was a central feature of his autism.

Identical pairs: soldiers, witches and kittens

Sam drew a pair of identical soldiers, one on each side of the castle. Anxiously, Sam mumbled to himself: 'Attacking the castle . . . something very bad . . . don't want to hurt the castle . . . their own . . . fire into the sky!' I said he seemed to be afraid of the damage he might do to the castle made from bits of me, and to the tiny people inside it. Responding, Sam produced the sound effect of a gun firing into the sky. Instead of being directed at me as before, the barrage was redirected up and away from me.

Next came two broomsticks on either side of the sky. Riding on each was a kitten. Witches were noticeably absent. Sam seemed unwilling to draw them and drew stars in the sky instead. I suggested his real concern wasn't about the stars in the sky but about the two who overlapped like the circles, the two who were just the same. Sam responded by adding on the right a moon with black spikes protruding from it; 'twitches', he called them. 'That', I said softly, 'makes me think of two witches.' 'Oh yes', Sam said, 'we were just about to draw them.' With evident trepidation Sam got on with it, but all the colour drained from his face. As if the drawing were beyond his control and he was unable to prevent what happened, 'stuff' exploded skyward from the guns of the soldiers. Desperate, Sam moaned: 'They're not shooting at the kittens'! None the less the kittens were so close to the witches it was impossible to shoot one without hitting the other. For Sam it was as if this catastrophe were actually taking place then and there. White with terror, he flipped the page over. The next drawing was the chilling result.

Figure 16.2 Sam: drawing two

DRAWING TWO (FIGURE 16.2): STILL SESSION 16

Compulsively, Sam produced robot after robot as if he could never amass enough of them. When pressed to tell me about them, without stopping Sam muttered tersely: 'They used to be people.' I replied that the frightening troubles on the other side of the paper seemed to make Sam like a robot as well. Stick-figure rescuers, which Sam volunteered were a television hero and heroine, appeared at the top of the page. Fortunately, I knew the programme and episode this drawing was re-telling. The plot was that a greedy man had tried to take over the universe, but an explosion resulting from errors in his plans had left him horrendously crippled. He survived thereafter only by encapsulating his body in a hard, metal life-support system. Sam confirmed this was the story and drew the man in the upper left-hand corner. For additional protection, the man had designed a race of killer robots. Clearly, for Sam, this story had not been an imaginative fabrication but live-action reporting of the world in which he lived, and a vivid portrayal of events he felt had happened to him.

DRAWING THREE (FIGURE 16.3): SESSION 18

Later the same week Sam continued the overlapping theme. At the beginning of the session, Sam tried to usurp my chair. I told him that I could not allow this because if I did he would feel I was like the shop (of drawing one), deprived of my goods with nothing left to give him.

Figure 16.3 Sam: drawing three

Figure 16.4 Sam: drawing four

Next, Sam wanted to stand on my toes with his back to me while he drew. I told him gently that together we would help him to learn to stand on his own feet, but that I could not let him stand on my toes in this way because it hurt me, and also because he would feel that we were the same person and thus not pay any attention to me at all. I suggested that he wanted to borrow my big grown-up feet, just as he had taken things from me to make the yellow-stone castle in order to feel big and grown up. But this prevented him from growing up as a separate person using his own good feet, and kept him small like the people inside the castle. Upset, Sam drew why he felt he needed to use my feet: at the end of a row of flowers and trees with their roots was a tiny person cut off from a circle meant to be *his* roots. With deeply felt bitterness Sam complained, 'Flowers and trees can grow because they have roots. People don't have roots, so people can't grow!' [The early infantile situation in which the mother acts for the child had been perpetuated for Sam in a crude way. The therapist had to help him to see that instead of lending him her feet she would give him her 'understandings', which would help him to grow psychological roots. This will be discussed more fully in the following chapter on 'Thinkings'. F. T.]

DRAWING FOUR (FIGURE 16.4): SESSION 22

This drawing eloquently conveys the desperate insecurity Sam felt as a person without 'roots'. It was one of many similar drawings that poured from Sam whenever he had a pencil in his hand, whether at school, at home or in a therapy session. The idiosyncratic nature of these drawings worried and puzzled everyone. Sam fended off all attempts to discuss them with him.

The only clue Sam gave about this particular drawing at the time he did it was that in the centre was 'a wobbly house that might fall down'. When we discussed it many months later, the rest of the drawing turned out to be about his efforts, through protective manoeuvres, to prevent that collapse. On the far right three soldiers in an army jeep sped to the rescue of the house. An army 'unit' acts collectively for the superior strength it confers. Sam had been seeking such strength by taking my bigness for his castle, and by wanting to stand on my toes. In many of his behaviours a desire for overlapping was evident: for example he used 'we', never 'I', when speaking. Inevitably, overlapping failed at times and, when it did, Sam fell apart catastrophically.

On the far left of the picture is a person entrenched in an armoured tank. Sam seemed to believe he could prevent collapse by hiding away inside a hard protective covering. But such rigid protection led to the dilemma of the little fellow to the right of the house. He wanted to grow like a flower but could not because the hard protective armour of the tank constricted growth. Finally Sam hoped to be winched above all danger by helicopter. One of the 'tricks' that enabled Sam to feel he *could* get above it all was the application of his intelligence to foster hypersensitive alertness. He tried to pick up extra clues which might give him an overview of what was taking place. We see this in action in the next drawing.

DRAWING FIVE (FIGURE 16.5): SESSION 86

From Sam's remarks on the house in this drawing, it was clear that he felt the extraordinarily large window allowed him to oversee everything that happened. The extra light-bulbs in the street-lamp were to illuminate everywhere, so that nothing remained unknown. Sam pointed out that

Figure 16.5 Sam: drawing five

the ordinary-sized windows were blocked up. Meanwhile he drew an enormously over-sized television aerial which pointed in every possible direction, so that no broadcasts were missed. I said that he didn't listen or look at the things people wanted him to see and hear, for example to the meaning of what I was saying now, because he was so busy listening to the tones of my voice and watching how I sat in my chair for hints about how I was feeling. He used his eyes to search my jewellery and clothes, hoping to pick up extra information about my activities. As a result, I said, he missed out on chances to grow – not just here but at home and at school as well. Sam looked as if he knew only too well that this was so.

Now there was a different feel to the session. As if Sam were earnestly trying to tell me something, he drew a car with a hook on the front engulfed by its own exhaust. I said I thought that he was showing me that the window and the aerial were devices to hook himself to me, in order to know all about me. He felt that his extra information joined us together and gave him an overview of everything that took place, so nothing unexpected could occur. The trouble was that unexpected things did happen and felt like a big bump, as if we came unhooked. Even when things went as he expected, he still had trouble because he took in more than he could manage to deal with. Then all the 'extra' over-whelmed him, like the exhaust did the car. Instead of fuelling him, the extra made trouble. Sam looked relieved that I had understood how over-burdened he felt. For Sam, senses were actual hooks that caught pieces of me, and 'perceptions' were concrete pieces of me rather than abstract pieces of information.

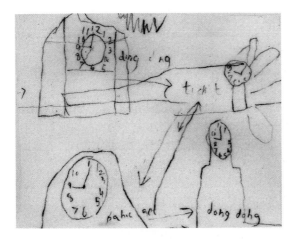

Figure 16.6 Sam: drawing six

DRAWING SIX (FIGURE 16.6): SESSION 131

One piece of me which Sam particularly wanted to hook up to was my wrist-watch. When he got one of his own he wanted to be certain that it synchronised with mine every time he came. In the sessions, he related to my wrist-watch rather than to me. He treated me as if I were completely redundant. Outside the sessions Sam filled the gap that would have been made by my absence with whatever 'timepiece' was available: the clock on the wall in his classroom, the alarm clock by his bed or, most importantly, his own wrist-watch. With this watch Sam believed that he 'kept' time and could magically 'watch' over me because our watches said 'the same' time. Learning to tell time supported the pathology of autism rather than healthy development, since he used timepieces as autistic objects. Instead of bridging the gap made by separation they obliterated his awareness of it. The use of such objects to the exclusion of all other activities consumed not just most therapy sessions but most of Sam's waking hours.

DRAWING SEVEN (FIGURE 16.7): SESSION 141

His reliance on autistic objects left Sam vulnerable, as this drawing shows. Before a holiday break Sam set out to fill a paper with sums and stories simply to have something to do. I suggested he was hoping the sums and stories could fill the holes in time made by the cancelled holiday sessions, just as they were filling the paper. Sam responded by

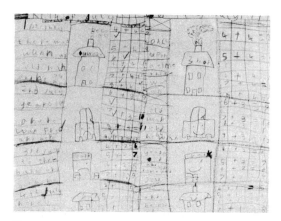

Figure 16.7 Sam: drawing seven

adding four pairs of objects: one of each pair was complete and happy while the other was incomplete and therefore miserable. I said he seemed to be showing me that when he did not succeed in magicking the holes away he felt as if part of his body were missing. I explained that this happened because he tricked himself into believing he had taken pieces of me and made them part of his body, like an arm or a leg. When the trick failed, he felt his body was broken. Then he was unbearably miserable and longed for me as if I were a missing arm or leg. I stressed that to stop feeling broken he would have to accept that I was not part of his body, and work with me to learn a better way to manage being alone. At the very mention of the word 'alone', Sam went white with terror. Wide-eyed he turned to stare at me and bravely said 'Yes'.

DRAWING EIGHT (FIGURE 16.8): SESSION 166

Increasingly, Sam was becoming aware that his protective manoeuvres did not serve him well. As he drew and we talked, it was apparent that this drawing of a road system with a traffic roundabout in the centre was Sam's way of telling me how trapped he felt by his autistic tricks. He wanted to reach the 'treasure island' in the lower right-hand corner, the only part of the drawing which had any colour to it. But he could not escape from the deadening, colourless whirl of his 'roundabout' autistic behaviour. 'The roundabout', Sam told me with horror, 'has no exit!' During this phase there were outbursts of very disturbed behaviour at home, at school and in the therapy sessions. His frustration at being trapped was breaking out everywhere. He longed for the 'treasure', as he spoke of me, feeling that I could free him from the trap.

Figure 16.8 Sam: drawing eight

Although Sam was now trying to see me as a separate person and wanted my insights, he still conceived of these concretely as extra bodily bits taken from me and added to his body. In a fever of greed about what he could get from me, as the treasure island, Sam coveted and tried to have more than his fair share of me. Sam saw other children as rivals who also preyed on me in this way, and feared attack from them. Hence the school playground became a terrifying place, and Sam spent all his time there spinning in circles. In the waiting room an electrical socket left in the 'on' position was viewed by Sam as an attempt by another patient to electrocute him. And, in the therapy room, someone was felt to have left slime on the floor so that Sam would slip and fall. Thus, Sam jumped from table-top to couch and back because he was too frightened to step on the floor. Firm management, such as arranging that mother bring him even though he pleaded he was too ill with a 'headache', was necessary in order to mitigate the fantastic nature of his terrors and relate them to his infantile needs where they originated. The next drawing shows this process taking place.

DRAWING NINE (FIGURE 16.9): SESSION 200

The session began with Sam pacing back and forth on the couch like a trapped wild animal and muttering to himself. I said firmly that only discussing what was frightening him would help him find a way to be less scared. Getting down to work, Sam drew a monster named Earthlifter, who was supposed to protect him. Sam told me Earthlifter's story: 'He began life as a tiny crab, but when he lost his mother he became a

Figure 16.9 Sam: drawing nine

monster. He grew too big for earth and went to live on a planet all on his own many miles away.' Sam marked the tail and the tummy with an 'X'. Then he partitioned off each segment containing the 'X' from the rest of the body. When questioned about the tail, Sam said it was 'full of pooh'. He mumbled uncertainly that 'the overflow could go out the hump above'. I questioned him about the segment containing the 'X' in the tummy. He replied, 'It's the extra piece to prop the monster up.' Then Sam climbed on the table, spun himself round and round on his stomach and rubbed himself back and forth against the table-top.

Talking it over, Sam could see that he tried to prop himself up with tricks to reach an Earthlifter size. Sometimes he felt that he hooked bits from people bigger than he was and stuck them on to himself. Sometimes he used the full sensation of pooh in his bottom or in his tummy, and sometimes he spun or rubbed himself to feel excited and full. He wanted to feel bigger and more powerful than anyone else, so that he need not feel so afraid. But these extra sensations made him feel he would explode and he was unsure what could be done about this overflow. Desperately Sam pleaded for help, 'Earthlifter has all pooh inside him and doesn't know what to do!' I replied that what Earthlifter really needed was his mother, who would take away the overflow and teach him how to use the loo, just as Sam needed me to clean up the overflow of his feelings and teach him a proper way of managing them. But first he must stop trying to be bigger than he really was, and be an ordinary size, so that an ordinary amount of help in growing up properly from his mother, his teacher or myself would do. Grudgingly, Sam supplied Earthlifter with a small faceless mother to whom he 'lent' over-sized wing-breasts. [This material about Earthlifter having 'all pooh inside him' echoed his assessment session with the psychologist, where, on being asked to draw a

Figure 16.10 Sam: drawing ten

person, he had drawn a giant with his head where his bottom should have been and his bottom where his head should have been and 'all pooh coming out of him'. F. T.]

DRAWING TEN (FIGURE 16.10): SESSION 252

Sam had gone on thinking about what we had been talking about because in this session, purposefully as a communication, he drew a loo which recycled its own water by pumping water from the bottom to the top. There was no outlet to the outside and no clean input. Sam wondered if the water at the bottom was clean or dirty. Anxiously, he separated each substance into its own compartment, 'One for wee, one for pooh, one for toilet paper, one for water'. But then he felt compelled to make further isolations by separating, as he said, 'good poohs from bad with a wall of pooh and good wees from bad with a wall of bricks'. 'Bricks are necessary', he informed me, 'because you can't separate wee from wee with wee.' [This material illustrates a striking difference between encapsulated children and confusional children. A confusional child would feel that good and bad pooh were all mixed up and confused together, as with the schizophrenic patient of Dr Herbert Rosenfeld

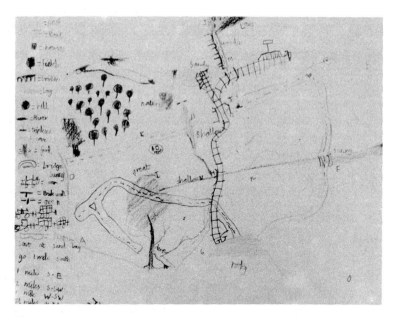

Figure 16.11 Sam: drawing eleven

(1950) who had a dream that he was stirring both good and bad pooh together in a cooking pot. F. T.]

Behaving as if he were as self-contained as the loo meant that Sam shut out help from everyone. But on his own he could not learn to make sense of the jumble of feelings that welled up within him. The best he could manage was separating them obsessionally and walling them off. Sam tried now to draw my attention to this problem by saying repeatedly 'I can't think' and 'I can't remember'. He wanted to bring things together but felt everything inside him was in separate compartments he could not open. Sam had not allowed thoughts to meet other thoughts, feelings to meet other feelings, or thoughts and feelings to mix. Each remained an encapsulated segment of experience. This kept him from building a sense of 'I-ness'. To have colour of his own, his own treasure, he would have to sacrifice his protective isolation on 'a planet of his own'. In a series of island drawings Sam worked towards doing just that.

DRAWING ELEVEN (FIGURE 16.11): SESSION 324

In this drawing, the large island with its bays named 'Sandy' and 'Rocky' represented the therapist. The small island, Sam agreed, stood for him. So that the little island would not be isolated, he drew a bridge connecting the two. The story Sam told was this: People from the small island travelled to the big one to enjoy it as a natural place; but then they built so many roads, railways, dams and such, that the big island was spoiled by over-use; eventually there was no place left for living creatures. Listing items in the key began to absorb Sam entirely. The islands and the events taking place there were forgotten in his obsession with the list. I put a halt to this so that we could discuss what was happening: the overview offered by the key let him withdraw above it all; then the treasure of his own liveliness was lost sight of. Sam wanted that treasure.

In the ensuing weeks Sam learned to trust me to regulate contact between us so he did not feel that greedy over-use took place. To do this, I insisted that the bridge between us consist of words or pictures rather than the tricks and atmospheres which Sam habitually used to make it seem we overlapped. Sam joined me in watching out for these 'old tricks' that interfered with proper relating. Since his own contact with me could now be regulated by watchfulness on both our parts, Sam was less frightened of other predatory over-users, and worried less about damage to the island. Hence he was increasingly willing to sacrifice his overview for a place on the ground with everyone else. And the 'island' was allowed to return to 'her' natural role of providing conditions that facilitate life and growth.

DRAWING TWELVE (FIGURE 16.12): SESSION 331

This last drawing is of an island as well, but it is no longer viewed from a remote vantage point as was the previous one. Sam had come down to earth. Unlike the former drawing with its 'everything in its place' character, the full cycle of life's happenings was allowed to take place. Sam had begun to be able to stand on his own feet amidst the rough and tumble of life. Rather than withdrawing, Sam was now joining fully in family life, playing with friends of his own age in the neighbourhood, and beginning to do well at school.

But the reversal of the autism was not yet complete. The one idiosyncrasy in the drawing reflected this. Sam had started by colouring the sun yellow, but decided this meant it was too distant from the island, leaving the island too cold. Switching to red, he again was dissatisfied, saying it made the sun too close. Sam worried that 'not just the island would be too hot but the sun itself'. Uneasily, he settled for colouring the sun orange, 'for a warm summer day'. We could both see, as we talked it over, that like the sun he was learning to be neither so distant from people as to feel out in the cold, nor so close that the fusing overlap made him feel too hot and over-excited. But I was still troubled by

Figure 16.12 Sam: drawing twelve

Sam's need to see himself as the sun. It seemed he still partially clung to the magical notion that he was above it all with his extra inform-ation. The basis of the trick was that 'SUN' and 'son' sound the same. He wanted to trick himself into believing he was as powerful as the 'SUN' rather than just an ordinary human 'son'. Sam confirmed this was so. It emerged that his toys and colours, while overtly being used as a medium of communication, were covertly felt to be, in Sam's words, 'magician's tools for creating the world and to control everything that happens'.

At my suggestion, Sam courageously agreed to give up using his toys, in order to tackle the problem of learning to be 'just human'. Now nine years old, for the remaining half year of treatment he lay on the couch talking to me. At first this was extremely frightening for him, not just because he had given up 'magic', exposing himself to all of life's uncer-tainties, but also because the toys as tangible objects were not interposed between us to serve as a secret physical barrier. Out of his shell Sam felt extremely vulnerable. However, he took the risk of leaving it behind and came to value in its place the healing to-and-fro of talking openly to another person. In the shelter of the therapeutic relationship Sam discovered, to his surprise, that the quiet 'alone' moments need not feel like bottomless chasms, but could become spaces where ideas might come together. He began to realise that thoughts could bridge the 'holes' in time and, when shared, the distance between 'I-lands'.

Chapter 17

'Thinkings'

A marked characteristic of encapsulated autistic children is that the early infantile stage in which the mother acts for the child has been perpetuated in a crude and pathological way, long past the time of normal usefulness. For example, they will use the limb of another person as if it were their own, with no acknowledgement of their indebtedness and little or no recognition of the separateness of the other person. Thus, they will pull a grown-up person's hand to make it open a door for them instead of using their own hand for this purpose. John, in the assessment session described in Chapter 5, did not attempt to turn back the cuff of the sleeve of his pullover which had become turned down so that it hampered the movements of his hand – it was as if he expected me to do it for him. Sam, the subject of the clinical study of the previous chapter, stood on the therapist's feet as if to use them as part of *his* body. In this mode of behaving, the children are only aware of the outside of the body and what they can stick onto the outside of it. They are averted from being fully aware of the inside of the body. In Sam's case, this seems likely to be because, as he told the psychologist in the assessment session, he felt that a 'family of pains' lived inside him. Other children have shown that they felt that their insides and, in adhesive equation, the mother's insides, were damaged. This inhibition of awareness of the inside of the body restricts curiosity about the inside of the mother's body and, by extrapolation from this, curiosity about the outside world. As infants they will sit virtually motionless where they have been put down. Thus, learning is inhibited, and, as I hope to show in this chapter, the development of thinking is similarly impeded.

An important part of Miss Stone's work was to make clear to Sam that instead of lending him her feet she would lend him her understandings so that he could learn to stand on his own feet. It gradually became clear that he needed to lean on her in this way in order to be a giant. He felt that he had to be a giant because he was beset by nameless terrors. The therapist's understanding of his plight enabled him to face and to formulate his terrors, but first of all he had to be helped to give up his perverse and ineffectual way of dealing with them. This mediation of understanding, rather than acting for them in a crude way, enables the children to begin to think about their situation rather than being impulse-driven. It is an important part of effective therapy with them if they are to be moved from their unduly materialistic approach to life and their over-concretised notions. In effect, the therapist demonstrates by words and actions that 'rather than lending you a limb of my body to do things for you that you can well do for yourself, I will lend you my "thinkings" so that you can develop "thinkings" of your own.'

This is important because the lack of psychological connection with the nurturing parents is the source of their traumatic sense of being disconnected from their 'roots', the 'fracture-dislocation', as one of Balint's patients aptly expressed it. It is the origin of the 'basic fault' (Balint, 1968), of the 'psychological catastrophe' (Bion, 1962b), the 'psychotic depression' (Winnicott, 1958), the 'primal depression' (Bibring, 1953), 'the black hole with the nasty prick' (John in *Autism and Childhood Psychosis*, Tustin, 1972), the 'nothingness' of the existentialists. Awareness of this phenomenon is not restricted to mental health workers. As we become aware of it both in the children and in ourselves, we cry (with E. M. Forster), 'only connect and live' – because lack of psychological connection leads to *undue* insistence on a constant physical presence, and on the *over*-valuation of sensation-giving material objects. This makes unbearable the reality of individual separateness, of absences and ultimately of death. The clinical study of Sam illustrates how the therapist helped him to begin to come to terms with some of these inescapable realities.

This chapter seeks to carry further our understanding of the development of psychological functions which help the child to emerge as a separate individual who can begin to come to terms with the inevitable facts of life. To do this, a session from the treatment of Peter (some of whose further sessions are presented in the next chapter) will be given in full. This session hints at how the development of thinking takes place and also raises questions about it. For me, as his therapist, the session was a particularly vivid and dynamic one. In order to convey this to the reader, the actions of the child will be paralleled by an account of the trains of thought which were stimulated in myself, as I struggled to understand and to talk to him in his idiom. In this session, it was not the situation of a therapist trying to get in touch with a non-communicating child, as it had been at the outset of treatment; rather it was that we were two responsible people *discussing* how he could be helped 'to grow up properly'. A good deal of what I said was in the form of questions, but it seemed to make sense to Peter who replied, not in a passive conforming way, but as if he found that I was helping him to give tenable form and shape to his experiences.

A brief account of Peter's early history will be given in the next chapter. It is sufficient to say here that when he came into psychotherapy, aged six years, he was so autistic as to appear brain-damaged. However, physical investigations did not reveal anything untoward. In terms of the classification presented in Part I, he was an encapsulated child who had become segmented. He was seen twice a week and the presented session occurred after he had been in treatment for two years. Peter was now eight years old and, although when he started treatment he had been virtually mute, he was now speaking fluently.

To understand the session, the reader must know that in the consulting-room each child has his own drawer or drawers in which the provided toys are kept. Peter had both the top and bottom drawers in a chest of five drawers. Each child had a key to his drawer, which would not open any other drawer, so the drawers in between Peter's top and bottom drawers were locked and he did not have access to them.

SESSION 77

Activities of child and therapist

Trains of thought

Peter decided to move the contents of the bottom drawer to the top drawer. The bulk of the contents of the bottom drawer consisted of toy animals, 'the beasts' as Peter called them. They were hauled up one by one by fastening them to a long piece of string which was pulled slowly upwards. He began by hauling up the giraffe.

I said, 'Are you thinking about the giraffe which has fallen down?' (for an explanation of this, see adjoining column).

He said, 'Yes, they're trying to *raise* it up' (see adjoining column).

I said, 'Do you feel there is a part of you that has fallen down – that has "flopped" like the poor giraffe, and which needs raising up?'

He nodded.

I said, 'You seem to be talking about being raised up from being fallen down.'

From the outset, I was intrigued because he bustled into the room in a business-like way as though quite decided about what he was going to do. This was in contrast to the lackadaisical way in which he sometimes came, as if undecided what to do; on these occasions the contact between us seemed limp and tenuous.

When he hauled up the giraffe I was reminded of a news item which was gripping the public interest at this time and which had been reported in the papers and on television. It concerned a giraffe which had fallen down with its long legs splayed out and which could not get up again. Many methods were tried of raising it from the ground and one of them had been to put ropes around it. It was stated that if it could not be raised, it would die, and in fact this eventually occurred. At the time of Peter's activities it was still alive.

However, after he had 'raised' a few animals, his attention was deflected to a paper aeroplane he had made several weeks ago and which he now found in his drawer. He started to fly this around the room.

His attitude was very different from the purposeful one he had had whilst hauling up the animals. He seemed dreamy and almost as if in a trance.

The paper plane banged into the walls and the windows and into me. His attention seemed unfocused and there was a loose, empty 'feel' to the session (see adjoining column).

I said, 'You are behaving as if there were no walls, no boundaries to the room nor to me. I think you wish we flowed into each other and that we needn't trouble to *attend* to what each other said and did, because we were rippling (vibrating) with each other and so were part of each other.' He said dreamily, 'It's a spaceship.'

When he said, 'It's a spaceship', it stirred me to say, 'I think you want endless space and endless time and to feel that there are no such things as endings or boundaries. You want to feel that you need not bother about concentrating on growing up properly because you have all the time in the world and that it doesn't matter when you start because there will never be an end. For example, that this session will never come to an end.'

At this, he became focused and attentive again and turned back to the 'beasts'.

When he said, 'raise it up', I was reminded of the phrase, 'I have raised (*x* number of) children', meaning to 'bring up'.

Later, I realised that he felt that he had the whole responsibility of 'raising' himself. He could not turn to me (or his parents) for help. The terrors which prevented this became clear later in the session.

I found my thoughts wandering. It was with an effort that I came back to what Peter was doing.

At first I was struck by the way in which the plane banged into the walls, etc., as if they did not exist, and so I framed the next interpretation in terms of this.

I was reminded of a case study by Eleonora Fe d'Ostiani (1979) where she coined the phrase 'spaceless space and timeless time'. This was with reference to a pyschotic child who also behaved as if he were a space-man.

Later in the session, I realised that he oscillated between the extremes of no boundaries and states of narrowed constriction. (These latter states come later in the session and illustrate the cruel and rigid way in which he dealt with his uncontrolled behaviour as compared with

As he laboriously hauled the animals one by one to the top, I was at first lost for what to say, so I said, 'What are you doing, Peter?' To which he replied, 'I'm taking the *shapes* from the bottom to the top.' (The word 'shapes' stimulating a train of thought in me. See adjoining column.)

In the light of these trains of thought, I said, 'You mean you're moving the "sensation shapes' you make in your bottom up to your head?'

He nodded.

I said, 'Is this your idea of how to grow up?' He nodded.

After a while I said, 'Is the chest of drawers like your body?' Again he nodded. I continued, 'It looks as if the middle part is your tummy.' He replied dismissively, 'That part is missed out.' (This made a strong impression on me. See opposite.) I said, 'Oh dear, your hard top part (your head) is not connected to your soft bottom. There is a gap – a nothingness – an emptiness – where your tummy should be.'

He made no reply but continued hauling up the 'shapes' in a grimly determined way. I sat there thinking. I talked reflectively, both to Peter and to myself. I said pensively, 'The missed-out middle part of the chest of drawers is the part you share with other children. You don't know what is in there, just as you don't know what is in your tummy. It's the part you don't know about. It's also the part you share with other people – the part that is not just you – not just Peter.' I felt he was listening although his back was still turned towards me. After a while I continued, 'I think you're afraid of the

the firm but kind control offered by the therapist.)

The word 'shapes' set a train of thought going in me. The week before the presented session we had had several sessions where we had talked about 'shapes'. He had told me that he and his sister made 'shapes' by bubbling their spit in their mouths, and by wriggling the poohs in their bottoms. I had talked about these to him as 'sensation shapes' and he later told me that he and his sister had begun to 'draw' shapes in each other's bodies with their fingers, i.e. that it had become a 'shared' activity.

The determined way in which he said, 'That part is missed out' was as if he were obdurate about having anything to do with that part. I sensed intractable resistance both from what he said and from the fact that his back was turned towards me.

When I am puzzled about what is going on I express my thoughts out loud.

part you don't know about – the part you have to share with others – that part feels as if it is not you – as if it is not Peter. I think perhaps you're a bit scared of me today because I'm not you. You feel I'm a stranger.'

At this, as if he were going on to another train of thought, he started to move some of the animals back from the top to the bottom.

I commented that it looked as if things went round and round with no changes taking place. The same animals came down as went up. That didn't seem to me to be a good way to grow up.

He said, 'It's changed inside my tummy.'

I was puzzled at first until, as he put the animals on the string at the top, he moved his mouth as if he were eating. This gave me a clue, so I said, 'Is it like food going in at the top – into your mouth?' He nodded. So, as the animals reached the bottom drawer, I said, 'And out at your bottom as poohs?'

He did not nod or speak to confirm this and as his back was turned towards me I could not see his face, but I had the impression that I was on the right lines. I think later material confirms that this was so.

After a good deal of thought (as instanced in adjoining columns), I said thoughtfully, 'You know, I think you feel that you know what goes into your mouth (at the top) because you can see it and touch it. You also feel that you know what comes out at your bottom because you can see and touch your poohs. You don't know what goes on in the middle part – in your tummy – because you can't see it or touch it. So you miss out that part. But

---

This was very constricted and constricting behaviour. I thought with some despair, 'Oh, here they come again, the autistic vicious circle of endless repetition with no possibility of change' (the 'traffic roundabout' of Miss Stone's presentation).

I felt shut out and puzzled. I wished I could see his face. I wanted to touch him and turn him around to face me so that I could know whether what I said made sense to him. This feeling led to my next interpretation.

I now felt more focused on Peter

it's the part where changes take place. How these changes happen is mysterious to you. It's a bit frightening. It's unknown and you can't control it.'

He said, 'They might get out.' He turned and looked at my stomach and rubbed his own where his tummy button was. As he delicately traced the outline of his tummy button with his finger, I had an inspiration and said, 'Do you feel that the tummy button buttons up the tummy and that if that came undone all sorts of frightening, strange, unknown things might pop out to startle you?' He turned to look at me, with relief on his face, and nodded.

I said, 'Perhaps you were also frightened about what might pop out of *my* tummy.' He replied, 'Monsters.'

and resorted less to what thoughts were being stirred up in myself. This earlier thinking had been in order to find connections between the child's activities, and also to make connections with him. He was talking more freely now and providing the links himself. We were more spontaneous with each other.

I said, 'But that's a nightmare or a fairy-tale. It's stopped you from growing up properly because you were afraid of what would come out of your mummy's tummy and out of your tummy.'

I went on, 'I do agree that it's very puzzling as to how, when you eat cheese and biscuits or lollipops, they are changed in your tummy to come out as poohs.'

He said, 'They're digested.' I said, 'Yes, eight-year-old Peter knows that, but there's a bit of you that doesn't know these things and has been very frightened and worried about tummies and the mysterious changes which go on there. To that part of you all the outside world seems like a big tummy full of dangerous things, so you shut yourself away in order to feel safe. You turn your hard back to protect your soft front and you don't feel that your back is connected to your front, just like you don't feel your hard head is connected to your soft bottom. *The middle connecting part where changes take place is missed out.* Everything is either very hard or very soft.'

He had now changed to raising the shapes to the top drawer again but he seemed less tense as they went past the middle of the chest of drawers. There was a different 'feel' to the session. The atmosphere was relaxed and friendly, so I said, 'You know I watch what you are doing. Sometimes I just *describe* it like saying, "You are pulling up the animals with a piece of string." I just talk about the outlines of things – about the *shapes* of things.' He was listening with interest now and had stopped hauling the 'shapes' up the string. We sat talking in a face-to-face way. I continued, 'Sometimes I turn it over in the tummy of my mind just as though I were digesting it. Then we are sharing it. You share what you are doing with me and I share what I am doing with you, and from this shared middle thing, something new comes out. It may surprise you and it often surprises me. It's something we didn't know before. It's something new.'

To my surprise and delight he said, 'I suppose that's thinking.' I replied, 'Yes, and you can't see or touch or handle thoughts. They're different from things like chairs and tables.'

He said, 'I know.' When I said it was time to go, he put the toys away and waited impatiently whilst I locked the drawer. However, as soon as this was done he started to rush out without saying 'Goodbye'. So I stopped him and said, 'We both know that you try to ignore the ending of the session by rushing away, but if you say "Goodbye" it helps to end it in a way in which we are connected with each other before we go apart. Then while we are away from each other we can think of the things we have done together and it helps us to wait until the next session comes.'

AFTERTHOUGHTS

It was inevitable that the scheme of understanding offered to Peter was affected by the scheme of understanding I was building up from experiences with other children, but I tried to avoid being arbitrary in my use of it. I had to give form and shape to his unutterable thoughts, but I put much of what I said in the form of questions so that I could keep in touch with his individual way of expressing things and so that I could keep myself open to the 'jolts' when my scheme did not fit his. Language itself imposes a constriction on these inarticulate states which distorts them. We have to bear this inevitable lack of consonance. After all, to get in touch with 'real' 'reality' is a hopeless task. The way in which the human mind is constructed imposes a particular sort of construction upon 'reality', and since our minds have many things in common, we can communicate with each other about 'reality'. Then the individual mental quirks can add piquancy and zest. The 'reality' of a small child and the 'reality' of a psychotic child are different from ours because the apparatus which makes the construction is in a different state of formation. Part of the art (or science) of therapy is getting in touch with these different modes of construction. The criterion as to whether we are achieving this is to sense whether what we say seems sufficiently meaningful to the child to set a discussion going between us. Of course, this can only occur when the child has started to talk. Prior to that, the criterion is whether what we say affects the child's behaviour and also whether the child begins to turn to us and to respond to us. We can never be sure whether we have learnt his language or have followed his particular kind of logic absolutely accurately. However, we can tell whether it is good enough to effect changes in his responses. Myths and allegories also help us to know whether we are on the right lines. In the presented session I felt I was well enough in touch with Peter's particular idiom and logic because there were positive changes in his attitudes.

At first, it seemed as if there were an inarticulate pantomime on Peter's part. Actions were taking place instead of thinking. (Such material throws light on the 'acting-out' of neurotic patients.) During this period I had to do most of the thinking, and the right-hand column was well used. As Peter began to think for himself I did less thinking for both of us and the right-hand column was no longer needed. We talked to each other, 'digesting' our thoughts as we went along.

The clinical material illustrates that the psychotic child responds to the world on the model of a schematic picture of the human body. Learning proceeds by going from the known to the unknown. Bodies are known and familiar. The autistic child remains stuck at the known (the body). Peter shows us that it is terror of what will come out of the stomach-part of the body which prevents him from going any further. He does not dare to explore the mother's body, which is the basis for curiosity about the outside world.

Much clinical material has brought home to me the importance to children of the stomach, which often seems to be chest and stomach combined. As discussed in previous chapters, outside objects which have a rough-and-ready similarity with bodily parts are felt to be the same as those bodily parts. For example, a five-year-old patient who was being treated by Paul Barrows called the stomach part of his body a 'pouffe-top'. Children in autistic states invariably feel that cupboards and drawers are stomachs. Autistic children sometimes bring 'hard things' or 'prickly things' to put into a toy oven which, inadvertently at times, they call a 'tummy'. This is to 'soften' them or to 'take away the prickles'. Similarly, such children feel that they put their hard, prickly feelings into the ovens of our stomach-minds to take away the discomforting bits.

For Peter, the stomach 'was missed out'. I had to 'stomach' those things which were strange and discomforting, until he could 'stomach' them for himself. When children become aware of stomachs, they are fascinated by the changes which can take place in there; for example, bacon and eggs can get changed into poohs. They feel that there is an exciting object in the cavern of their stomachs, like an internal belly-button (an Aladdin's lamp), which can be rubbed to make these changes take places. This exciting object in the middle of the stomach seems likely to be an extrapolation from the earlier infantile experience of soft mouth encircling the hard exciting cluster of sensations aroused by the nipple-tongue. To the suckling infant, this sensation-object brought magical changes, in that discomfort was changed into bliss. It also becomes a magical 'button' which holds the child together by keeping him 'buttoned up'.

Jung's work on alchemy would seem to have relevance to these elemental states. In the elemental depths, the gestalt of the cluster of nipple–tongue sensations associated with the shining eyes of the suckling mother could be felt to be a kind of philosophers' stone which transmutes base things into sublime perfection. The disturbing prick of the loss of perfection which *had* been, but which is now gone, stimulates the search for the philosophers' stone, as also the Holy Grail or the crock of gold at the end of the rainbow. It becomes part of our feeling for beauty and aesthetic sensitivity so that we do not make impossible demands either on ourselves as fallible human beings or on the fallible human beings who surround us. But the psychotic child (and the psychotic child in all of us) has to learn that earthy, co-operative efforts at ordinary everyday tasks, rather than absorption in unduly romantic spaceship wanderings in search of magical objects, will bring about the basic integrity within himself which helps to 'breast' the fact of loss and the fact of 'death' ('goneness'). It becomes a stimulus to exploration, scientific investigation, creative and therapeutic endeavour, but not a futile search. With this ability to bear disillusionment comes the capacity to emerge from the death-trap of repetition-compulsion to the enjoyment of a world that is a fount of possibilities. In this world, romance, magic and the search for perfection take their appropriate place but are not pursued to the exclusion of everything else.

The psychotic child has experienced the outside world in the bizarre body-centred terms of an 'unbuttoned' stomach from which dangerous things can fall out. The arch of the sky, the cracks in the ceiling of his room can rain terrible things down upon him, such as explosive poohs and hard and prickly things. In his grandiose state, either very malevolent or very benevolent unidentified flying objects can come out of the void (the arch of the sky, the arch of the belly). Cupboards and drawers, experienced as stomachs, can send out an avalanche of horrors to torment him. (As witness Dr Etchegoyan's patient in Chapter 9, who thought that there were 'monsters' in the cupboard in which his equipment was kept.) Psychotic children are often afraid of taking equipment from their drawer or cupboard. Thus, for children in an autistic state the stomach-world becomes a witches' cauldron of Hieronymus Bosch-type creatures which threaten him, instead of being a crucible in which blissful transformations can occur. In saying 'That part is missed out', Peter has the illusion that he is blocking out those terrors. It is in the pit of his stomach that he feels the terrible sense of loss of sublime perfections which, being lost, turn into unutterable horrors. He has retreated from this, but it comes up again and again, to be blocked out with more intensity each time.

By 'stomaching' this for him until he can 'stomach' it himself, the therapist helps him to face the loss of the sublime and perpetually satisfying autistic objects, and to experience his need of other people. I have not studied eastern philosophy in any depth, but it occurs to me that, in urging concentration on the empty circle in their stomachs rather than on the cerebral elaborations in their heads, the Zen Buddhists are intuitively aiming to bring their novitiates in touch with this elemental sense of need. Going around with a begging bowl would also bring this home to them.

To be able to bear this exaggerated sense of need, the child has to have some capacity for retaining memories of good things in the past and imaginations and thoughts of good opportunities to come. At first the container for these mental possibilities seems to be located in the stomach. For the child, 'mind' is a physical container, as is a stomach! The child does not have the sophisticated notion of 'mind' being a convenient illusion which helps us to deal with mental events. As the stomach provides connections between his 'hard head' and his 'soft bottom', he feels he has a container for his thoughts. He begins to think. The hard head and the soft bottom become linked together and become integral and co-existent parts of the experience of the body-self. Sensation-shapes in his bottom can become thoughts in his head. But first of all they have to go through a process of transformation in the stomach. This was expressed allegorically in a television series called *Monkey*, which brought Chinese allegories to the Western screen. In one of the sequences, the young man who symbolises pure thought loses his 'irrepressible' money and also a strange faceless being called 'shape-changer'. They go into the stomach of the monster who makes volcanoes and earthquakes. After being transformed there, they are reunited with the young man who symbolises thought.

Peter's material and the foregoing allegory pose as many questions as they answer. Are they talking about the transformation of sensations into percepts and concepts by the activities of a stomach-mind in which digestive processes have to occur? Are they also saying that, to be thoroughly assimilated, experiences have to be felt in the gut before being worked over in the head? Clinical work with psychotic states in children has brought home to me that the child has to have awareness of 'insides' if fantasies and thoughts are to develop. Obviously, until this awareness occurs, incorporation and introjection cannot take place, nor can projective identification as described by Klein (1963). The child lives in the bi-dimensional terms of surfaces, in which state adhesive equation is operative.

In this state, until the child has developed some capacity to 'stomach' the frustration of loss, he will feel, in Bion's words, that 'the needed object is a bad object. All objects that are needed are bad objects because they tantalize' (Bion, 1962b, p. 84). He will also feel that he does not want 'a good breast' but that he wants 'to evacuate a bad one' (Bion, 1962b, p. 84). At this stage, the therapist is experienced as an inanimate object to 'contain' his evacuations.

As the years have gone by, other children have helped me to understand Peter's material with more depth. I have come to realise that the stomach is the place into which outside 'not-me' things go. Transactions take place there between the 'me' and the 'not-me', but, first of all, the 'not-me' food has to be worked upon to become tolerated. (This understanding is very significant in anorexia nervosa.) Children have told me that the stomach is a waiting place. Food does not go straight through them; it has to wait there to be changed before it can leave the body. Material such as Peter's has demonstrated to me the importance of the waiting-room in the setting we provide for patients, and also the importance of not allowing children to rush into and out of the consulting-room. I have come to see that being able to wait, to restrain impulsivity sufficiently to go through the usual courtesies of one human being to another, is a necessary basis for interactive, creative endeavours. For someone like myself, with an unconventional background and progressive ideas, to come to see the value of doing things 'properly' has been a revolutionising experience.

The session around which this chapter has been focused has stayed in my mind over the years. I felt at the time that it was a significant session, and later sessions proved this to be the case. It obviously provided Peter with connections which had previously been missing. After this session, Peter became much less obsessional and repetitive in his activities. He lived less in terms of surfaces and of outside supports. The sessions now took an on-going course leading to the presented session of the next chapter (session 71). It will be seen from that session that the ordinary, everyday family had begun to fill the empty middle space. With his delusory terrors relieved, he could now allow the nurturing possibilities of ordinary family life to play upon him. His esoteric, other-worldly notions could now become the stuff of imagination, romance and the feeling for the perfection of beauty. Prior to this, they had been an all-pervasive means of *evading* reality, instead of a means of working upon it and patterning it in order to come to terms with it.

Chapter 18

The struggles of an autistic child to develop a mind of his own

In this chapter some of the struggles of one autistic child (Peter of the previous chapter) to develop a mind of his own will be described. The presentation will be a simple description rather than a scientific account. It seeks to portray the insights which psychotic child patients have revealed to me over the years, some of which are not an established part of current psychotherapeutic practice with psychotic children. The picture of these insights in operation will be painted through some particularly refreshing and interesting sessions.

BACKGROUND

When Peter was two and a half years old he was seen by Anni Bergman, who at that time was Margaret Mahler's senior psychotherapist. She has told me that she considered Peter to be one of the most severe cases of autism she had ever seen. He had no speech whatsoever, he was extremely withdrawn and had bizarre hand movements. He walked on his toes and avoided looking at people.

Peter came into treatment with me when he was six years of age. The family lived in Oldham and he was brought by mother and father to see me every weekend in the small Buckinghamshire village in which I then lived. Thus, he had two sessions, one on Saturday and one on Sunday. Previously, I had seen other autistic children much more frequently.

Prior to coming to see me, Peter had had some cognitive therapy. He was speaking in a very restricted way and could hold a pencil, but he did not draw or write spontaneously with it.

When I first saw Peter he was coming towards the cottage in which I live, carrying an enormous key-ring on which there were one hundred keys of varying shapes and sizes. The parents told me that he would not be parted from keys, and carried them everywhere. He had a smaller key-ring for more general use, but needed the large one when he was doing anything new and anxious-making, like coming to see me for the first time.

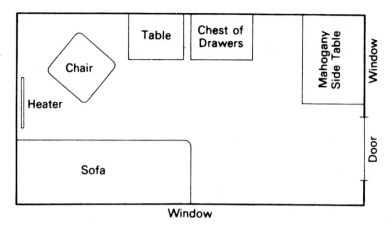

Figure 18.1 Plan of the therapy room

It would have been funny, if it had not been so pathetic. His stiff little body was bent over to one side with the weight of the keys. His white, anxious face with pinched tight lips looked out from a sideways angle above his cumbersome burden. He was unsmiling, and his eyes looked like black pits, as his pupils were dilated in what I conceived to be terror. He certainly aroused therapeutic feelings in me as I escorted him up the garden path, to the pony shed which my husband had converted into a therapy room. This was a brick-built shed with a stable door. Figure 18.1 shows how the room was arranged.

In this room, each child had his own drawer of toys with a key which would not open any other child's drawer. The keys were kept in a wooden box with a sliding lid and each key had a label with the number of the drawer on it and the child's first name. This box was kept in the drawer of a side-table.

I put Peter's toys into a round plastic bowl, which was kept in his locked drawer. In the bowl was a bag of wild animals, a bag of tame animals, felt-tip pens, pencil-crayons, a rubber, a pencil, a pencil-sharpener, and a humming-top. Under the side-table there was a bag of wooden bricks which were shared by all the children who used the room.

This case presentation is going to be as unorthodox as Peter's entry into treatment had been: I am not going to give a developmental or family history other than to say that Peter was the first-born son of an intelligent middle-class Jewish couple. With hindsight, they realise that Peter seemed remote and odd from the beginning of life. There were no traumatic events such as hospitalisations, but the mother was depressed when Peter was a small baby and father had to be abroad frequently because of his work. The baby was a poor sucker. Mother had a great desire to be a perfect mother and tried to breast-feed him, but after a few weeks he was put to the bottle because her milk became less and less, possibly in part owing to lack of stimulation from the baby. Like many parents of autistic children, they wondered whether Peter was deaf and took him to an audiology unit. Peter has a sister whom I will call Rosalind. She is two years younger than he is and is relatively normal.

THE SESSIONS

In describing Peter's sessions the novelist's device of 'flashbacks' will be used. In this way it is hoped to convey the ebb and flow of Peter's developing feelings as they intertwined with his cognitive developments. A session has been selected in which he looked through the drawings in his folder and by this means remembered certain significant happenings in the course of his psychotherapy. (Peter had been in treatment for just over a year at the date of the present session.)

The session in which Peter looked back over the course of his psychotherapy occurred on Saturday, 21 February 1976. It was the 71st session and took place before a gap of three weeks of non-attendance due to the parents going on a skiing holiday. The children were to be left at home, so that, as well as an impending separation from me, there was to be separation from the parents. The children were to be looked after by the mother's help, called Heather. The following is as I recorded it immediately after the session:

> Peter came in, took off his anorak and hung it on the peg provided. As he hung up his coat, I found myself saying, 'You must be worried about mother and father going away and not coming to see Tustin.'
>
> He said in an artificial, high-pitched voice, as if parroting what had been said to him, 'Oh no, Heather will look after me.' As he said this his face had that ethereal, translucent, other-worldly look I've come to know so well in certain psychotic children.
>
> I replied in a very ordinary tone of voice. 'Yes, but you'll miss your mother and father and you'll miss Tustin.'
>
> At this he said quite simply and naturally, 'Yes, I shall.' His face had become that of an ordinary seven-year-old boy.
>
> He came over to sit on the sofa facing me in the armchair. When he does this I know we are going 'to have a conversation' as he once expressed it.
>
> He said with a malicious twinkle in his eyes, 'Do you know this poem?' He then recited:

'Twinkle, twinkle, little bat!
How I wonder what you're at!
Up above the world you fly,
Like a tea tray in the sky.'[1]

Of course, this is a mocking parody (by Lewis Carroll) of the well-known verse, which you will remember goes as follows:

Twinkle, twinkle little star,
How I wonder what you are
Up above the world so high,
Like a diamond in the sky.

I reminded him of the proper version and also reminded him of certain of his characteristics which we had discussed many times in varying contexts. Because I was summarising what had been talked about many times before, I was able to convey to him more briefly the following thoughts, which for the sake of clarity will be amplified here. I conveyed the following thoughts:

We both knew that there was a part of him which wanted to be such a bright star that he shone like a diamond, that wanted to be Jesus Christ Superstar (we'd had much material about this musical), that wanted to be the most perfect baby and child that anyone had ever seen. This part of him felt 'let down' when his parents and Tustin weren't ultra-perfect in the way that he felt they should be. To be parents to a Jesus Christ Superstar, they should never do unexpected things. In short, they should never 'misbehave' according to the rigid scheme of expectations he had of them. Nor should he 'misbehave' in terms of his rigid expectations of himself and of those he felt were theirs.

If they, and he, weren't precious, clean, shining stars fused together in a sublime oneness, then they were broken apart to become dirty, brown bats – brown 'poohs' put in the wrong place like the tea-tray in the sky. If unexpected and disappointing things occurred, like daddy and mummy going away, and Tustin going away, it made him feel like saying and doing the wrong things. He disappointed as he had been disappointed. He became sulky and uncooperative. He put things in the wrong place. He mocked at me and his parents. He gave wrong answers although he knew the right ones.

After I had said something of the above to him, although obviously not all of it, he went to his drawer and got out his folder of drawings, which he brought to the sofa where I sat. He began to look through the drawings. As he put the first one on the table, he wet his finger and smudged one of the brown lines on the drawing, saying, 'Just a smear.' It was one of his good drawings. I said, 'When you feel sad and angry like you do today, you want to smear and spoil the work we've done together, to mock at it and say it's no good.'

He began to look through his drawings in a somewhat obsessive way, counting them as he used to count his keys and his coins.

I said I thought that he was anxiously collecting together his good things to keep them safe from the dirty smearing feelings he felt he had. Gradually, his obsessive leafing through the pictures turned to interested scrutiny and he started to show them to me, talking about them to me and obviously asking me to talk back to him. His mood was very different from the resistant, uncooperative mood at the beginning of the session. As the session went on, he became interested and animated.

The first few pictures were undated because I had only started to date them after he had asked for and been given a folder in which to keep them. When he first started therapy in January 1975, he had done very little other than counting and looking at his keys. When he first put pencil to paper he merely drew around the outline of the keys (*session 4, 1 February 1975*).

In the session I am reporting, he looked at these outlines of his keys, saying, 'I don't need them now.'

I said, 'No, you needed them when you first came because you felt you needed an extra bit to your body to plug your holes to keep your good things safe inside you.' (This was something we had talked about in other sessions for which there had been much evidence.) Continuing this theme, Peter said, 'The keys made me feel like a grown-up.'

I said, 'Yes – do you remember that you thought grown-ups were children with special extra bits stuck on their bodies?' He replied, 'They're grown-up because they've grown.'

I hadn't said this to him at any time – and it seemed to me a neat summary of insights we had talked over in relation to seeds and their growth – about which more later.

[At this early stage of therapy he merely drew around the outlines of the keys. This was an example of his state of imitative fusion. He could not experience his bodily separateness from the keys. They were part of his body. Consequently, they were not looked at as separate objects, held in the mind, and then represented on paper. At that stage, he had not developed the capacity for abstraction and representation.]

The next picture he brought from the folder *was* a representation (Figure 18.2). It was the chest of drawers in the therapy room in which the children's toys were kept (*session 11, 18 March 1975*). It will be seen that keys are still very important to him, but these are drawn from a construct in his mind. Nor are they isolated keys, detached from

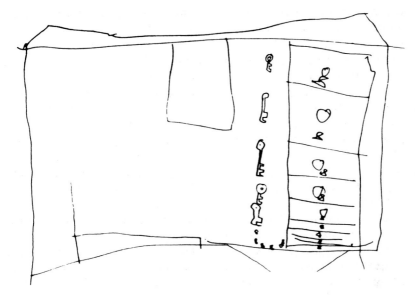

Figure 18.2 The chest of drawers

their reality-function. Instead of being used for an autistic purpose –
to give his body an extra grown-up bit – they are related to an object
for which they have a real purpose and which had significant emotional
associations. This drawing showed that Peter was developing a capacity
for abstraction, representation and recollection. Things, and himself,
were becoming less idiosyncratic and were becoming meaningful in a
functional way which could be shared with other people. (This was
the 18th session.)

At this point in our somewhat nostalgic going over the past, he
remembered the occasion when he had put the tops of the felt-tip pens
onto his fingers in an attempt to make his fingers longer than they
actually were. We remembered together that this misuse of the pen-
tops had meant that his felt-tip pens became dried-up and unusable
(*session 23, 22 March 1975*).

I reminded him of how he had misused me, trying to feel that I was
a mechanical extra bit to his body – a 'vending machine' as he had
called me. As this 'vending machine', he put questions to me to which
he well knew the answer, and to which he well knew that I knew the
answer. Then, the expected answer would pop out just like a cup of
coffee after the coin has been put in and the button pressed. (It did,
until I realised what he was doing!). But this had made me dried-up
and unusable. I wasn't a real, live, responsive human being who could
love and understand him. We didn't adapt and adjust to each other's

unpredictabilities, but we went through mechanical procedures which made everything dull and boring – and dead.

At this point in the presented session, we came to the drawings of the crocodile. He now became very animated because this was a time when he had come to life as a person. In order to understand the crocodile material it is necessary to go back to the early days of Peter's psychotherapy.

As with every other patient, I had provided a crocodile in his set of toys. From the beginning of his therapy, this had obviously been a disturbing animal for him. He would push it away out of sight. At the end of each session, I, or the child and myself, would gather up all the toys and lock them away in the drawer before the child left the room. Several times after this had been done and Peter had gone, I found that he had pushed the crocodile down the opening in the sofa where the back joins the seat. At other times, I would find it hidden under a piece of furniture. Once he told me he did this to upset Paul. (Paul is another child, whose name he had seen on a key label.)

After the summer holidays of 1975, I found that Peter's crocodile had completely disappeared. I searched the therapy room. I had the room cleaned from top to bottom. I asked the parents if it had been taken home. Peter expressed ignorance of its whereabouts. It was nowhere to be found.

On 13 September 1975, I provided him with another crocodile, feeling that the crocodile part of Peter was too important a part for him to lose. Here is an extract from 13 September 1975 (session 37), the day on which I gave him another crocodile. I recorded as follows:

> He put the doll family on the floor and said that the crocodile might eat them up. Because of this, he decided to wrap the crocodile in a plastic bag and put him at the bottom of the bowl, as he said, 'in prison'.
>
> He then took a large hunk of Plasticine. Unbeknown to me, on the last day before the summer holiday, he had secreted this in one of the other drawers which was empty and unlocked. The psychotherapist who shared the room with me brought it to me after the summer holidays. I put it back into Peter's drawer.
>
> This hunk of Plasticine was composed of all the Plasticine I had provided for him and had many colours all mingled together. With his fingernail, he now put a face on this thick column-like piece of Plasticine and said, 'That's God.' I said, 'Does He take care of you?' To which he replied, 'No! I take care of him!' After a pause he said, 'Then he takes care of me.'
>
> He then broke a fairly large piece of Plasticine from the body of

God and said, 'That's the guard.' [Peter, like other autistic children, had the notion that words which sound alike must be connected in some way. This is part of the autistic disposition to classify the world in terms of superficial 'clang' similarities rather than in terms of meaning.]

To return to Peter – having made God and the Guard, he said, 'It's dark now and all the family are going to bed.'

He then put a piece of cardboard as a floor to separate the family from the crocodile in the bottom of the bowl.

It will be remembered that the crocodile was imprisoned. God and the Guard also protected the family. So they were trebly protected against the ravages of the crocodile. Figure 18.3 is a picture of the bowl as it was left in his drawer. There is also a drawing by William Blake (Figure 18.4) which has a striking similarity to the arrangement of Peter's bowl. At the top, where Peter has God and the Guard, Blake has God and two guardian angels. In the bottom, where Peter has the crocodile, Blake has the dragon. In the middle part, where Peter has the good family, Blake has a strange animal with human ears. This is the part where ordinary humanness seems to be coming into focus to offset the polarities of bestiality and hyperspirituality. It is the beginnings of a transitional area.

But let us return to what Peter tells us about the crocodile. The record of the session on 13 September continues in the following way:

> Selecting a black felt-tip pen Peter wrote, 'Do not touch the crocodile it will eat you all up', and put this in his bowl.
>
> With a brown felt-tip pen he wrote, 'Do not put your hands down at the bottom.'
>
> I said, 'I think the bowl is arranged like you feel your body to be. You've told me that the hard poohs when they come out of your bottom feel as if they were biting you. I think they feel like a crocodile with a hard prickly skin.' I asked, because I was puzzled, 'Why do you feel that God and the Guard are in your head?'
>
> He said, 'Because my eyes and ears are there.' I said, 'You mean they help you to be on your guard?' He nodded. I asked, 'Is the good family in your tummy?' Again he nodded.

Here endeth the first lesson by Peter on the crocodile!

The next 'crocodile' session occurred on Saturday, 27 September 1975 (session 41). I had told him that I would be away the following weekend. His parents had told him I was going to Rome.

> He said, 'I'm going to bite Rome.' He then said, 'If I bite Rosie [his sister], she bites me back.'
>
> I said I thought perhaps he was afraid that Rome would bite him back.

GOD
AND
THE GUARD

THE FAMILY

THE CROCODILE.

Figure 18.3 Peter's bowl

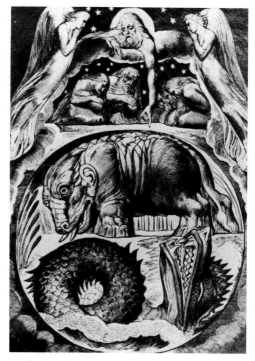

Figure 18.4 'Behemoth and Leviathan', engraving by William Blake

He then wrote some words and drew lines round them so that they were in boxes 'to keep them safe', as he said.

I said, 'I think you are keeping your good words safe from being bitten by Rosie and by Rome and by the other children you feel you've bitten. You bit them because you felt that they were taking something precious away from you.'

I said, 'I think you have put your good words into boxes to keep them safe because you are afraid that there is no mummy and daddy and no Tustin to take care of you.'

He said, 'Rosie did a splashy pooh all over the floor. Wasn't that naughty?'

I said, 'I think you feel that Rosie's pooh is a crocodile that's slipped out of control and is misbehaving. You're afraid it might eat up all your good family. You're parcelling up all your good things to keep them safe from the other children's crocodiles. If Tustin isn't always with you as a part of your body, like your eyes to guard and protect you, you're afraid that the sly, slippery crocodiles that pass my guard will come to hurt you.' [It will be remembered that the crocodile had slipped past my guard in that it had got lost.]

At the end of the session as he put his toys away, he put a notice in his drawer which said 'Keep out Crocodiles.'

The next day, Sunday, 28 September 1975 (session 42), he was very high-handed, unlistening, impenetrable and bossy with me.

At last he said, 'I've put on the crocodile's skin. I *am* the crocodile.'

I said, 'I think you feel you've got to be a crocodile to fight the other children, particularly Paul. But you've made him into a crocodile by feeling you have slipped your hard crocodile poohs into him to be rid of them. So you make him much more frightening than any ordinary child could really be.'

At the end of this session he fetched God and the Guard, saying that they were daddy and mummy. He now sat on the floor on the green rug, which he said was a cabbage patch, and played like an ordinary six-year-old. Daddy (God) and mummy (the Guard) were sending the crocodiles away who were trying to eat up the cabbages and the seeds.

The following weekend, 5 October, I was in Rome. After this the parents were in the USA for some weeks. Peter came back on 8 and 9 November.

A session will now be described which followed this long gap in coming to see me. It was a session of great beauty (session 45, Saturday, 15 November 1975).

He brought a carrier-bag full of seeds. He showed me a large horse-chestnut nut. It was a beautiful one, gleaming like a piece of well-polished antique mahogany. He explained that it had come out of a prickly green skin, and he showed me one of the cases. He agreed with me when I said that it was a bit like a crocodile's skin. He said, 'It doesn't need the prickly skin any more. It has been *borned* out of it.'

I said, 'I think you feel you've been born out of your thick, prickly crocodile skin.'

He said, 'Yes, I don't need it. Daddy and mummy take care of me.' He put his hand into his large carrier-bag of seeds and got out a sycamore key, which he threw into the air. He watched delightedly as it spiralled gracefully to the ground. His hand played around his mouth with gentle stroking movements as he watched it. He said, 'They go round and round.' Now and again he lost the sycamore key as it spiralled away under pieces of furniture and was lost from view. When this occurred he became anxious. I said, 'You seem worried when you lose the thing which gives you such lovely round-and-round feelings in your mouth.'

He said, 'Round-and-round wind seeds.'

I said, 'You seem to feel that the round-and-round sensations in your mouth are like seeds – beautiful "creations" which as a baby you felt you could make with your mouth.' He looked at the chest of drawers and said, 'Paul has drawer number 4.' As he said this he farted and then talked about how skunks 'sent out bad smells as a protection.' He then said that Rosalind had stolen some of his seeds.

I said, 'You are afraid that the other children want to take these beautiful round-and-round sensations you make with your mouth away from you. So you send out bad smells to protect yourself.'

He said, 'When they took the round-and-round thing away I made my own bubbles.' He bubbled with his spit which spread around his mouth. With relish his pointed pink tongue licked it away. He looked at me and laughed roguishly.

In another session he prefaced everything he said with a little whistle. Eventually I asked him why he did this. He replied, 'It's a bubble of joy inside me.'

When I came to write up this 'bubble of joy' session, I imitated the type of whistle he had made and found that as the air was gathered together in the puckered mouth and then gently expelled by the soft whistle, it spread around the lips in a sensually satisfying way.

In other sessions, he drew pictures in which there were 'puff-balls' which were poisonous.

Gradually he showed me that these puff-balls were poisonous bubbles (farts) sent out by skunks (himself and other children) for their protection.

So now we had 'joy bubbles' and 'stink bubbles'. The fear now arose that the 'stink bubbles' would poison and explode the 'joy bubbles' (his seeds – his beautiful creations – his ecstasies).

Every source of frustration (and gaps in coming to see me were a major source of this) was a threat because so many ugly 'stink bubbles' were felt to be bottled up inside him that the beautiful 'joy bubbles' were threatened.

In the session being used to give 'flashbacks' of significant phases in Peter's psychotherapy, we had reached the drawing of 'joy bubbles' which he had drawn for his mother as Christmas approached (session 51, 6 December 1975). He so much wanted to be a source of joy and delight to her (and to me and his teachers also) that the 'stink bubbles' which he felt he needed for his protection were feared. In other words, he was continually trying to get rid of his crocodile, sometimes by pretending it didn't exist, sometimes by feeling that he surreptitiously slipped it into his rivals, who then seemed to become more dangerous because of it. (The mechanism of 'projection' took place in quite a concrete way.) The 'joy bubbles' were fairly solid-looking 'bubbles', which also looked like a heap of brightly coloured balloons. On a more primitive level, they could be faeces, since dots were put round them to show that they sent out a 'radiance' – or a smell!

In the session being described (Saturday, 21 February 1976) I said something of this to Peter. He replied by saying, 'They *resemble* balloons. They *resemble* poohs, but they're bubbles.'

This, of course, made me rejoice because it was clear that he had firmly moved from autistic 'as if' functioning to a more differentiated perception in which things which resembled each other were not felt to be one and the same thing. One thing could be a *substitute* for another thing to which it had a resemblance, but it was not used 'as if' it were that thing. That is, it could not *be* it, or *replace* it, but it could be a *substitute* for it. The basis for symbolism was becoming established.

In the past, I feel I have hampered these developments by making interpretations which presuppose symbolic capacities which these children do not have. But Peter's symbolising capacities were now becoming well established. The fact that these cognitive developments went hand in hand with an increased capacity for experiencing feelings was illustrated by what Peter did next. With an orange-coloured felt-tip pen he now inserted, 'love from Peter'. Originally it had said, 'To mummy', written with a turquoise-coloured felt-tip pen, and surrounded by wavy lines, not the rigid straight lines with which he did his protective 'boxes'.

But this relaxed, responsive, loving state of mind-cum-body began to be disturbed by other feelings which were welling up within him.

When there were only ten minutes left of this session, he began to become very anxious. (It will be remembered that his parents were going away for two weeks and he would have three weekends when he did not come to see me.)

He closed the folder and drew rigid lines around each of his first names and around his surname to enclose them in boxes. His behaviour also showed that he was encapsulated from the more tender aspects of himself and of me. He became hard and domineering. He said, 'Write these spellings.' When I wouldn't comply he banged on the mahogany table with a wooden brick. He asked intrusive questions about me and the cottage in which I lived.

He then started to write 'news' as he did at school. Having finished, he ordered me to put the date on it. I refused to do it immediately at his command, but said I would put the date on it when I was ready to do so. He then wrote 'more news'. He was in a panic when he could not feel I was under his iron control. I talked about this sympathetically to him, whilst maintaining my position as a separate person who had his long-term welfare at heart and so could not give in to his short-term demands.

As I was getting the key to lock his drawer, he saw a microscopic bit of paper sticking out of Paul's drawer. He pulled at it and part of it came out further.

I said, 'I think you're wanting to take Paul's things because you're jealous of him. You think he can leave things sticking out of drawers – leave things in the wrong place – do his poohs and wees anywhere. You feel cross that you are expected to control yourself and to put your poohs and wees in the proper place, and that you are expected to control your feelings. You think that Paul doesn't have to do this. You think he is allowed to have all his own way.' (In short, he was frustrated at having to be toilet-trained both physiologically and psychologically.)

He said, 'I'm a crocodile. I'll bite him.' But he said it in a 'playing' sort of way with a twinkle in his eyes. He rubbed his bottom with his hand and made as if to throw something out of the window. He then looked at me with a grin.

When he went to the waiting car he went to sit in the front seat. His sister Rosalind, who was in the back seat, leaned forward towards him in a pretended menacing attitude. She had covered her teeth with white bubble gum and she bared these at him in a ferocious way. As her teeth gleamed white in the gloom of the interior of the car, she looked to me very much like a crocodile. If Peter saw her as I did, he must have felt he was facing the rivalry we had talked about in the session. However, I felt confident that he was more robust to cope with it.

CONCLUSION

In conclusion, I will tell what has happened to Peter since the sessions which have been reported in this chapter.

He finished treatment a year before the first edition of this book was published. At that time, he was a charming, original and intelligent little boy aged eleven. The parents telephoned me that year to say that he had passed the quite stiff examination for entrance to a very good local private school, but in addition to this he had also passed the 11+ examination to the local grammar school.[2] Naturally, we were all very pleased. However, on this issue of intellectual progress I would like to add a few words.

In reading the reports of the sessions, you may have felt that my remarks were less sane than those of the child. At this stage of the analysis, when the child is coming out of his autism and beginning to communicate lucidly, I have found that it is important to keep him in touch with the elemental levels from which he has emerged. If this is not done, we get a kind of 'egghead' autism by which the child cuts himself off from his basic elemental origins. Thus, the pathological autism is transmogrified into another form which is often very acceptable to parents and teachers, but which means that the child is cut off from his roots. Thus, his personality is built on shaky foundations and he is forever insecure. Such a child becomes a good conforming child in school, though very rebellious underneath. He is a good 'learner' but his originality is lost. He is liable to various kinds of phobia. In later life he is liable to swing from excessive conformity to extreme rebellion. It seems fairly certain that this will not be the fate of Peter.

A NOTE ON FEELINGS ABOUT BEAUTY AND UGLINESS

Peter's material, as with all work with autistic states in childhood, inevitably brings one to consider feelings about beauty and ugliness. Let me explain what I mean.

In a study of the wild boy of Aveyron (Itard and Malson, 1972) who, as we have seen, had many features in common with autistic children, we are told of his 'ecstatic' trances on drinking clear water, on feeling snow, on experiencing moonlight, on being naked in the rain. It is common for psychotherapists to encounter such experiences with autistic children. For example, one child I had in treatment went into ecstasies about the motes in a shaft of sunlight. Another child, having poured water from a jug into a bowl, went into ecstasies about the dancing ripples and the gleams of light and shade in the water – at least, this is how the water appeared to me. I do not know how the child saw it, but it obviously provoked an ecstatic response. His whole body quivered, his gaze was riveted upon the water, and he jumped up and down in obvious delight and excitement. When such children can talk, they tell of the 'ugliness' of the tantrum. For them, beauty seems to be associated with ecstasy, ugliness with tantrums.

I have come to realise that, for these elemental children, the ecstasy of beauty is associated with moments of bodily completeness in which there is an experience of ecstatic fusion with the 'earth mother'. These children's despairing search for an 'extra bit' to their bodies seems to be part of their need for perfect sensuous completeness (which means that it is perpetually present and available). Gradually, as therapy progresses, they come to see that a sense of satisfying completeness does not come from auto-sensual experiences nor from material objects used to plug the gap. Rather, it comes from the transformations brought about by hard-working and reciprocal interchanges with people and experiences outside themselves. But before this can take place, they need support in bearing their extreme states of ecstasy and tantrum. After this, their 'good-enough' achievements can help them to bear the hard fact that, in this world, the perfection of completeness is not attainable, although inevitably the striving for it goes on. However, although 'man's reach exceeds his grasp', transitional activities help to make this bearable.

NOTES

1 A useful example of the difference between working with an autistic and a neurotic child was provided when another therapist suggested that Peter might be thinking of my going to Rome in an aeroplane. For him 'Rome' was another child, like Rosie, who took me away from him.

2 In a letter written to me twelve years later, Peter wrote: 'Thank you for your expert help on releasing me from the prison of autism. I deeply appreciate the job you have done to make me feel better. I still remember those days when I would spin a humming top, play with farm animals, and tell you ludicrous stories.'

Chapter 19

Autistic elements in neurotic disorders of childhood

The usual distinction between psychosis and neurosis is that in psychosis awareness of commonly agreed reality is massively blocked or distorted, and in neurosis it is less so. However, in working with neurotic children, I have invariably come upon a 'pocket' of functioning in which awareness of reality was so blocked or distorted that it justified the term 'psychotic'. What I have learned from psychotic children about the autistic processes which blocked awareness of reality (encapsulated children), or distorted it (confusional children), has enabled my work with neurotic children to be more effective.

In order for more normal processes to be set in train by psychotherapy, the repetitive, perseverative processes of the pathology of autism have to be modified. It has been suggested that the artificiality of autism has arisen to counter the lack of connection with, or the too-wounding disconnection from, the mother of early infancy. It was a surprise to me when I found that this 'broken-away' phenomenon, experienced as a hole or a wound (usually in relation to the mouth) and the associated deviant sensuousness, was also an invariable feature in the analysis of neurotic children. I found that the phobic and inhibited neurotic children had a capsule of autism. Other neurotic children had a jumbled tangle of reactions which were associated with confusion with other people and with objects in the outside world. In treatment, one of the earliest struggles was to help both types of child to live within their own body outlines, and to work through the disillusionment that they had not an 'extra bit' to their body (particularly to their mouth), that gave them omnipotent control and power over the outside world. They also had to learn to live with the limitations of their body, for example, that they could not fly, nor could they draw an exact representation of the picture they had in their mind, nor could they always do the things the grown-ups could do.

The *infantile transference*, which is the major instrument of psychoanalytic therapy, is crucial to helping the child to come to terms with these hard realities. In autistic states, the mother has come to be used as if she were an organ or limb of the child's body, instead of coming to be recognised as a separate being on whom the child depends for allaying discomfort and for enabling him to achieve things which are beyond his physical powers. This pathological response is repeated in his use of the therapist. This makes it possible for the therapist to modify his behaviour and to help him to bear the fact of his bodily separateness and all that this entails, in particular, the *tantrum* in which grief, panic and rage are experienced together. He also needs to be helped to bear his moments of ecstasy about 'beautiful' things. (Autistic children have taught me that the 'incompleteness' which provokes the tantrums is felt to be ugly, whereas the sense of 'completeness' which provokes the ecstasy is their experience of beauty.)

Another feature which is characteristic of the 'pocket' of autism in neurotic children is the lack of appropriate and effective regulation of impulses and responses, such lack of regulation being the essence of madness. In this 'pocket', the turbulence of elemental sensuousness has not been regulated and modified by becoming focused upon real parents who exist in space and time and so impose limits. In this alienated aspect of their functioning, the neurotic children have become attached to their own bodily parts, organs and rhythms, which are experienced in an inanimate mechanical way. Thus, in this part, they are just as deviant and at risk as the ethological goslings who imprinted a cardboard box instead of the mother goose! Their behaviour is regulated in terms of an unchanging, inanimate, mechanical object rather than in terms of a growing and alive one. Such regulation lacks the appropriateness and flexibility necessary for dealing with human situations and people. Work with psychotic children has brought home to me the need for being an alive, active and responsive person in therapeutic work with autistic states in neurotic children. In doing this, we need to be on the alert to point out to them the occasions when humane flexibility and kindness is interpreted in their mechanical terms as 'weakness' and 'softness', to be exploited and despised. They also fear it, because it means, in their 'all-or-nothing' terms, that the people who care for them are 'weak', soft and silly.

Work with the autistic elements in psychotic children has also made me aware of the importance of bringing together the basic sensuous contraries such as hard and soft, weak and strong, etc., and to hold the child through the explosions and implosions of the tantrums and ecstasies occasioned by this. (This was discussed in Chapter 9.) In 'stomaching' these for him we help him to 'stomach' them for himself. As we have seen, at these elemental levels, 'mind' is conceived in terms of the stomach or gut, which 'digests' and brings about transformations and changes. To help the child to tolerate and grow from change is the major aim of therapy, but we need to be in touch with his primitive notions about how this takes place. We have to understand concretised, body-centred, sensation-dominated levels which are basic to the abstractions which the child will make later. To talk in terms of abstractions before these basic levels are established is meaningless to him, and can result in imposing an unduly cerebral set of responses and clichés which are as artificial as the pathological autism. To impose placating conformity on the primal split between sensuous contraries means that the 'self' is a house divided against itself. In these divided states, the weak or soft part feels predatory and destructive towards the strong or hard part and wants to steal or destroy its strength and hardness. This understanding is helpful in dealing with neurotic disorders, on the occasions in which progress and success are felt to be dangerous because destructive elements in one part are aroused to destroy the possibility of success and progress occurring in another part.

In all types of autism, the sensuousness which is biologically so valuable has gone disastrously awry. Instead of being the bait to nature's hook which encourages activities which make for survival, it becomes a snare and a delusion. The normal and progressive use of the sensory apparatus becomes blocked or distorted by excessive sensuality.

I will now summarise some of the foregoing autistic elements as they are encountered in neurotic syndromes, after which their occurrence in clinical situations will be illustrated.

SPECIFIC NEUROTIC DISORDERS

The relevance of the foregoing hypotheses to psychosomatic disorders and hypochondria will be fairly obvious. For various reasons, sensuousness has become unduly directed towards bodily organs and processes. This has remained unregulated and untransformed into dreams, fantasies and play. One function of the psychosomatic illness seems to be to release and deal with the violence associated with unregulated sensuality, as well as to give form and shape to formless, raw auto-sensual elements.

The relevance to encopresis and enuresis may also be fairly obvious. The child obtains surreptitious, and oftentimes unconscious satisfaction from the contents of his bladder and bowel. This bypasses the mother-and-father who are limited and separate and so impose limits. Part of these limits is the child being 'toilet-trained' both physiologically and psychologically.

There are two forms of encopresis. In one, the child retains his faeces and there is overflow and staining of clothes from this overflow. In another type of child, the faeces are not retained but are deposited in inappropriate places in a random manner; for example, one child hid them in a piano. Dr Mary Lindsay (personal communication) describes these two types of child by the picturesque terms of 'retainers' and 'ploppers'. The ploppers invariably have a very mixed-up and muddled family setting, and are confused and entangled with the outside world. The retainers are obstinate, pseudo-self-sufficient, controlling children who block awareness of painful realities with hard autistic objects. Thus, the retainers manifest encapsulated autism, and the ploppers have the features of confusional autism.

The relevance to learning difficulties may also be obvious. If, in a part of the personality, sensations have not been transformed into percepts and concepts, this will mean that learning will he hampered. School-phobic children have invariably been using outside rhythms as if they were the rhythms of their own body. Thus, when school 'breaks up', as we significantly phrase it, they feel at depth that their body is breaking up. Also, they use outside regularities to feel that wild and explosive feelings are being controlled by these constantly occurring regularities. As we know, such children often become phobic before or after a school holiday, i.e. when outside rhythms and regularities break down. Such breaks in routine also bring home to the child that he does not live in a timeless universe and that he has to be 'schooled' to accept limitations and 'to grow up properly'. Also, these children are very preoccupied with death and sometimes the phobia occurs after hearing of someone's death. Death, to them at elemental levels, means bodily break up and annihilation. It also brings home to the child that 'endings' are a fact of life. These children have great difficulty with their unregulated violence. They have 'caged it in' and 'battened it down' with autistic objects. This makes them very good, conforming children in school, but it is a pseudo-adaptation on the basis of pathological autism, and, finally, the child goes 'on strike' in a flurry of non-conformity.

In anorexia nervosa, as with other disorders in which some form of *inhibition* is the source of the trouble, a capsule of encapsulated-type autism is encountered. In this pathological state, the notion is very operative that growing up takes place by stealing or destroying taller people's inches (or centimetres!), or their strength, or their words, or their qualities or their grown-up appurtenances. This makes each mile-stone in their development (and in adolescent girls who develop anorexia nervosa it is often the onset of menstruation and the development of the breasts) an experience which is ringed around by threatening predators who want to bite back or destroy the 'things' which have been 'stolen' from them or destroyed.

Extracts from my own psychotherapy notebooks will now be presented to illustrate the operation of pathological autism in some of the most common forms of neurotic disorder in children. On the whole, the children will speak for themselves. I do not pretend to understand all that they had to say, but it will be clear that they are struggling to free themselves from the shrouds of pathological autism and to emerge to

more authentic ways of responding to themselves and to the outside
world.

SESSION FROM A FOURTEEN-YEAR-OLD GIRL SUFFERING FROM SCHOOL PHOBIA

This fourteen-year-old girl had been a severe school phobic for the past
three years, during which time she was seen in a family group with her
mother and father by the child psychiatrist and the psychiatric social
worker, who began to think that the girl should have individual psychotherapy. I was asked to take her on for once-weekly psychotherapy. She
was a girl of average intelligence from a working-class family. The session
given here was session 12.

Laura said that she had stopped head-banging. (Since I did not know
that she was a head-banger, I looked questioningly at her but said
nothing.) She went on to explain that she always had to bang her head
against the headboard of her bed in order to get to sleep. Her parents
had padded her headboard with an old blanket so that she did not
damage herself. Last night, for the first time, she had not needed to
bang her head. She did not know when she had first started to bang
her head but it must have been when she was a very little girl. She
had never known a time when she did not need to bang her head in
order to get to sleep, so that last night when she had not done so was
a momentous occasion.

(I sat in my chair facing her, looking attentive and interested, but
I did not feel the need to comment or to interpret since she had
obviously come with a great deal that she wanted to tell me. In
previous sessions I had talked a good deal because the infantile transference had quickly become established with this girl and I had felt
the need to explain and discuss with her the unassimilated infantile
feelings and sensations which distorted and inhibited her fourteen-
year-old functioning.)

On this occasion, she looked at my face as if to reassure herself of
my interest and attention, and then went on to say that she had seen
a television programme about a gramophone record of the beating of
a mother's heart which was played to newborn babies in the nursery
of a maternity hospital. Some of the babies had been crying but they
stopped when they heard the beating of the mother's heart and this
had happened several times. She went on to say that this had made
her think about what I had been saying to her in her sessions with me
about the way in which she sometimes used the rhythm of the beating
of her own heart to comfort herself when she felt lonely. Seeing the
television programme about the babies' reactions to the beating of the

mother's heart had made her think about her head-banging, and she had thought that perhaps she did this to feel that her mother was close to her and that she could feel the rhythm of the beating of her mother's heart and this comforted her and helped her to sleep. Last night she had found that she didn't need to do it and she thought it was because she had begun to understand why she did it. (I said perhaps it was also because she was beginning to be able to bear the fact that her mother was separate from her and not attached to her in a physical way as part of her body.)

She said, 'Yes. I had a dream last night about that.' (I asked, 'The night you didn't bang your head?', and she confirmed that this was so.) She said, 'I was standing beside a lake. It was still and silvery from the moonlight. Suddenly the middle of the lake started to pulsate like the beating of a heart and sent out large circular ripples which came towards the shore. As the first one touched the shore where I was standing, I suddenly felt very cold and as if I was like a statue – not a flat picture – and surrounded by space. A huge shiver went from top to bottom of my body like a streak of lightning and I felt very lonely. Suddenly from the pulsing bit in the middle there came a voice which was speaking in Bible language. It said, "Thou canst not have all thine own way." '

(I said I thought that the dream had helped her to relive the time when as a little baby she had first realised that her body was separate from her mother's body. She had felt the beating of her mother's heart to be like a disciplining daddy kind of thing inside the mother, imposing limits upon her. The beautiful, calm, silvery time with the moon-mother had to be disturbed to give way to a time when she realised that she was separate from a mother with whom she could not have all her own way. As well as recalling the beating of her mother's heart, the head-banging also expressed her destructive anger about the disciplines associated with separateness.)

The girl returned to school after this session. The three years she had had in family therapy had prepared her to use individual psychotherapy, so that salutary changes could take place quite quickly.

ANOREXIA NERVOSA

A piece of writing will now be presented which was given to me by a sixteen-year-old girl who was referred for psychotherapy suffering from anorexia nervosa. At the time of referral she was at death's door. She was seen three times a week. The piece of writing was given to me after she had been in treatment for three months and had recovered sufficiently to return home and was strong enough to put pen to paper. In it, she tried to describe her feelings about the hospital which, incidentally, was a very caring and humane place. She had been grumbling to me about the hospital, in particular saying that they had always been talking to her about food and eating when she was feeling that she was going through a spiritual crisis. (She came from a religious family.) She was a highly intelligent girl who enjoyed writing and the idea arose between us that it might be helpful for her to write about her reactions to the hospital. Mary handed the following piece of writing to me.

On reflection she couldn't remember ever having known 'where it all began.' The indefinable 'they' had tried to 'con' her that there must have been a fixed moment of decisive beginning, and had exercised their little ploys of stimulation to trick confession for her: it was fortunate that most of them had remained within the timeless, shapeless hollow that was memory, yet lay beyond the limits of concentration, or she might have found it in herself to hate. This was the extension of her rebirth, and when the gap came, or at least the one officially recognised and sanctioned on the printed list of dates she had seen somewhere, she would slowly ponder and commence the critical self-analysis that was an obligation to self and the mysterious Mother Earth figure in whose embrace she had rested, cradled, for a while. She could see herself suddenly touched in recollection, and laughing – a gentle expression of the bubbles inside – and, in anticipation, she felt the tightness which could flow out in streams so readily to songs, leaving the shell of her body intensely tired and aching.

A little before the gap though, there came the chance to grasp the shadows and hold them up to the light of naïvely profound reflection: one necessarily transient moment in which to contrast the torments and brief, brief exultation – the diamonds and rust.

She had been frightened into the webs of silence, having caught glimpses of their outrage when she was in danger of revealing the imperfections in the mask which she had given up removing, even during the time she spent, stiff-limbed, in dark contemplation. She recognised the symptoms of spiritual estrangement and knew herself torn between sweet, blissful, altruistic love and the numbness of steely indifference: knew that she would continue to fall from peak to pit until she had reached the harmony of heart and mind. It took the final retreat to do that, and even then they had misunderstood, trying to make their, oh! so good reasons, fit her.

She struggled now, still uncomfortable in supposed victory. The child cried for life and she wished only for oblivion. Her lovers made her, the loveless, lovely and yet she was untouched. They made her attributes and gave her grace and yet she remained the self-despised. The question was left unspoken, and the answer a small, hard-twisted knot in her side.

On another occasion, Mary quoted the following Paul Simon lyric to explain to me her state of being:

I am a Rock
A winter's day
In a deep and dark December,
I am alone,
Gazing from my window
To the streets below
On a freshly fallen, silent shroud of snow.
I am a rock
I am an island
I've built walls,
A fortress steep and mighty
That none may penetrate
I have no need of friendship
Friendship causes pain
The laughter and its loving I disdain
I am a rock, I am an island.

ANALYSIS OF A SCHOOL-PHOBIC BOY

Finally, a very condensed summary of the analysis of a school-phobic boy will be presented, up to the time when his tantrums about the many frustrations of reality limits were becoming restrained, to culminate in two interesting drawings.

Paul was referred at six and a half years of age, because of a reluctance to go to school and fairly severe eating difficulties. The eating symptoms began during a six-month hospitalisation of his mother when he was five years old.

There was a good deal of evidence that he came into analysis with unduly high expectations of its being a place where he could do as he liked and have what he pleased. This was in line with his father's description of his abnormally exaggerated expectations of birthdays and Christmas. During the first year of analysis it became clear that he had hopes that the 'bad bit', as he phrased it, would be eradicated by analysis. This 'bad bit' emerged as being the part of the outside world which did not fit in with his expectations, and which he could not control. It was also the part of himself which did not fit in with other people's expectations of him and which was uncontrollable. It was the part which did not achieve 'perfection', either his own views of this or those of other people. This 'bad bit' was felt to be 'mad' as well as 'bad'. It became clear that the sublime perfection he visualised was to be part of the mother and for her to be part of him, and that there should be no separation between them, separations being felt as a 'hole'.

During the first year, on those occasions when awareness of his bodily separateness from me (as the mother in the infantile transference) could not be avoided, he refused to come into the therapy room. As the analysis proceeded, it became clear that he had marked oscillations of mood. These were shown in his skin tone and colour rather than by facial expressions, tones of voice or communication by speech. When he felt empty and disillusioned, his skin looked grey and crumbling. He slid into the room as if merging with the shadows. At other times when he felt that everything was going his way, he looked strikingly different. His eyes and skin had a shining, translucent, other-worldly quality. His associations sparkled with such wit and charm that they tended to make me feel grey, no-good and empty. In both states he hardly seemed to hear what I said and seemed impenetrable. Towards the end of his second year of psychotherapy, this translucent 'shining' appearance was associated with crude, highly coloured pictures concerned with teasing and destructiveness. This coincided with a period of intense acting-out at home. He was cruel to his younger brother, who had displaced him in the mother's lap at eleven months of age, and his tyrannical and greedy behaviour reduced his mother to despair. However, this seemed to be a 'last-ditch stand' before giving up the notion that the desired sublime perfection of being physically part of the mother's body and she of his body could be achieved. When this had been worked over yet again in the transference to me (it was a constantly recurring theme), this 'acting-out' gave way to more co-operative behaviour and his skin changes were a thing of the past. The emotional turbulence still rumbled underground, but instead of reacting in the sensuous way of skin changes, he was beginning to 'think' and to have fantasy images about his recalcitrant state of mind.

He now drew pictures concerning undercurrents of uncontrolled destructiveness and cruel teasing that went on beneath the polite exterior. He drew people with bubbles coming out of their heads, with the word 'thinks' introducing what they had to say. This was invariably mocking or teasing. He drew scenes which were peaceful above the ground, but underneath there were scenes of destruction. In one such picture, there were little rodent-like animals eroding the ground from the peaceful scene above. In another there were horrible birds of prey feeding on dead bodies. In another below-ground picture there were seductive ice-creams with a cherry on top, which were tantalisingly whisked away when the man at the table came to eat them. Also, during this stage I often found that, whilst he had been sitting at the table in a seemingly friendly mood, he had picked the rush seat of the chair on which he was sitting and the bits of rush were scattered over the floor. As I became alerted to this underground resentment about having to give up his sublime expectations of never having to learn to share his mother with other people and to be separate from her, there came pictures of lions. It became clear that these represented his tantrum of disillusionment about his unfulfilled expectations. Finally, there came the picture of a lion which was on a leash and was straining towards a joint of meat (Figure 19.1). At this time he admitted his need and his longing for the analysis when he did not come at the weekend. He strained for it with all the strength of the lion for the joint of meat.

He began to come to his analysis on his own. Up to now his mother had brought him in the car. Coming on his own involved a long journey by Underground, but he persevered with this. During this time he drew a map of his journey to get to analysis (Figure 19.2). It will be seen that the contours of the lion straining towards the meat which was drawn on 15th February were outlined in the contours of the map which was drawn on 24 March of the same year. This would seem to demonstrate his eagerness to get to his session. (I am indebted to Dr Donald Meltzer for the detection of the striking resemblance between the two pictures.) The amazing congruence of the two pictures might be dismissed as coincidence, if it were not for the fact that the material of the session on 15 February and that of 24 March were also congruent. In both sessions he was working over his grumbling and resentment about the fact that he was separated from the school and from me by space, distance and time. In the session of 15 February he was concerned about the coming half-term holiday, and on 24 March he was concerned about the coming Easter holiday.

The map is an attempt to bridge the gap between us and it seemed to me that the ferocious lion tantrum about disillusionment was now a source of energy and perseverance. He no longer needed to block awareness of his need by the artificiality of pathological autism. It could be tolerated because it was becoming a hunger for things which ordinary human beings could supply. His expectations were coming within the range of available possibilities. In my experience it is crucial to work over with encapsulated children the painful sense of loss and suffering on which they feel impaled, and by which confusional children feel bewildered and confused.

Paul's images about his struggles with his elemental nature are reminiscent of Richard Livingstone's description of Plato's famous picture of human nature, as quoted by Guntrip. Livingstone writes:

'He' [Plato] describes human nature by a smile. On the outside men look like human beings, but under their skin three creatures are concealed: a monster with many heads, some wild, some tame . . . the

Figure 19.1 Paul's lion

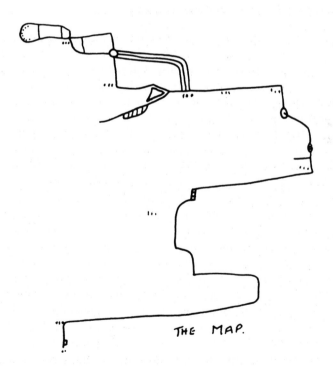

Figure 19.2 Paul's map

desires and passions. A lion – the spirited quality which will fight . . . and a human being – the rational element . . . Plato urges us to make the man supreme and see that, helped by the lion, he controls the many-headed monster.

(Guntrip, 1961, pp. 140–41)

As Paul was freed from the artificiality of autism, he began to develop genuine independence and self-respect. Reciprocal relationships with other people could develop when other human beings were no longer experienced as mere instruments to cater to his never-to-be-satisfied needs. He began to show consideration to other people – for example, in sparing his mother the long journey to my consulting-room. He stopped teasing his brother as a regular ploy, and the teasing that he did had more of a humorous quality and was less malicious. (Follow-up reports over the years show that he has maintained these and other changes which took place at this time.)

In conclusion, certain features which I consider to be desirable to the outcome of psychotherapy with both psychotic and neurotic children will now be summarised.

THE OUTCOME OF PSYCHOTHERAPY

When the child reaches the stage of being aware of his ecstasies and his tantrums and realises that he needs help in managing them, he is no longer cut off and isolated in a false self-sufficiency (as exemplified in Mary's writing and Paul Simon's lyric), where he is solely dependent on his own resources. There is an area which is shared with other human beings who are also fallible. But the faults and failings that are shared with these other human beings provide opportunities for sympathy, kindness, forbearance and mutual helpfulness. In short, the 'holes' can be filled, the 'wounds' can be healed, but they are not one individual's sole responsibility. Tender, sensitive areas can be used as avenues of awareness instead of being blocked or muffled. They are places where fulfilling connections with other people can be made instead of seeming to be places where mutilating disconnections, or lack of connection, have occurred and where inimical influences can enter. Normal shyness and wariness of strangers is preserved, but massive withdrawal and recoil is mitigated. Reciprocal relationships and creative activities offer means of fulfilment. In these, the connecting links between the sensation parts of the body-self and with other people are fundamental. As a result, a resilient inner core of self-hood is established which makes for stability and integrity.

With this development, the realisation that 'man's reach exceeds his grasp' becomes a stimulus to endeavour rather than a bottomless pit into which they will fall. Realistic achievements make the unattainable vision a bearable experience. Poignant experiences of frustration due to inability and incompleteness become the prelude to creation and psychological growth. The harvest of the world in which they live is there for them to reap. Like Luther, after he had broken away from 'mother-church', at times they may say 'I'm afraid of the darkness and the hole in it and I see it sometime every day' (quoted by Dare, 1969), but established inner resources enable them to 'breast' this devastating experience and to press on with hope and courage. With both psychotic and neurotic children, the therapist's main task and privilege is to help them to become aware of, and to bear the pains of separateness, with the ensuing disillusionment of losing the celestial bliss of seeming part of the mother. Instead of these being a source of evasion, intractable inhibition and confusion, they herald the dawning of a sense of reality. Thus, an authentic individual is born who has a mind of his own.

Concluding remarks

This book has sought to study autistic states in children, which have been very little investigated. In the process of writing it, the realisation has emerged that knowledge in the psychological field is different from that in the physical sciences, in that it does not consist of discovering physical objects and processes that are already in existence to be uncovered. Rather, it is detailed observation of, combined with empathic responsiveness to another person's states, so that a *construction* which has sufficient consonance with the nature of those states can be formed, making it possible to describe them to other people who have had something like the same experiences. Thus, those readers who have not had deep experiences with psychotic children may have found this a somewhat incomprehensible book, for we have been immersed in states which are not part of everyday experience. What has been written here cannot slip into the reader's mind with the easy familiarity of thoughts worn smooth by constant use. These ideas are bound to seem rough and strange. But, since they have been hewn out of the rock of basic experiences, other readers who have encountered similar experiences may have found it worth the struggle to take in the thoughts embodied here, in spite of their being jagged and difficult.

The primary aim has been to increase our capacities for being in touch with the children we are trying to help. An effort has been made to speak from the child's point of view, so that in a disciplined way we could 'get into the skin' of such a child and sense what it is like to be in a psychotic state. In order to foster this understanding of the child's state-of-being, evocative descriptions rather than abstract formulations have been used. There are limits to the extent to which it is possible for differentiated human beings to empathise with undifferentiated states, but the effort is worthwhile in that it fosters a human approach to these children. For one thing, we realise that behind their often mask-like faces there are boundless terror-stricken rage and overwhelming ecstasy and anguish. This needs to be understood if we are to help them.

Although this quest for understanding arises from therapeutic ambition and intention, the quest has therapeutic value in itself.

It is hoped that the book will be useful, not only to psychotherapists and to those who are caring for psychotic and deeply disturbed children, but also to those who want to understand human functioning more deeply. For example, work with psychogenic autistic children brings home to us how we become a person in our own right. Such children have missed the first essential step in this process, that is, the toleration of the awareness of their bodily separateness and difference from the mothering person, as the first representative of the outside world. For various reasons, for these children, such awareness has been a traumatic catastrophe which has skewed their psychological development in an aberrant direction to an almost total extent.

Clinical work with certain neurotic children also indicates that for phobic children or for those with psychosomatic disorders, a segment of their personality has gone in an autistic direction due to their having achieved psychological birth only partially. In an enclave of their awareness such children have felt that they have remained fused with the mother's body. In this part of their awareness they have never tolerated their bodily separateness and difference from her. This constitutes a block to their psychological development and to psychoanalytic work with them. The study of the almost *total* block in psychogenic autistic children helps us to understand this *partial* block in neurotic children. To a more limited extent, this block to achieving psychological birth as a separate individual is present in even relatively normal people. For all of us, individuation is a lifetime's task.

This book has endeavoured to demonstrate that in work with psychotic children subtle and perceptive assessment of the child's experience of bodily holes, of his use of objects in autistic and confusional ways, and of the factors which impede his psychological birth, combined with an understanding of primary sensuous differentiations and integrations, have increased the effectiveness of therapeutic work with both psychotic and neurotic children. Clinical work has shown that as they escape from being immobilised and frozen, or confusedly immured in their auto-sensual moulds, they feel that they face death-dealing dangers, both from within and from without. It is a life-or-death struggle. In this struggle they need someone alongside them who is both stern and accepting, strong and sensitive. In short, they need a stable setting and a well-balanced therapist.

As therapists, we need to be aware that it is a serious responsibility to lift the autistic covering to disclose the open hole or the unhealed 'wound' beneath. As the patient experiences this he will be over-sensitive and will over-react. At this stage, we need to be able to protect him by helping him to realise and to trust his inherent capacities for growth and healing. His auto-sensual manoeuvres begin to diminish as co-operative, effortful activities with other people develop. As the impeding pathological elements cease to dominate the whole of the child's functioning, and autistic expectations of sublime perfection become part of aesthetic sensibility and a feeling for beauty, rather than making impossible demands on everyday life and ordinary human beings, the child develops trust in parents to whom he learns to adjust as they learn to adjust to him. As he develops skills which enable him to channel and pattern his impulses, he begins to develop a growing medium for communication and expression, the flexibility of which will stand him in better stead than the rigid barriers of the extremes of autism by which he has avoided individuation and separateness. But self-realisation is difficult and painful, especially when the volcanoes of overwhelming tantrum and ecstasy have been covered by the ice-cap of autism. The heart-aches of loneliness associated with bodily separateness and self-identity have to be encountered as its icy grip melts away. We need to bear this in mind when we embark on remedying autistic states in children.

Afterword

As I take a last-minute look at the revised version of this book before it is prepared for the printers, I begin to fear that I may have given the erroneous impression that appropriate psychotherapeutic treatment for psychogenic autistic children is readily available. This is not the case. Psychotherapy with even young autistic children is long-term and difficult. However, if it is successful, fundamental changes will have taken place and the healing process will go on throughout the child's life. With young encapsulated autistic children, treatment is likely to take at least six years of dedicated work and the child will need to be seen at least three times a week, and more if possible. The marasmic type of child who has not developed a protective shell will take much longer and the outcome is more uncertain. Also, not all psychotherapists are suited to work with autistic children, although they may be extremely skilful with other childhood disorders. In addition, most psychotherapists cannot stand the strain of having more than one or two autistic children in treatment at the same time. Thus, appropriate psychotherapeutic treatment is likely to be in short supply.

A successful outcome depends upon having a suitable psychotherapist who uses appropriate methods of treatment, combined with co-operation from the parents and also from the teachers. Metaphorically speaking, all the carers need to hold linked hands around the child whilst he or she goes through the difficult process of beginning to grow up. Even when and if autistic children manage to achieve this, they will still feel some lacks; as a former severely autistic child patient of mine, whom I met recently as a 24-year-old man who now had a good science degree and was about to embark on an interesting professional career, said to me, 'One of my greatest regrets is that the autism blanked out my childhood'. This patient was six years old when he came into psychotherapy. He came twice a week and finished when he was eleven years old. Without the psychotherapy this young man would have been in an institution. As it is, he is a friendly and helpful member of society. However, he knows, and I know, that he has still quite a lot of growing up to do. The psychotherapy helped to set the growing-up processes in train.

It is hoped that the findings embodied in this book will help those who care for autistic children in ways other than by psychotherapy. A particularly important finding is that these passive, non-communicating children are traumatised and terror-stricken. Such understandings can help us to have the patience to care for these seemingly stubborn children, who can be extremely frustrating and irritating. Although they need to be treated in an unsentimental, firm, 'no-nonsense' sort of way and need our constant vigilant attention to modify their aberrant tendencies, methods of education which are based on a system of crude rewards and punishments are to be deplored, for they can brutalise those workers who put them into practice in a simplistic way. It is hoped that this book will help to humanise the care of autistic children, for it is only by such care that they can become more human.

References

Alvarez, A. (1977), 'Problems of Dependence and Development in an Excessively Passive Autistic Boy', *J. Child Psychotherapy*, vol. 4, no. 3.

Alvarez, A. (1980), 'Two Regenerative Situations in Autism: Reclamation and Becoming Vertebrate', *J. Child Psychotherapy*, vol. 6.

Anthony, J. (1958), 'An Experimental Approach to the Psychopathology of Childhood: Autism', *British J. Medical Psychol.*, vol. 31, no. 3 and no. 4.

Anzieu, D. (1986), *Le Moi Peau*, Paris, Dunod.

Anzieu, D. (ed.) (1987), *Les Envelopes Psychiques*, Paris, Dunod.

Anzieu, D. (ed.) (1990), *Psychic Envelopes*, London, Karnac.

Asberger, H. (1944), 'Die Austistischen Psychopathen in Kindesalter', *Archiv. fuer Psychiatrie und Nervenkrankheiten*, vol. 177, pp. 76–137.

Balint, M. (1968), *The Basic Fault*, London, Tavistock.

Balint, M. (1969), 'Trauma and Object Relationship', *Int. J. Psycho-Analysis*, vol. 50.

Barrows, A. (1988), *Asberger's Syndrome: A Theoretical and Clinical Account*, Ph.D. dissertation submitted to the Wright Institute Graduate School of Psychology, U.S.A. (as yet unpublished).

Bemperad, J. R. (1979), 'Adult Recollections of a Formerly Autistic Child', *J. Autism Develop. Disorders*, vol. 9, no. 2.

Bender, L. (1956), 'Schizophrenia in Childhood: Its Recognition, Description and Treatment', *Amer. J. Orthopsychiatry*, vol. 26, pp. 499–506.

Benjamin, J. D. (1963), 'Further Comments on Some Developmental Aspects of Anxiety', in Gaskill (ed.), *Counterpoint*, New York, International Universities Press.

Bergman, P. and Escalona, S. (1949), 'Unusual Sensitivities in Young Children', *Psychoanal. Study Child*, vol. 3, no. 4.

Bettelheim, B. (1967), *The Empty Fortress; Infantile Autism and the Birth of the Self*, New York, Free Press (London, Collier-Macmillan).

Bibring, E. (1953), 'The Mechanism of Depression', in P. Greenacre (ed.), *Affective Disorders*, New York, International Universities Press.

Bick, E. (1964), 'Notes on Infant Observation in Psycho-analytic Training', *Int. J. Psycho-Analysis*, vol. 45.

Bick, E. (1968), 'The Experience of the Skin in Early Object Relations', *Int. J. Psycho-Analysis*, vol. 49.

Bick, E. (1986), 'Further Considerations on the Function of the Skin in Early Object Relations', *Brit. J. Psychotherapy*, vol. 2, no. 4.

Bion, W. R. (1962a), 'A Psycho-Analytic Study of Thinking', *Int. J. Psycho-Analysis*, vol. 43.

Bion, W. R. (1962b), *Learning from Experience*, London, Heinemann Medical.

Bion, W. R. (1963), *Elements of Psycho-analysis*, New York, Basic Books.

Bion, W. R. (1979), *A Memoir of the Future. Book 3: The Dawn of Oblivion*, London, Karnac, 1990.

Bleuler, E. (1913), 'Autistic Thinking', *Amer. J. Insanity*, vol. 69.

Bonnard, A. (1960), 'The Primal Significance of the Tongue', *Int. J. Psycho-Analysis*, vol. 41.

Boston, M. (1975) 'Recent Research in Developmental Psychology', *J. Child Psychotherapy*, vol. 4, no. 1.

Bower, T. C. R. (1978), 'The Infant's Discovery of Objects and Mother', in E. Thomas (ed.), *Origins of the Infant's Social Responsiveness*, Hillsdale, N.J., Erlbaum.

Bowlby, J. (1969), *Attachment and Loss*, vol. 1. London, Hogarth Press.

Brazelton, T. B., Koslowski, B. and Main, M. (1970), 'The Origins of Reciprocity: The Early Mother–Infant Interaction', in M. Lewis and L. Rosenblum (eds), *The Effect of the Infant on its Caretaker*, New York, John Wiley & Sons.

Bressler, B. (1965), 'The Concept of the Self', *Psychoanal. Review*, vol. 2, pp. 425–45.

Brodey, W. M. (1965), 'On the Dynamics of Narcissism: Externalization and Early Ego Development', *Psychoanal. Study Child*, vol. 20.

Brontë, E. (1972), *Poems*, Denis Thompson (ed.), London, Chatto and Windus.

Chomsky, N. (1976), 'Language and Unconscious Knowledge', in J. H. Smith (ed.), *Psychoanalysis and Language*, vol. 3 of *Psychiatry and Humanities*, New Haven, Yale University Press, 1978.

Copeland, J. (1973), *For the Love of Ann*, London, Arrow.

Corbett, J., Harris, R., Taylor, E. and Trimble M. (1977), 'Progressive Disintegrative Psychoses of Childhood', *J. Child Psychol. Psychiat.*, vol. 18, no. 3.

Creak, M. (1961), 'Schizophrenic Syndrome in Childhood', *Brit. Med. J.*, vol. 2.

Dare, C. (1969), 'An Aspect of the Ego Psychology of Religion' (a comment on Dr Guntrip's paper), *Brit. J. Med. Psychol.*, vol. 42, no. 4.

Darwin, C. (1892), *Expression of the Emotions*, London, John Murray.

Day Lewis, C. (1943), *Word over All*, London, Jonathan Cape.

Deutsch, H. (1942), 'Some Forms of Emotional Disturbance and Their Relationship to Schizophrenia', *Psychoanal. Quarterly*, vol. 11.

Docker-Drysdale, B. (1972), *Therapy in Child Care*, London, Longman.

d'Ostiani, E. Fe (1979), 'Analytical Space and Time: The Dimension of Representation' (unpublished).

d'Ostiani, E. Fe (1980), 'An Individual Approach to Psychotherapy with Psychotic Children', *J. Child Psychotherapy*, vol. 6.

Eliot, T. S. (1909–62), 'East Coker', in *Collected Poems*, London, Faber.

Erikson, E. (1950), *Childhood and Society*, New York, Norton.

Fairbairn, W. R. D. (1941), 'A Revised Psychopathology of the Psychoses and Psychoneuroses', in *Psychoanalytic Studies of the Person*, London, Tavistock, 1952, pp. 28–58.

Fitzgerald, E. (1958), From the 'Rubáiyát of Omar Khayyám', in A. P. Wavell (ed.), *Other Men's Flowers*, London, Cape.

Fordham, M. (1966), 'Notes on the Psychotherapy of Infantile Autism', *Brit. J. Med. Psychol.*, vol. 39.

Fordham, M. (1976), *The Self and Autism*, London, Heinemann Medical.

Freud, S. (1911), 'Formulations on the Two Principles of Mental Functioning', in *Standard Edition of the Complete Psychological Works of Sigmund Freud*, vol. XII, London, Hogarth.

Freud, S. (1915), 'Observations on Transference-Love', in *Standard Edition of the Complete Psychological Works of Sigmund Freud*, vol. XII, London, Hogarth.

Freud, S. (1920), 'Beyond the Pleasure Principle', in *Standard Edition of the Complete Psychological Works of Sigmund Freud*, vol. XVIII, London, Hogarth.

Freud, S. (1921a), 'Group Psychology and the Analysis of the Ego', in *Standard Edition of the Complete Psychological Works of Sigmund Freud*, vol. XVIII, London, Hogarth.

Freud, S. (1921b), 'The Ego and the Id', in *Standard Edition of the Complete Psychological Works of Sigmund Freud*, vol. XIX, London, Hogarth.

Freud, S. (1922), *Introductory Lectures on Psycho-analysis*, London, Allen & Unwin.

Freud, S. (1930), 'Civilisation and Its Discontents', in *Standard Edition of the Complete Psychological Works of Sigmund Freud*, vol. XXI, London, Hogarth.

Frith, V. (1985), 'Does the Autistic Child Have a Theory of Mind?', *Cognition*, vol. 21, pp. 37–46.

Gaddini, E. (1969), 'On Imitation', *Int. J. Psycho-Analysis*, vol. 50, part 4, pp. 475–84.

Gaddini, R. (1978), 'Transitional Object Origins and the Psychosomatic Symptoms', in S. Barkin and M. Berger (eds), *Between Fantasy and Reality*, New York, Jason Aronson.

Gampel, Y. (1988), 'Facing War, Murder, Torture and Death in Childhood', *J. Psychoanal. Psychoth.*

Giannotti, A. and De Astis, G. (1979), 'Autismo Infantile Precoce: Considerazioni sulla psicopatologia e sul processo psicoterapico', *Neuropsichiatria Infantile*, Rome University.

Giannotti, A. and De Astis, G. (1980), 'Birth and Autism: Some Considerations about Early Mother–Child Psychotic Relationship' (unpublished).

Gillberg, C. (1989), 'Asberger Syndrome in 23 Swedish Children', *Dev. Med. Child Neurol.*, vol. 31, pp. 520–31.

Goldberg, L. (1979), 'Transference–Counter-Transference', *Int. J. Psycho-Analysis*, vol. 60, part 3.

Gomberoff, M. J., Noemi, C. C. and Pualuan de Gomberoff, L. (1990), 'The Autistic Object: its relationship to narcissism', *Int. J. Psycho-analysis*, vol. 71, pp. 249–59.

Greenacre, P. (1970), 'Fetish Objects', *Int. J. Psycho-Analysis*, vol. 51, pp. 447–56.

Grotstein, J. (1980), 'Primitive Mental States', *Contemp. Psycho-analysis*, vol. 16, pp. 479–546.

Guntrip, H. (1961), 'The Manic-Depressive Problem', *Int. J. Psycho-Analysis*, vol. 43.

Hamilton, V. (1989), 'The Mantle of Safety', *Winnicott Studies*, vol. 4, pp. 70–95.

Hayman, A. (1962), 'Some Aspects of Regression in Non-psychotic Puerperal Breakdown', *Brit. J. Med. Psychol.*, vol. 35.

Hobson, P. (1986), 'The Autistic Child's Appraisal of Expressions of Emotion', *J. Child Psychol. and Psychiat.*, vol. 27, pp. 321–42.

Hopkins, J. (1977), 'Living under the Threat of Death', *J. Child Psychotherapy*, vol. 4, no. 3.

Hoxter, S. (1972), 'A Study of a Residual Autistic Condition and Its Effects upon Learning', *J. Child Psychotherapy*, vol. 3, no. 2.

Itard, J. and Malson, L. (1972), *Wolf Children. The Wild Boy of Aveyron*, trans. Fawcett, Ayrton and White, London, New Left Books.

Jacobson, E. (1964), *The Self and the Object World*, New York, International Universities Press.

James, M. (1960), 'Premature Ego Development. Some Observations upon Disturbances in the First Three Years of Life', *Int. J. Psycho-Analysis*, vol. 41.

Kahn, M. (1964), 'Ego Distortion, Cumulative Trauma and the Role of Reconstruction in the Analytic Situation', *Int. J. Psycho-Analysis*, vol. 45.

Kanner, L. (1943), 'Autistic Disturbances of Affective Contact', *Nervous Child*, vol. 2.

Kanner, L. (1944), 'Early Infantile Autism', *J. Paediatrics*, vol. 25.

Kennedy, R. (1980), 'The Function of Language in a Borderline Psychotic Boy', *Bulletin Brit. Psychoanal. Ass.*

Kernberg, O. (1965), 'Notes on Counter-Transference', *Amer. Psychoanal. Ass.*, vol. 13.

Klaus, M. and Kennell, J. (1976), *Maternal-Infant Bonding*, Philadelphia, C. V. Mosby.

Klein, M. (1930), 'The Psychotherapy of the Psychoses', in *Contributions to Psycho-Analysis* (1950), London, Hogarth.

Klein, M. (1937), 'Love, Guilt and Reparation', in M. Klein and J. Riviere, *Love, Hate and Reparation*, London, Hogarth.

Klein, M. (1950), *Contributions to Psycho-Analysis (1921–45)*, London, Hogarth.

Klein, M. (1952), 'Notes on Some Schizoid Mechanisms', in M. Klein, P. Heimann, S. Isaacs and J. Riviere, *Developments in Psychoanalysis*, London, Hogarth.

Klein, M. (1957), *Envy and Gratitude*, London, Tavistock.

Klein, M. (1963), 'On Identification', in *Our Adult World and Other Essays*, London, Heinemann Medical.

Klein, S. (1980), 'Autistic Phenomena in Neurotic States', *Int. J. Psycho-Analysis*, vol. 61, pp. 395–402.

Kohut, H. (1971), *The Analysis of the Self*, Monograph Series on Psychoanalytic Study of the Child, New York, International Universities Press.

Kretschmer, E. (1936), *Physique and Character*, London, George Routledge and Sons.

Laing, R. D. (1971), *The Divided Self*, London, Tavistock.

Lawrence, D. H. (1960), *The Fox*, in *Three Novellas*, Harmondsworth, Penguin.

Lichtenstein, H. (1961), 'Identity and Sexuality', *J. Amer. Psychoanal. Ass.*, vol. 9, pp. 179–260.

McDougall, J. (1974), 'The Psychosoma and the Psychoanalytic Process', *Int. R. Psycho-Analysis*, vol. 1, pp. 437–59.

McDougall, J. (1982), 'Alexythimia, Psychosomatosis, and Psychosis', *Int. J. Psychoanal. Psychoth.*, vol. 9, pp. 379–88.

McDougall, J. (1986), *Theatres of the Mind*, London, Free Association Books.

McDougall, J. (1989), *Theatres of the Body*, London, Free Association Books.

Mahler, M. (1952), 'On Child Psychosis and Schizophrenia: Autistic and Symbiotic Psychosis', *Psychoanal. Study Child*, vol. 7.

Mahler, M. (1958), 'Autism and Symbiosis: Two Extreme Disturbances of Identity', *Int. J. Psycho-Analysis*, vol. 39.

Mahler, M. (1961), 'On Sadness and Grief in Infancy and Childhood: Loss and Restoration of the Symbiotic Love Object', *Psychoanal. Study Child*, vol. 16.

Mahler, M. (1963), 'Development and Individuation', *Psychoanal. Study Child*, vol. 18.

Mahler, M. (1968), *On Human Symbiosis and the Vicissitudes of Individuation*, New York, International Universities Press.

Mahler, M., Bergman, A. and Pine, F. (1975), *The Psychological Birth of the Human Infant*, New York, Basic Books.

Meltzer, D. (1967), *The Psychoanalytical Process*, London, Heinemann.

Meltzer, D., Bremner, J., Hoxter, S., Wedell, H. and Wittenberg, I. (1975), *Explorations in Autism*, Strath Tay, Perthshire, Scotland, Clunie Press.

Meltzoff, A. and Barton, R. (1979), 'Intermodal Matching in Human Neonates', *Nature* (November).

Milner, M. (1955), 'The Role of Illusion in Symbol Formation', in Melanie Klein (ed.), *New Directions in Psycho-Analysis*, London, Tavistock.

Monchaux, C. De (1962), 'A Psychoanalytic Study of Thinking', *Int. J. Psycho-Analysis*, vol. 43.

Ogden, T. H. (1989), *The Primitive Edge of Experience*, Northvale, N.J./London, Jason Aronson.

O'Gorman, G. (1967), *The Nature of Childhood Autism*, London, Butterworths.

O'Shaughnessy, E. (1964), 'The Absent Object', *J. Child Psychotherapy*, vol. 1, no. 2.

Park, C. C. (1972), *The Siege*, Harmondsworth, Penguin.

Pérez-Sánchez, M. (1990), *Baby Observations*, Scotland, Clunie Press.

Piggott, L. R. (1979), 'Overview of Selected Basic Research in Autism', *J. Autism Develop. Disorders*, vol. 9, no. 2.

Piontelli, A. (1987), 'Infant Observation From Before Birth', *Int. J. Psycho-Analysis*, vol. 68, pp. 453–63.

Pribram, K. H. (1969), 'Neuro-physiology of Remembering', *Scientific American*, vol. 220, no. 1.

Rank, B. and McNaughton, D. (1950), 'A Clinical Contribution to Early Ego Development', *Psychoanal. Study Child*, vol. 5.

Richards, M. P. M. and Bernal, J. F. (1976), 'An Observational Study of Mother–Infant Interaction', in N. Blurton Jones (ed.), *Ethological Studies of Child Behaviour*, Cambridge, Cambridge University Press.

Ricks, D. (1975), 'Vocal Communication in Pre-Verbal, Normal and Autistic Children', in N. O'Connor (ed.), *Language, Cognitive Defects and Retardation*, London, Butterworths.

Rimland, B. (1964), *Infantile Autism*, London, Methuen.

Rolland, R. (1930), *Prophets of the New India*, New York, Boni.

Rosenfeld, D. (1986), 'Identification and its Vicissitudes in relation to the Nazi phenomenon', *Int. J. Psycho-Analysis*, vol. 67, pp. 53–64.

Rosenfeld, H. (1950), 'Notes on the Psychopathology of Confusional States in Chronic Schizophrenia', *Int. J. Psycho-Analysis*, vol. 31.

Rosenfeld, H. (1965), *Psychotic States: A Psychoanalytic Approach*, London, Hogarth.

Rosenfeld, S. and Sprince, M. (1963), 'Borderline Children', *Psychoanal. Study Child*, vol. 18.

Rubens, B. (1979), *Spring Sonata*, London, Sphere Books.

Rubinfine, D. L. (1962), 'Maternal Stimulation, Psychic Structure and Early Object Relations', *Psychoanal. Study Child*, vol. 17.

Rutter, M. (1966), 'Behavioural and Cognitive Characteristics', in J. K. Wing (ed.), *Early Childhood Autism*, Oxford, Pergamon.

Salk, L. (1973), 'The Role of the Heartbeat in the Relationship Between Mother and Infant', *Scientific American* (March).

Sandler, J. (1960), 'The Background of Safety', *Int. J. Psycho-Analysis*, vol. 41, pp. 352–6.

Sarason, S. B. and Gladwin, T. (1958), 'Psychological and Cultural Problems in

Mental Subnormality: A Review of Research', *Genet. Psycho. Monog.*, vol. 57.

Saussure, F. de (1972), *Course in General Linguistics*, trans. W. Baskin, London, Fontana.

Searles, H. F. (1965), *Collected Papers on Schizophrenia*, London, Hogarth; New York, International Universities Press.

Sechahaye, M. A. (1956), 'The Transference in Symbolic Realisation', *Int. J. Pscho-Analysis*, vol. 37.

Segal, H. (1957), 'Notes on Symbol Formation', *Int. Rev. Psycho-Analysis*, vol. 38, no. 6.

Shartuck, R. (1979), *The Forbidden Experiment: The Story of the Wild Boy of Aveyron*, New York, Farrar, Straus & Giroux.

Spensley, S. (1989), 'The Diagnosis and Treatment of Autism', paper given at a conference on autism in Sweden.

Spitz, R. (1949), 'Auto-erotism', *Psychoanal. Study Child*, vol. 3, no. 4, pp. 85–120.

Spitz, R. (1950), 'Relevancy of Direct Infant Observation', *Psychoanal. Study Child*, vol. 5, pp. 66–73.

Spitz, R. (1960), 'The Primal Cavity. A Contribution to the Genesis of Perception and Its Role in Psychoanalytic Theory', *Psychoanal. Study Child*, vol. 10.

Stein, L. (1967), 'Introducing Not-Self', *J. Analyt. Psychol.*, vol. 12, no. 2.

Stern, D. (1986), *The Interpersonal World of the Infant*, New York, Basic Books.

Stevenson, O. (1954), 'The First Treasured Possession', *Psychoanal. Study Child*, vol. 9.

Stroh, G. (1974), 'Psychotic Children', in P. Barker (ed.), *The Residential Psychiatric Treatment of Children*, London, Crosby, Lockwood, Staples.

Taylor, G. (1987), *Psychosomatic Medicine and Contemporary Psycho-Analysis*, New York, International Universities Press.

Tischler, S. (1979), 'Being with a Psychotic Child: A Psychoanalytical Approach to the Problems of Parents of Psychotic Children', *Int. J. Psycho-Analysis*, vol. 60, pp. 29–38.

Trevarthen, C. (1979), 'Instincts for Human Understanding and for Cultural Cooperation, in *Human Ethology: Claims and Limits of a New Dicipline*, London, Cambridge University Press.

Tustin, F. (1958), 'Anorexia Nervosa in an Adolescent Girl', *Brit. J. Med. Psychol.*, vol. 31, no. 3 and no. 4.

Tustin, F. (1963), 'Two Drawings Occurring in the Analysis of a Latency Child', *J. Child Psychotherapy*, vol. 1, no. 1.

Tustin, F. (1966), 'A Significant Element in the Development of Autism', *J. Child Psychol. Psychiat.*, vol. 7.

Tustin, F. (1967), 'Individual Therapy in the Clinic', in *Proceedings of 23rd Child Guidance Inter-Clinic Conference*, London, National Association of Mental Health.

Tustin, F. (1967), 'Psychotherapy with Autistic Children', *Bulletin Ass. Psychotherapy*, vol. 2, no. 3.

Tustin, F. (1969), 'Autistic Processes', *J. Child Psychotherapy*, vol. 2, no. 3.

Tustin, F. (1972), *Autism and Childhood Psychosis*, London, Hogarth; New York, Jason Aronson, 1973.

Tustin, F. (1980), 'Autistic Objects', *Int. R. Psycho-Analysis*, vol. 7, pp. 27–38.

Tustin, F. (1984), 'Autistic Shapes', *Int. R. Psycho-Analysis*, vol. 11: 279–90.

Tustin, F. (1987), *Autistic Barriers in Neurotic Patients*, London, Karnac Books; Yale Univ. Press. U.S.A.

Tustin, F. (1988), 'Psycho-therapy with children who cannot play', *Int. R. Psycho-Analysis*, vol. 15, pp. 93–105.

Tustin, F. (1990), *The Protective Shell in Children and Adults*, London, Karnac Books; New York, Brunner Mazel.

Tustin, F. (1991), 'Revised Understandings of Psychogenic Autism', *Int. J. Psycho-Analysis*, vol. 72, no. 7, pp. 585–91.

Weil, A. P. (1953), 'Certain Severe Disturbances of Ego Development in Childhood', *Psychoanal. Study Child*, vol. 8, pp. 271–87.

Williams, A. H. (1960), 'A Psycho-analytic Approach to the Treatment of the Murderer', *Int. J. Psycho-Analysis*, vol. 45, parts 4 and 5, pp. 532–9.

Wing, L. (1981), 'Asberger's Syndrome: A Clinical Account', *Psychol. Med.*, vol. 11, pp. 115–29.

Winnicott, D. W. (1958), 'Transitional Objects and Transitional Phenomena', in *Collected Papers*, London, Tavistock; also in *Through Paediatrics to Psychoanalysis*, London, Hogarth (1975).

Winnicott, D. W. (1971), *Playing and Reality*, London, Tavistock.

Wolff, S. and Barlow, A. (1979), 'Schizoid Personality in Childhood: A Comparative Study of Schizoid, Autistic and Normal Children', *J. Child Psychol. Psychiat.*, vol. 20, pp. 29–46.

Wolff, S. and Chick, J. (1980), 'Schizoid Personality in Childhood: A Controlled Follow-Up Study', *Psychol. Medicine*, vol. 10, pp. 85–100.

Wolff, S. and Cuth, A. (1986), 'Schizoid Personality and Anti-Social Conduct: A Retrospective Case Note Study', *Psychol. Medicine*, vol. 16, pp. 677–87.

About autism

I would like to recommend two recently published books: *Little Boy Lost* (Bloomsbury Press, 1990) by Bronwyn Hocking, the mother of an autistic child; and *Nobody Nowhere* (Doubleday, 1992) by Donna Williams, a former autistic child.

About baby observations

I would like to draw readers' attention to a recently published book containing detailed observations of babies, called *Closely Observed Infants* by Lisa Miller, Margaret and Michael Rustin and Judy Shuttleworth (Duckworth, 1989), and also to *Through the Night* by Dilys Daws (Free Association books, 1989), in which interactions between parents and infants are described.

Name index

Subject index